Advance Praise

"In *Stress Test*, Kay White Drew speaks insightfully and honestly about her personal journey through medical school in an era where very few women were in her ranks. She then widens the aperture to illuminate what it means to be both a woman in medicine and a woman in the larger landscape of motherhood, work, and wellness. This book moved me to my core with its wisdom, compassion and grace for the people portrayed and the human flaws faced, which is to say it's a book for all of us."

— Christine Koubek Flynn, essayist and fiction writer with work featured in *The Washington Post; Poets & Writers; Brain, Child; Washingtonian, Bethesda, Arlington; Chautauqua;* and *Hypertext*

"A touching and at times painful memoir of a young woman's journey from a small town to a big city, from an all-girl's college to a medical school class with only a handful of women, and from an idealistic notion of medicine to the grim realities of hands-on care. A fascinating and heartfelt story."

— Paul Offit, MD., Chief of Infectious Disease and Director of the Vaccine Education Center at the Children's Hospital of Philadelphia, author of *You Bet Your Life: From Blood Transfusions to Mass Vaccination, the Long and Risky History of Medical Innovation*

"Kay White Drew's frank and honest memoir lays out the challenges she encountered in medical school in the 1970s—from facing her first cadaver, to the heartbreak of losing patients, to losing her mother to cancer—woven together with the joys of building meaningful relationships, solving complex problems, and saving lives. Holding nothing back, she delves into the intimate details of her life: her emotional difficulties and therapy, and her struggle to gain respect in a field dominated by men. And throughout the story, she demonstrates resilience, internal strength, and compassion for herself and others. During a period when women's rights are being stripped away in decisions such as Dobbs vs. Jackson and women still make up less than half of the medical profession, this story will show today's women that the challenges faced by those who went before them were not that different, give them insight into the power of pushing back, and inspire the courage to press on."

— Ariele Sieling, a prolific science fiction and speculative fiction writer who also speaks, writes, and gives workshops on craft, publishing, and marketing.

"*Stress Test* is an excellent title for an excellent memoir. Kay White Drew writes an incisive, unsparing account of her years training to become a doctor. Any woman who's ever been underestimated, devalued, or doubted her capabilities will understand and empathize with Drew's journey and the misogyny she encountered. Her story is also a coming-of-age narrative, well told, of a medical student whose relationships and personal struggles changed and challenged her, and ultimately shaped her into the strong and resilient woman – and physician – she became."

> — Celia Wexler, author of *Catholic Women Confront Their Church* and *Out of the News*

"*Stress Test* is as charming as it is vital in telling the story of a woman becoming a doctor during the national upheaval and civil unrest of the '60s and '70s. The book captures important moments in our country's history and reveals the misogyny women in the medical field still face in striving for equality. Kay White Drew writes with clarity and humor a deeply personal, redemptive story that satisfies. *Stress Test* is a delightful read of grief, ambition, and love."

> — Melissa Scholes Young, Professor of Literature, American University; author of award-winning novels *Flood* and *The Hive*

Stress Test

A Memoir

Kay White Drew

Apprentice House Press
Loyola University Maryland

First Edition

Library of Congress Control Number: requested

Hardcover ISBN: 978-1-62720-522-1
Paperback ISBN: 978-1-62720-523-8
Ebook ISBN: 978-1-62720-524-5

Cover Design by Jack Stromberg
Design Editing by Claire Marino

Published by Apprentice House Press

Apprentice
House Press
Loyola University Maryland

Loyola University Maryland
4501 N. Charles Street, Baltimore, MD 21210
410.617.5265
www.ApprenticeHouse.com
info@ApprenticeHouse.com

To my mother, Rachel Harriet Wheat White

CONTENTS

AUTHOR'S NOTE

Knowing that memory is selective, distorted, and often inaccurate, I've relied on my journals and calendars from the years 1973 through 1978, as well as letters and other documents, to supplement my memories in the writing of this memoir. I've tweaked or added details as necessary for the sake of narrative, but I've tried to be as truthful and factually accurate as possible.

I am indebted to Larry Pitrof's *The University of Maryland: The First Two Centuries*, published by the Medical Alumni Association of the University of Maryland, Inc., Baltimore, MD, 2006, for the section about the history of the medical school in Chapter Two, "Incipit Vita Nova."

Chapter Seventeen, "Baptism by Fire," appeared in a slightly different form in *Grace in Darkness*, Melissa Scholes Young, ed., American University Press, 2018.

Part of the epilogue appeared in a slightly different form in a flash essay, "The House on South Stricker Street," in *Loch Raven Review*, Fall 2023.

Most names and some identifying details have been changed in an attempt to protect others' privacy. The names of my family members have not been changed.

PROLOGUE

"Shhh." He put a finger to his lips. We tiptoed down a dark, concrete-floored hallway. Turning the handle slowly so as not to make any noise, he opened the door, took my hand, and led me into the empty space. I blinked as I stepped inside. The dim corridor opened onto a large semicircular room flooded with light from a wall of windows.

It was late August 1968, and the country was still reeling from the assassinations of Martin Luther King, Jr., and Robert F. Kennedy. Cities were going up in flames. Protests against the Vietnam War, forcefully quelled by Mayor Richard Daley and over twenty thousand police officers and National Guardsmen, were stealing the spotlight at the Democratic National Convention in Chicago. I was pretty much oblivious to all this, being seventeen and ready to start my senior year of high school. My boyfriend, Lance, a sandy-haired, six-foot-six-inch pre-med college junior, had brought me to this place. Lance must have figured I wasn't likely to be squeamish; my brother was in medical school, and I enjoyed Lance's anecdotes about his vertebrate anatomy course. I'd dressed with care that morning, choosing a white dress I'd recently made on the family sewing machine, paired with some new earrings. Lance arrived at my house shortly before noon, wearing khakis and a short-sleeve button-down shirt, redolent of English Leather cologne.

"You look great," he said, beaming at me.

The drive to Baltimore seemed a lot shorter than the hour or so it was supposed to take. While I was usually a quiet person,

Lance always had a lot to say—about his dad's clothing business, about "playing the ponies," and sometimes about his aspiration to become a doctor. When I asked him how we would get into the hospital, he waved his hand dismissively.

"I know a guy," he said with a grin.

Sure enough, his medical-student buddy Jim, a former fraternity brother, was waiting for us outside the main building of the Johns Hopkins Hospital. He greeted us, shook hands with Lance, and gave me a look of frank appreciation. Then he told us where to go and how to get there. We tiptoed down the hallways, not speaking above a whisper. I held my breath. Unaccompanied non-medical people weren't supposed to be in the observation area above the surgical suite.

After sneaking through the maze of corridors, it took a while for our eyes to adjust to the operating room's stark brightness. I hung back until Lance gestured me forward.

"Let's sit up front," he whispered, pointing to two plush fold-out chairs, like those in the movie theaters where he usually brought me on dates.

We slipped silently into our seats, and, wide-eyed, I leaned over to take in the vast surgical amphitheater on the other side of the windows. Lance placed a hand lightly on the small of my back and his voice resumed its normal boisterous volume.

"Jim said this was a gallbladder operation. It looks like they just opened her up."

I recoiled at first: a human being, cut open on the operating table, her internal organs exposed to view. A faceless, inert, draped figure surrounded by busy anonymous people in gowns, masks, and rubber gloves, wielding surgical instruments like a bunch of car mechanics with wrenches. I flashed on images of sides of beef in butcher-shop refrigerators, or coroners examining corpses on

TV crime shows. But then Lance pointed out the woman's liver, deep red and glistening, as the surgeon started to tie off the small greenish-brown sac attached to it, the gallbladder. My revulsion gave way to curiosity and a sense of wonder.

"Wow! So *that's* what we look like inside."

"Yeah, pretty neat, huh?"

I was stunned by the scene unfolding below us. The patient was anesthetized, asleep on the table, and yet—blood kept coursing through her body, fluids kept moving through her intestines, even while the doctors and nurses were getting rid of the expendable organ that wasn't working right. What did her beating heart look like? Was it the same shade of red as her liver? And her lungs, rising and falling gently within her chest to the rhythm of the ventilator: did their surfaces gleam, too? Did they really look like sponges, as we'd been taught in 10th grade biology? There were occasional glimpses of bright red blood as vessels were cut and then stitched or cauterized. The blood, the organs of a living human being—they were beautiful, in a way I never would have expected. And a few hours from now, the woman on the table would be awake and talking, relieved of the pain that had brought her here. If this wasn't a miracle, what was?

I reached for Lance's hand and gave it a grateful squeeze as I kept my eyes on the scene below. I wanted to know more about what went on inside our bodies. I wanted to know what to do when something went wrong, how to fix it.

I wanted to learn what those people in the operating room knew.

1

THE EYE OF THE STORM

My mother spent the summer of 1973 lying on the family-room sofa, watching the Watergate hearings with my two younger sisters. I was the only one of the three of us who held a job that summer, a time in which everything seemed suspended—for me, a tranquil hiatus between college and medical school. My twenty-year-old sister Sarah was staying home so she could drive our mother on the roughly ninety-mile roundtrip to her chemotherapy and radiation appointments at Johns Hopkins Hospital. Seventeen-year-old Mary Alyce had taken over the family cooking responsibilities. Our brother Phil, five years older than me, was a military doctor, an Army flight surgeon trained as an ophthalmologist and currently based on the West Coast.

While my mother and sisters spent their days watching the Watergate drama unfold, I assisted with rat autopsies in a veterinary research facility connected with Fort Detrick, the army cancer research installation located a dozen or so miles from our family's home in Libertytown, Maryland. My father and I rode to work together each day. He would drop me off at my job in Walkersville, a few miles from the plastics plant in Frederick where he was vice president in charge of operations.

I worked with Dick Gantt, the grizzled Black veterinary technician at Walkersville. Weighing tiny rat hearts, livers and kidneys gave me lots of time to reflect on the events that had brought me to the threshold of medical school.

As a child, my interests had oscillated between medicine and writing. In grade school, I'd adapted science experiments from my brother's *Mr. Wizard* book, which I performed in a walk-in closet; and I'd assembled a doctor kit, complete with my very own pair of stainless-steel bandage scissors. Throughout high school, I'd retained a largely unspoken desire to become a doctor, though much of my energy was focused on writing articles for the high-school quarterly and contributing a weekly column to the local newspaper. Once I arrived at Wellesley College, where there were no boys in the classroom—no more high-school popularity issues to contend with—I went public with my intention to go to medical school. My career choice was met there with support, even admiration.

In keeping with my pre-med aspirations, I loaded up on science courses my first semester. But the siren song of English literature wouldn't let me go. At the end of my sophomore year, it was hard to decide whether to major in English or Biological Sciences. I loved literature, reading and writing, but I was still as fascinated with the workings of the human body as I'd been while watching that gallbladder operation with Lance, so my dream of being a doctor wouldn't let me go, either. Biological Sciences won out. By the end of my junior year, in the spring of 1972, I was preparing for a summer at the Jackson Laboratory in Bar Harbor, Maine, a world-class genetics research facility whose summer program paired research scientists with promising college students from all over the country, giving the students a taste of what they could do with a more advanced degree in one of the life sciences.

On a lovely late-May afternoon, I strolled back to the dorm after my last exam, reveling in my freedom and dreamily wondering what my summer at the Jackson Lab would be like; its Mt. Desert Island location was reputed to be stunning. The sun warmed my face and the breeze lifted my hair. Everything on the beautifully landscaped campus was bright green and blooming. When I reached the dorm, a note with my name on it was tacked to the bulletin board behind the bells desk, the dorm's communications hub. "Call your father," the message read.

Frowning at the note's peremptory tone, I headed straight for one of the lobby's pay phones. My dad had never called me at college before. What followed was the longest conversation I'd ever had with him, on or off the phone.

"It's your mother," he began. My heart sped up.

"She had surgery yesterday and the results came back today." He paused. "Mom has cancer." Dad had never been one to mince words.

"Whaaaat?" I braced myself against the side of the phone booth.

"She's had this lump in her groin since Thanksgiving. I tried to get her to see a doctor about it, but she wouldn't go. She wanted to finish the school year first." I could hear the exasperation in his voice. My mother had started teaching first grade at Libertytown Elementary four years ago and got her teaching certificate two years later. She hated missing a day of class.

Her diagnosis was non-Hodgkin's lymphoma, a cancer of the lymph nodes and lymphatic system, a blood cancer related to leukemia. My usually taciturn dad rambled on about tumor staging, radiation, and chemotherapy, as if someone had flipped a switch. He could not stop talking, but it was all wasted on me. He'd lost me at "Mom has cancer." Eventually we said goodbye, awkwardly but earnestly exchanging I-love-you's. Those words between Dad and any of us kids had always been reserved for special occasions.

"Give my love to Mom." I hung up the phone in a daze and spent the rest of that night pacing the floor and packing up the contents of my dorm room.

• • •

Mr. Gantt deposited another tray of rat entrails for weighing in front of me. "You doing all right?" he asked with a smile. He didn't miss much.

"I'm fine." I smiled back.

This wasn't true, of course. Remembering how I'd heard about my mother's cancer diagnosis took me back further, to a late-winter afternoon when I was nine years old. Our father had sat us down in the living room—my older brother, my two sisters, and me—to tell us that he would be taking Mom to the hospital the next day, so she could have an operation to remove a "cyst." She'd been acting a little weird, wearing a preoccupied look and dropping occasional hints that there might be a new baby on the way. I'd been mystified by the whole thing, but I hadn't been worried until Dad mentioned the hospital. Besides wondering whether Mom would be okay, I was anxious to know how I'd get to Janet Bergsten's birthday party at the bowling alley that Saturday, which I'd been looking forward to with breathless excitement for weeks.

My father drove me to the party, of course, where I bowled with a vengeance and stuffed myself with cake. My mother's surgery ended up going fine, as our parents had assured us it would. An unusually large tumor had been removed from one of her ovaries. Years later, my father would tell us it was a teratoma, a bizarre but benign cystic mass containing strands of hair, teeth, and bits of bone.

While I meticulously logged that day's quota of rat-viscera

measurements into the ledger, my mind flashed back to my last few weeks at Wellesley, a year after my mother's diagnosis. In the midst of finishing my honors thesis, there'd been a couple of wonderful surprises: I was inducted into Phi Beta Kappa as well as Sigma Xi, the science honor society. My grades were good, but it hadn't occurred to me that I might make Phi Beta Kappa. I phoned my mom in the middle of the day, as soon as I got the letter in the campus mail.

"Phi Beta Kappa? Oh, sweetie, that's wonderful! I'm so proud of you!" It felt really good to give her something happy to think about while she was in the throes of radiation and chemotherapy.

A couple of weeks later, I packed up my dorm room for the last time. While boxing up books and papers, I felt a pang of apprehension tinged with nostalgia as I looked out the picture window into the lush dark boughs of a large evergreen tree. What would the next stage of my journey bring? The previous summer at the Jackson Lab had shown me that, exciting as research might be, I lacked the kind of innovative mind-set needed to make a career of it as my beloved Jackson Lab mentor, Dr. Elizabeth Russell, had done. My mother's serious illness had reinforced my desire to help people in a more direct and tangible way than research would permit, tipping the scales in favor of medicine, so I'd applied to medical school in the fall of my senior year. After a few nerve-wracking rejections, I was, to my great relief, accepted at my state school, the University of Maryland in Baltimore.

My mother traveled to Massachusetts from our Maryland home for my graduation, reclining in the back seat of the blue family station wagon with my father as her chauffeur, husbanding every ounce of strength she could salvage from the latest round of chemotherapy. She'd been a music major at Wellesley herself. Her studies had been interrupted by the exigencies of

World War II and resumed after the war's end; my brother attended her graduation ceremony in a baby carriage. My mom was inordinately proud of me, and of herself for having produced a daughter who'd surpassed her own academic achievements.

June 2, 1973, a lovely cloudless day, marked Wellesley College's ninety-fifth annual commencement. There's a haunting family photograph taken after the ceremony in which I'm standing under a tree, diploma in hand, beaming, though my face is in shadow. Dad is on my left, wearing a seersucker suit and bowtie and a severe military bearing. He and I are looking directly at the camera. Mom is on my right, dressed in a pale aqua suit. She looks unexpectedly solemn as she gazes at some distant point to the right of the camera, like she's looking at something the rest of us can't see.

After commencement, my mother and I attended a formal mother-daughter tea at the college president's home. When we got to the head of the receiving line, she clasped the woman's hand in both of hers and said, "I'm class of '44. And I'm so happy!" She smiled beatifically for what felt like minutes—one of the few times I'd ever seen her at a loss for words. Just when it was starting to get awkward, I prodded her gently to move on. The fact that she needed to walk with a cane because of her bone pain hadn't diminished her joy.

• • •

Helping Mr. Gantt tidy up the lab at the end of the day, I considered my upcoming transition. At a time when medical schools were still in the process of abolishing quotas for female students, coming from a small women's college like Wellesley might be a mixed blessing. On one hand, we Wellesley graduates had experienced the big-girl equivalent of what little girls were starting to hear more and more during the 1970s: you can be anything you want to be! We'd received an excellent education and had been taught, and expected, to think for ourselves—to be successful in our own right, not just appendages to high-achieving men. As graduates of a prestigious institution, the premedical students among us were well-positioned for acceptance into medical school. We'd been nurtured and supported by the faculty and each other, a far cry from the cutthroat competition we heard about at other schools, which meant—on the other hand—that we were sheltered, even pampered. Our campus was one of the loveliest in the country. We'd been watched over "in loco parentis"—unobtrusively, of course—by young house parents, with tea in the dorm on Friday afternoons and peppermint-fudge pie for dessert at least once a semester. We weren't accustomed to being patronized, overlooked, or treated with disdain. Would that change in medical school when most of our instructors and classmates would be men?

• • •

Dad and I got home from work to find Mom napping, Sarah reading, and Mary Alyce preparing dinner. I quickly changed into my bathing suit and swam several laps in our backyard above-ground pool, then sat down, rubber-limbed, with a gin and tonic to top off the exercise-induced endorphin boost. Soon the others joined me. Dad swam a few laps, Mom dog-paddled a bit, and my sisters splashed each other. There's a photograph from that summer which tugs at my heart even now. My father stands at the side of the pool in his navy swim trunks, his thinning, once-black hair now completely gray. My mother is on the ladder in a skirted bathing suit smaller than any she'd been able to wear since the early days of their marriage. She's smiling, but she's a pale shadow of her former self, her once-dark hair now a washed-out grayish brown.

● ● ●

My mother had a largely unhappy childhood, running interference between parents who were continually at odds. Her father, a clarinetist with unfulfilled symphonic aspirations, made her practice piano for at least an hour a day. This stood her in good stead once she started at Walnut Hill School as a day student. Her yearbook characterized her as "an outstanding member of the Glee Club and a talented pianist, whose playing at school occasions we have all greatly appreciated." The yearbook also described her as "conscientious and ambitious;" but once she got to Wellesley, where she again matriculated as a day student, she claimed to have gotten all Bs and Cs. She'd wanted to pursue a premedical curriculum; but her father, who paid the tuition, insisted she major in music. She continued choral singing until the last few years of her life, and she always maintained an uncanny ability to play an impromptu piece by Brahms or Mozart or Beethoven without a single mistake, while we kids listened in awe.

Mom was a devoted wife and mother. This is how she described her life in a Wellesley alumnae booklet, "Class of '44 in '64": "I read a great deal and make no apologies for not having a long list of accomplishments and activities. I'm doing the best job I know how to do with my family, and" with characteristic exuberance, she added, "—am as happy as it is possible to be in this life!"

But as we girls grew into adolescence, another side of our mother emerged. Though she scorned Betty Friedan's book, *The Feminine Mystique*, she started showing signs of what Friedan called "the problem that has no name." We came home from school one day to find the lazy Susan in two pieces on the dining table. Our mother admitted, with an air of guilty defiance, that she'd thrown it on the floor while dusting the dining room because she was fed up with housework that day. Fortunately, when I was a junior in high school she had an opportunity to teach kindergarten, which led to a position as a first-grade teacher. Four years later, the large lump removed from her groin at the end of the school year turned out to be lymphoma.

• • •

The first few weeks of the summer passed uneventfully for all of us. My sisters held down the home front, driving our mother to her appointments, taking her to the grocery store when she felt well enough to do the shopping and doing it for her when she didn't. My father and I continued to ride to work together, usually with a minimum of conversation. One morning, he turned to me and said, "You know, I'm afraid Mom's not going to make it."

"Dad! How can you say that? Of course, she's going to make it! You know what a fighter she is…" He shook his head.

A couple of weeks later—on Friday, July 13th —I had a piercing epiphany while assisting with rat autopsies: I knew in the most visceral and irrefutable way that my mother would die of her cancer, and soon. Mr. Gantt heard me sniffling in front of the scales as I weighed a rat liver.

"What's the matter? Did I say something to upset you?" His forehead creased.

"Oh, no, Mr. Gantt, it's not you. It's my mom." And I told him about my mother's cancer, how her oncologist said her treatment was taking her one step forward and two steps back, how I just knew she wouldn't live much longer. He shook his head.

"Aw, that's a real shame." He patted my hand. "Why don't you take a little break now?" I gratefully took him up on the offer, stepping outside the building for a breath of fresh air. If I'd been a smoker, I would've lit up.

One weekend afternoon as she lay on the sofa, my mother said in an offhand way, apropos of nothing, that she wanted us to read the poem "On Death" from Kahlil Gibran's *The Prophet* at her funeral. My sisters and I stared at her for a moment, then burst into a litany of denial: "Don't say that!" "You're not going to die!" As if to validate our protests, the twice-weekly trips to Hopkins continued uneventfully for a while. Throughout the course of her illness, she endured multiple rounds of chemotherapy with progressively more exotic and experimental agents, but radiation was the part she hated the most: moving this way, then that, was difficult because of her bone pain. She dubbed the radiation therapy unit, located in the bowels of the hospital, "the black hole of Calcutta."

One day in early August, while my father and I were at work, my mother became short of breath. At the direction of her Hopkins oncologist, Sarah drove her through unfamiliar streets to Baltimore City Hospital, a Hopkins affiliate east of the main hospital campus, for admission to an inpatient oncology unit. Despite all those months of radiation and chemotherapy, the cancerous lymph nodes in her chest had grown large enough to press on her airways and compromise her breathing.

By the end of August, when my mother had been in the hospital for almost a month, my father and Mary Alyce, who was starting her senior year of high school, were the only people residing at the Libertytown house. Sarah had left for her junior year at Simmons College in Boston, where she'd transferred after two years at Clark University in Worcester. At this difficult time in our family's life, she would find herself in a completely unfamiliar environment.

The Red Cross had flown our brother Phil back to Maryland

for "compassionate leave" from a ship in Pago Pago, where his army unit had been providing support services for a naval mission. He was reassigned to the army base at Aberdeen, which enabled him to spend several hours a week at Mom's hospital bedside. Phil, a history major in college, had gone into medicine mainly because of his interest in diseases of the eye. Though being an ophthalmologist didn't give him much expertise in oncology, he found himself in the difficult position of being the family's medical liaison.

Once our mother was hospitalized, my father made the 100-mile round trip between Frederick and Baltimore daily, managing to spend every weekday morning at work and every afternoon at her bedside.

As for me, I'd left the lab rats behind and embarked on a journey into utterly unfamiliar territory: starting medical school in Baltimore, living in a city for the first time in my life.

2

INCIPIT VITA NOVA

The place didn't look like much from the street. A three-story rowhouse of red-painted brick in need of repair, its marble front stoop—an iconic piece of Baltimore architecture—was its sole redeeming feature. My father and I gazed up at it with trepidation. Having grown up in suburban and rural areas, followed by four years of Wellesley's bucolic campus, I was overwhelmed by the prospect of living in a gritty city. Four years earlier, when I'd had an anxiety attack about leaving home for the first semester of college, my mother had concluded one of her shot-in-the-arm pep talks with a bright smile, saying, "Incipit vita nova—here beginneth a new life!" Her words were much more applicable that day in front of the row-house; but they were somehow more ironic than comforting now that she was in the hospital.

My room was on the third floor. Dad and I hauled my belongings up the narrow staircase: a small upholstered chair, the maple desk I'd received for Christmas when I was nine, a couple of suitcases, a few boxes of books, and my clothes—a collection of peasant blouses and bell-bottom jeans, plus a tweed wool skirt I'd made myself a few years earlier. The walls had recently been repainted a flat white. A scruffy brown shag carpet covered the floor. I'd recently purchased a bright-orange chenille bedspread on sale, with which I finished making the bed while my father fiddled with something at the desk near a window. "Here," he said, showing me the coil of rope in his hand. "Since there's no fire escape, you can use this if there's ever an emergency."

"Fire escape?" I walked to the window and looked down at the street. I'd never had to think about fire safety before.

"Here's what you do." He secured one end of the sturdy nylon rope to the desk leg closest to the window and tightened the stout knots he'd placed along it at one-foot intervals. "Just hang this out the window and climb down the knots. Hopefully you'll never need it."

I was touched by my engineer dad's practical thoughtfulness. He gave my new digs one last skeptical look as he walked to the door, headed for my mother's hospital bedside.

"You sure you're okay here?" Actually, I wasn't at all sure; but I was grateful he hadn't refused outright to let me move to 334 S. Stricker St. (Mom would have raised hell if she'd known about it.)

"Don't worry, I'm fine," I said shakily. "Tell Mom I'm okay."

Dad drove off in the blue Ford station wagon, leaving me to put my things away and settle into the place I would call home for the next several months. I stacked my medical textbooks on the desk and placed my microscope in its case on the floor. Classes would begin in a few days, and I was as ready as I would ever be—which is to say, not at all. Several things had conspired to throw me off balance besides Mom's hospitalization, including the last-minute scramble to find this apartment when it turned out I hadn't procured a place in the dorm after all. To add to my unease, my four housemates were all male, which exacerbated the culture shock of entering medical school from an all-women's college. Thankfully, two women lived a couple doors down in 330 S. Stricker, where our landlord lived. One of the women, Jane, was a first-year medical student like me; the other,

Sadie, was starting social work school. Bruce, the landlord, was an intern at University Hospital, and his sidekick Will—short for Willard—was a second-year medical student.

The first of my housemates to introduce himself was a physical therapy student whose room was across the landing from mine. We met when Dad was helping me move in. "Hi, I'm Andy," he'd said, with a warm smile and quick wave. Though he'd clearly been in a hurry when we first crossed paths, he would prove to be a cheerful and pleasant neighbor. Later that afternoon I met Tony, a pharmacy student from the room below mine, and Jack, a first-year social work student who occupied the other second-floor bedroom. As I walked through the living room with some things to put in the kitchen, Jack looked up from the couch where he and Tony were watching TV. "You must be the girl medical student," Jack said, with a noticeable Southern drawl. He rose and offered his hand with a smile. There was a twinkle in his eye, and he seemed genuinely pleased to meet me.

"She's a medical student?" Tony raised his eyebrows and drew back as if a bee had flown into his face.

"Of course, dummy! Bruce told us we were gettin' a girl med student, don't you remember? So, we need to mind our manners." Grinning, Jack clipped the back of Tony's head playfully with an open palm.

Tony looked flustered. "Oh, yeah, sorry, I forgot." Turning to me he said, "I'm Tony," and hesitantly offered his hand. Though I had to suppress an eyeroll at the term "girl medical student," it was hard not to laugh. They reminded me of *The Three Stooges* episodes I'd enjoyed as a kid.

The next day, the last of the merry band showed up—another first-year medical student, who was shoving a case of National Bohemian into the refrigerator when I met him.

"Howdy, classmate, I'm Charlie." He wiped his hand on his jeans and offered it to me for a hearty shake.

I tilted my head toward the fridge and smiled. "That should keep you going for a while."

Charlie laughed. "Yeah, I lived in a fraternity at College Park. Help yourself anytime."

"Thanks, I might take you up on that. And maybe we can study together sometime."

Adding to my discomfort on a more physical level was the stifling heat. The first night in my new home, I discovered that sleeping was nearly impossible on the third floor of a Baltimore row-house in August. My window fan barely made a dent in the hot, humid air during those last weeks of summer.

Then there was the strangeness of sharing a bathroom with four males. Located at the rear of the second floor, the tiny bathroom consisted of a toilet, a sink, and a metal shower-stall the size of a phone booth which proved to be a magnet for mold and soap-scum. The first few mornings, I made sure I was fully dressed for the day when entering and leaving the bathroom for a shower. But it was impossible to dry off completely in the steamy cubicle, especially when I could hardly turn around. After a week, I gave up and just wore my bathrobe, cinched tightly around my waist. Tampon disposal was another source of embarrassment in this living situation that was the antithesis of my Wellesley dorm.

And sharing a kitchen with a bunch of guys was a revelation. Within the first two weeks, the refrigerator filled up with ancient slices of pizza and more beer than I'd seen outside a liquor store. Days-old dishes piled up in the sink. At first, an occasional cockroach scurried across the floor; then, to my disgust, herds of them started running for cover over the sticky countertop. I was the only one who ever used the vacuum cleaner, and then only when I couldn't stand the dirt anymore.

My new home at 334 S. Stricker St. was the third rowhouse from the end. It overlooked Carroll Park, the Mount Clare Mansion—Baltimore City's oldest colonial-era structure— and a big white Montgomery Ward distribution center to the south. This was the Mount Clare neighborhood of Southwest Baltimore, an area that in 1973 was predominantly made up of white working-class families. The house fronts were brick or, more often, Formstone, a type of stucco manufactured locally and dubbed by Baltimore filmmaker John Waters "the polyester of brick." Even though there was litter in the gutters and some of the sidewalks buckled, most of the marble stoops gleamed from frequent washing. Children shouted at play and grownups shouted in anger. Televisions blared through screened front doors in those first warm weeks, accompanied by the dinnertime fragrance of frying onions. Many of the street corners featured a bar serving cheap beer and what was then known as "country and Western" music.

Occasionally a Black man drove a horse and cart down the street, calling, "Rags!" A few days a month, a different Black man with a similar cart, known as an "Arabber," would hawk his fruits and vegetables as if this were 1873 instead of a century later. Those old horse-drawn carts were a striking contrast to the hulking late-'60s sedans parked curbside.

An elderly Polish lady lived in the row-house next to ours. Every Sunday afternoon she played polka records, filling our end of the street with a kind of lost-world gaiety. She took a great interest in me, even though she spoke very little English and I spoke no Polish. As we became better acquainted, I told her about the challenges and struggles of medical school and my mother's illness. It was a little like talking to someone in a coma;

there's a kind of freedom you experience when you know they can't talk back. I was never sure how much she understood, but she certainly responded to my tone of voice and nonverbal cues. It was a comfort, receiving the nods and smiles and sympathetic looks of this unlikely yet motherly confidante.

· · ·

It was roughly a mile and a half from our end of S. Stricker St. to Howard Hall, the lecture hall where I spent most of the day for the first two years of medical school. When the weather was too cold or rainy, I took the city bus to the campus or caught a ride with someone, but most of the time it was a pleasant walk. Proceeding east along Lombard Street, I'd pass Union Square Park. Though the park itself was run-down, the neighborhood, where some of my classmates lived, was a lot nicer than S. Stricker St. Howard Hall itself was an unassuming early-1960s building behind the hospital, close to the campus's western boundary.

For the third and fourth years of my studies, the clinical years, University Hospital would become my home away from home. The hospital backed up to Penn St. and Howard Hall and faced Greene St., which was one-way southbound and the principal route of egress from that part of the city. Much of my world for those four years was contained between Penn St. and Paca St., Greene St.'s northbound neighbor. Just to the north of the campus was Lexington Market, a large, bustling venue for produce, meat, and seafood and one of the oldest continuously operating markets in the United States. I did some grocery shopping there, and my classmates and I sometimes went there for lunch. Somewhere along Pratt St., not far from campus, the McCormick spice factory released its marvelous aromas into the urban air. When the wind was right, the scent of cinnamon or clove lifted my spirits. At the corner of Fayette and

Greene Streets was Westminster Hall, formerly First Presbyterian Church, whose churchyard holds the remains of Edgar Allan Poe and other historical figures. Occasionally, I ate lunch there on warm days, alone or with a friend or two.

Exploring the city on foot on my way home from class, I was intrigued by its numerous old buildings and monuments. Within three blocks of Howard Hall stood the fifteen-story Bromo-Seltzer Tower, Baltimore's first skyscraper and an iconic landmark since 1915. One weekend I trekked up to the historic Mount Vernon neighborhood to take in the city's own Washington Monument, a giant Doric column with a staircase inside and an excellent view of the city from the top. Later I discovered that, though much of the downtown area had to be rebuilt after the Great Baltimore Fire of 1904, the city has more properties listed in the National Registry of Historic Places than any other city in the U.S. and more public monuments per capita than any other city in the country.

Early in the first semester, one of the anatomy professors gave my classmates and me a tour of Davidge Hall—a national historic landmark on the medical school campus and the oldest building in continuous use for medical education in the country—providing us with the historical background of the institution that would teach us the practice of medicine.

"The University of Maryland Medical School is the fifth oldest institution for medical education in the United States," the professor began. "It started out as a group of men in the early 1800s meeting secretly for lectures in John Beale Davidge's living room—a lot like the early days of the Christian church during the time of persecution by the Romans. Dissecting cadavers was forbidden, even though it was critical for learning about the human body. People could be beaten up, have their houses burnt down, even killed.

"At the end of 1807, the Maryland legislature conferred some legitimacy on these intrepid medical pioneers by establishing the College of Medicine of Maryland, a private institution for training physicians. Five years later, in 1812, the state re-chartered the school as the University of Maryland and authorized it to, as the statute says, 'constitute, support, and annex to itself faculties of divinity, law, and arts & sciences.'

"So, it became not only the nation's first public medical school, but the first university in America to be founded with a medical school at its educational core. Then Davidge Hall opened its doors to medical students, and here we are." I was impressed. I'd had no idea my school had such an illustrious past.

• • •

Before the official start of classes, there was an orientation program for a couple of evenings at the end of August. Not knowing what to expect, I donned a jacket over a blouse and dressy slacks for the first session. I was one of the first people to show up. Soon I was joined by a trim, compact guy with fine features, a neatly barbered black beard, and merry brown eyes. After we exchanged introductions, Eric asked, "Where'd you go to college?"

"Wellesley College in Massachusetts," I answered. Our class boasted graduates from several prestigious institutions, including Harvard, Princeton, Cornell, and Stanford; but most were from Maryland schools, especially the University of Maryland at College Park. I'd learned that most Marylanders required some indication of where Wellesley was, and many confused it with Wesleyan. To my pleasant surprise, Eric, a Vanderbilt graduate, said, "Wow! One of the Seven Sisters. Good for you."

We sat together for the rest of the orientation. Eric entertained me with anecdotes about the hospital and the university's

Baltimore campus, since his father was on the faculty. He knew his way around in a way that few of our classmates did, so his friendship was a great help during those first bewildering weeks. He had a dry, mordant wit, though he could belly-laugh with the best of them. He was also proficient at smoking weed, which—unlike many of my peers—I'd only tried a few times in college. And he introduced me to *Firesign Theater*, a West Coast comedy troupe that specialized in surreal satire. Their early-'70s radio show did for that medium what *Saturday Night Live!* would do for television a few years later.

It turned out that Eric, like me, had signed up for the Pediatric Tracking Program, an enrichment program for students considering pediatrics as a specialty. Once every week or two we met on the fifth floor of the hospital, where one of the attending physicians would demonstrate a physical finding on a child—a rash or a heart murmur, for example—and then lead a discussion of what we'd seen or heard. From this we would learn a bit of physical diagnosis and pediatric medicine, but we'd also learn how to relate to younger patients and what went into the making of a good pediatrician.

It was our first foray onto the pediatric ward, in the early days of medical school. We were all relatively dressed up, meaning there were no jeans or T-shirts, and we wore white coats with stethoscopes in our pockets. Eric gave me a quizzical look as we gathered outside the room of our small patient of the day.

"Are you an attending now?" he asked, with a little smile. When I looked confused, he said, "Attending doctors wear long coats; we're supposed to wear these short jackets." He indicated the difference in our hemlines with a gesture.

"Damn!" The color rose in my cheeks. On my first expensive trip to the university bookstore, I'd grabbed the first white coat I saw. The list of needed supplies had said only "white coat" without any indication of different lengths related to the medical pecking-order. I sighed as I contemplated returning to the bookstore, hoping the short white jackets wouldn't be sold out.

Throughout that first semester, we spent four afternoons a week wearing a different sort of white coat, one made of heavyweight material that covered as much of our clothing as possible, to protect us from globs of fat and bodily fluids—a coat that was kept in a separate locker in the Gross Anatomy lab. As it had been for our forebears at the turn of the 19th century, the dissection of the cadaver was at the heart of the first-year medical school curriculum.

Over the course of the next few months, we took a few deceased human bodies apart, limb from limb, in order to understand how all human bodies are put together. Yet some things had changed in the century and a half since the gross anatomy course had first convened in John Beale Davidge's living room. To our faculty's credit, the consciousness movements of the 1960s had given medical educators a greater awareness of the emotional and psychological significance of unveiling the cadaver. We had an entire class period dedicated to preparation for this event, culminating in assurances that there were people we could talk to if we found the process unduly disturbing.

With my mother lying in an oncology ward on the other side of town, my only thought throughout this drawn-out preparatory session was, "Please, don't let our cadaver be a white female."

We waited for the big moment, sitting on stools at steel tables bearing the indistinct draped forms of cadavers. I tried not to breathe too deeply. The formaldehyde odor—a smell like vinegar but much stronger, and without vinegar's redeeming vegetal note—was overwhelming, a smell that would permeate my clothes, skin, and hair for the next eighteen weeks.

Finally, it was time to remove the drape from our cadaver. One of my table mates did the honors and, sure enough, it was a white female.

I turned away. Once I'd collected myself, I could see that our cadaver, our principal teacher of gross anatomy, was older than my mother. Neither skeletal nor obese, she bore the redundant flesh of late middle age. There was nothing especially unusual about her. It wasn't obvious what had led to her demise, and I don't think we ever found out. We were to start our dissection with the muscles of the back. The face would remain covered for a few more sessions, to ease us gradually into this stark confrontation with mortality.

I looked around the table at the four other women comprising my cadaver group, the only all-woman group in the class, knowing that, at some point, I would have to tell them about my mother. There's a picture in the yearbook of four of us working on our dissection, with another female student looking on. I'm the tall one with crossed arms and a ponytail; the acne I'd struggled with throughout college is still evident.

A few days later it was time to uncover the cadaver's head and reveal her face. As disturbing as it was to be confronted with the visage of this erstwhile person who wasn't my mother but could have been, I was glad I wasn't part of the group whose table held the twenty-two-year-old white male cadaver, the same age as many of us. He was a slender young man with a few days' beard growth and no discernible signs of illness. How had he died? There was no evidence of wounding by bullet or knife; the arteries in his wrists were intact. His was probably a chemical death, most likely a drug overdose, perhaps a suicide. There was a drawn look on his face, as of some anguish that months of preparation in formaldehyde hadn't been able to eradicate. There was something magnetic about this dead young man. We would file past him, singly or in groups, and gaze at him like mourners in a funeral home. His table happened to be close to the door, so it was hard to miss him when leaving for a fresh-air break, or, for those so inclined—and there were many at that time—a cigarette break.

· · ·

Shortly after I started classes, my mother was discharged home for Labor Day weekend as a trial run to see if her recent modest improvement would hold. When I called her from the communal telephone in the Stricker St. living room, it took several minutes for her to pick up the receiver after Dad answered. It was painful to hear the laborious tapping of her cane on the floor in the background. I wasn't surprised when Dad called on Tuesday to say she'd been readmitted to the hospital.

For the rest of September, Dad picked me up a couple of evenings a week to visit my mother on the oncology ward. Mary Alyce joined us on weekend days. I always brought my textbooks—biochemistry, anatomy, histology—though I didn't usually get much studying done. When my sister was there, we sat with Mom together, chatting with her about high school and medical school as though we were sitting around the kitchen table at home.

One day I took a city bus to the hospital by myself. Suddenly, I was overcome by the realization I'd had earlier in the summer, that my mother couldn't go on like this much longer. Her cheerful, no-worries attitude of early August had given way to a forced gaiety mixed with querulousness; there were times when her attention wandered and she couldn't seem to concentrate on our conversation. Flashes of deep anger and despair broke through her façade with increasing frequency. We later found out she'd told a Roman Catholic chaplain on a well-meaning pastoral visit to "go fuck yourself."

Hunched in the cracked leather seat of the bus, my chest tight with fear and grief, I wondered if I should take a leave of absence from medical school or even drop out altogether, so I could spend every possible moment with my mother. But reason prevailed. I knew how much she wanted this, for me and for her. It wouldn't make sense to abandon the dream now. Fighting back tears as I looked out the bus window, I realized that no amount of time spent with her now could make up for the time I would soon have to spend without her.

3

SETTLING IN

By the third week of school, I'd settled into the routine: lectures all morning, several hours of Gross Anatomy lab four afternoons a week, Physical Diagnosis every Friday afternoon, an hour or two on the pediatric ward twice a month, and as much evening studying as I could manage.

The first two years of medical school, the preclinical years, were a time of book learning: anatomy, embryology, histology, biochemistry, physiology, pathology, microbiology, pharmacology. In our first-semester biochemistry lectures, we learned about the compounds, like DNA and proteins, that make up our cells. In the histology lab, we gazed for hours through our microscopes at the cells that comprise the body's tissues and organs. Dissecting our cadavers in the anatomy lab taught us about those organs and tissues on a macro level. Though we'd have to wait for the clinical years to begin applying all this knowledge, we started working with patients the first week of classes.

Physical Diagnosis, aka P.D., was our formal introduction to clinical medicine. In P.D. class, we learned how to take a patient's history and perform a physical examination. We were divided into groups of four and assigned to an attending physician, a member of the medical school faculty who provided us with patients to interview and examine, after which we'd discuss our findings. The other members of my P.D. group were fellow

Pediatric Trackers. The four of us dressed the part of those at the bottom of the medical food chain, wearing short white jackets over our street clothes.

On our first day of P.D. we milled around in front of the nurses' desk on one of the internal medicine wards, chatting nervously as we waited for our attending, a cardiologist named Dr. Silverman who was known for his obsession with heart murmurs. Finally, the good doctor blew in, his long white coat flapping in the breeze created by his rapid pace. For a moment it looked like the stethoscope draped around his neck might fly off. He stopped abruptly in front of the desk, paused as if for a round of applause, then rubbed his hands together like a man about to consume a good meal. I exchanged raised eyebrows with one of my classmates.

"Well, ladies and gentlemen, I've got some good cases for you today," the doctor said with a smile. He assigned each of us to a room and we dispersed. I entered Room 703 with my heart pounding and mind racing, like an actor about to take the stage for the first time in her life. Theoretically, I knew how to take a medical history, and I had the laminated cheat-sheet we were allowed to carry for the first few weeks. We'd also been taught how to do a complete physical exam, but the classroom demonstration hadn't prepared me for actually laying hands on a patient. I clutched my physical diagnosis handbook, the size of my old Catholic missal, like a talisman.

My patient, Mr. H., was an elderly white man whose skin was an unappealing fishy-pale color. (When I noted this, pediatrics seemed like a really good specialty choice.) He was a 69-year-old retired steelworker who'd been admitted to the hospital several times in the previous six months. When I introduced myself as a "student doctor," as we'd been instructed to call ourselves, he shook his head. "They're letting girls into medical school now? Great." I stifled a sigh and got to work. We began with his medical history. Besides the shortness of breath and fatigue that had led to his current hospitalization, I had to elicit information about other problems unrelated to his presenting symptoms, known as the "review of systems." In Mr. H.'s case, the review of systems was extensive and his delivery was rambling.

Finally, we got to the physical examination. I placed my stethoscope on his chest and listened to his heart and lungs, then palpated his abdomen for any enlargement of the liver and spleen or lumps that weren't supposed to be there. He grunted as I pressed on his belly. I checked the appearance of his neck veins, which didn't look distended. When it was time to feel his pulses, I carefully felt the ones in his neck, wrists, arms, and feet, but hesitated at the femoral pulses, the ones in his groin. It wasn't just because he was old, saggy, and wrinkled. It felt like an invasion of his privacy to place my hands so close to his genitals, especially after he'd made it so clear that he wasn't thrilled about being examined by a *female* "student doctor." *What am I going to do when I actually have to examine these old guys' genitalia?* I asked myself. *Guess I'll cross that bridge when I come to it.* In that moment I just couldn't go there, so I pocketed my stethoscope and skulked out of Mr. H.'s room to rejoin the others in the conference room.

Dr. Silverman leaned forward eagerly, his hands folded on the table. "So, what have we got?" he asked, piercing each of us in turn with his laser-like gaze.

Art, a quiet guy with a Prince Valiant haircut and a quirky sense of humor, went first. He was chewed out for missing some crackling sounds at the lowest part of his patient's lung fields— sounds the rest of us couldn't hear either, when the time came for all of us to check each other's patients under Dr. S.'s supervision. Angela, a petite, feisty woman from an Italian neighborhood in East Baltimore, received kudos for her thoroughness; but Silverman shot down her interpretation of her patient's heart murmur. Rob, a guy with movie-star good looks who was both smart and nice, didn't make any major gaffes, but he had to be prodded a couple of times for more detail about his patient's history.

Now it was my turn. I plodded through the history, knowing there was too much detail but not knowing what to do about it. I'd finished describing the physical findings and was ready to take a crack at explaining Mr. H.'s heart murmur when Silverman held up his hand.

"Wait a minute. You haven't told me about the femoral pulses."

My cheeks burned. "Um, I didn't check the femoral pulses," I murmured.

"You didn't check them?! That's completely unacceptable! What if that man's murmur is due to heart failure from a coarctation of the aorta? *You* would never know that, because *you* didn't check his femoral pulses!" He jabbed his index finger at me, his black eyes boring into mine. I hung my head and wished I could make myself invisible.

Dr. Silverman marched us all to my patient's room first. He felt the pulses in Mr. H.'s groin, then turned to me with an insincere, cloying smile. "Here, Dr. White, you feel these first."

The pulses seemed a little weak, but they were definitely there, so—no coarctation, thank god. No narrowing of the aorta that would strain Mr. H.'s heart and compromise blood flow to the rest of his body. Once we'd left the patient's room, Silverman said, "Fortunately for you, if you were the resident taking care of Mr. H., you would *not* have missed a critical physical finding and failed to do the imaging studies that would have allowed an accurate diagnosis and appropriate surgical intervention."

I would never skip anybody's femoral pulses again.

• • •

While anatomy lab and Physical Diagnosis were intimidating and sometimes unpleasant, life was by no means all work and no play. Free beer was available in the basement of the Student Union every Friday afternoon, something I looked forward to as a way to unwind after the stress of P.D. with Dr. Silverman. Art and I enthusiastically availed ourselves of this amenity every week, commiserating about our hard-ass attending. Over a few beers, I learned that Art had grown up on a farm and continued to deliver honey from the family's beehives in his pickup truck, a welcome change of pace from medical school.

Meanwhile, Eric, my friend from orientation, had instituted a weekly Tuesday-night get-together at the Campus Inn, a watering hole at the southeast corner of the medical school campus and a short walk from the Student Union. I became a regular at this gathering, along with some of Eric's undergrad friends and classmates from his P.D. group. We shared pitchers of beer and shot the breeze, exchanging gossip and complaints about our studies. A couple of the second-year students provided us first-years with timely tips and advice on how best to allocate our study time, including what items we were more and less likely to be tested on.

Besides Tuesday nights at the Campus Inn, Eric broke up the monotony of the medical school routine with an occasional hospital-cafeteria lunch with an assortment of people he knew as the son of a faculty physician. One day he introduced me to a professor he particularly admired, a man I recognized from one of our biochemistry lectures. Eric had told me a little about the professor before we met him for lunch that day.

"You really need to meet this guy. I know you'll like him," he'd said. "The baskets of his inbox are labeled 'In,' 'Out,' and 'Far Out.'" I laughed.

Dr. Hayward was the head of neuroscience research at the university. According to Eric, he also had wide-ranging interests outside of medicine, including jazz, theater, philosophy, and politics. He was an African American man in his early 40s, recently separated from his wife. While not particularly tall or large, he had an imposing physical presence, partly due to his strong jaw and impressive Afro; but it was his youthful energy and charisma that intrigued me.

At the first of these cafeteria lunches, Eric and I were accompanied by a handful of others from our class. One of my female classmates said, "I'd rather be interviewed by a man than a woman, so I can, you know, use my feminine wiles." She batted her eyes at Dr. Hayward. I had an uncomfortable flashback to my own medical school interview the previous fall with a microbiology professor whose eyes kept shifting from my face to my legs. Had I worn that short skirt with the unconscious intention of showing off my own feminine charms?

"Wait a minute," I said. "I don't think we should flaunt our 'feminine wiles' in a work situation. It seems, well, exploitative, of men *and* women." So far, my own default mode in medical school had been to play down my femaleness as much as possible—trying, however ineptly, to be one of the guys.

"Oh, really?" Dr. Hayward cocked an eyebrow at me. "Who appointed *you* arbiter of workplace interaction between the sexes? People are attracted to each other in the workplace all the time. Is it really so bad for them to be open about it?"

I wondered if he'd heard about my interview with the microbiology professor. What he said gave me pause: just how *was* I supposed to act around men in this male-dominated medical school world, anyway? Were my attempts at camouflage unwarranted, even unnecessary? This wasn't an academic question. I wanted to be more than friends with my constant companion, Eric; but my attempts to get him to ask me out were repeatedly rebuffed, and I was discouraged.

My femininity felt threatened enough in medical school without the conundrum of relationships, or the lack thereof, with male classmates. That very week, the emphysematous, chain-smoking head of the anatomy department had slipped a slide of a Playboy Bunny into his lecture, the first of several such episodes. Jane, my Stricker St. neighbor and anatomy-lab partner, met my shocked look with one of her own. "What the hell?!" I whispered.

"This is supposed to be medical school, not a college fraternity," she hissed through clenched teeth. I couldn't concentrate after that.

From the first day of class, I'd had the distinct impression that many of our male professors (and they were almost all male during the preclinical years) were uncomfortable having women on the team. These older men didn't seem to know what to do with the 27 women in our class of 169 souls—roughly 16% of first-year students—so they ignored us altogether, referred to the entire class as "men," or patronized us. If you wanted to make an impression as a female student, it wasn't enough to ace the quizzes and tests. You had to be perpetually ready to give the correct answer in anatomy lab, histology lab, or physical diagnosis class. You had to be better than your male classmates just to be considered as good. You had to prove, on a daily basis, that you had just as much of a right to be there as they had.

Though my classmates seemed more comfortable with us women than the professors did, I often felt like a girl invading the boys' treehouse. There were the jokes, the raunchy talk that you might expect guys to lapse into when women weren't around, which we were sometimes exposed to because we were their classmates. Most of this stuff wasn't deeply offensive, but it *was* awkward. I usually laughed along with the guys, even when it made me uncomfortable. Trying to be one of the boys seemed safer than letting them know how excluded and out of place I felt.

Sometimes our male classmates seemed to regard us—especially the more attractive, outgoing women—as mascots. Not like a sports team's good luck charm—more like *mascotas*, the Spanish word for *pets*. Many of the guys were genuinely rooting for us, and I wouldn't have been able to get through medical school without the friendships I developed with some of them. But I sensed that, underneath the camaraderie, a lot of them were really thinking, "She's pretty smart—*for a girl.*"

Occasionally, an older man, a professor or attending physician, would communicate a similar condescension, as if to say, "Look at her, studying to become a doctor—isn't she cute!" But our superiors were more likely to convey, usually indirectly but occasionally with painful bluntness, that any woman medical student was depriving a deserving male of a spot in medical school—because, of course, everyone knew that a woman would eventually leave the profession to have children.

Plus—and this really hurt—most of my male classmates, like Eric, weren't interested in dating a fellow medical student. Besides being the colleagues I would train with and perhaps swap referrals with later on, I assumed that the guys I studied with in medical school and would later work with in residency would constitute a major part of the pool of men from which I would one day select my life-partner. My classmates' lack of eligibility was very disheartening.

On the female front, I took comfort in a growing closeness with Jane and Sadie, my Stricker St. neighbors from two doors down. We got together for coffee in the kitchen at 334 shortly after school started. I hastily cleared a couple of empty beer cans off the discolored Formica kitchen table and set out milk, sugar, mugs, and spoons. Jane and Sadie pulled up a couple of chairs, scraping the linoleum with a piercing squeak. I filled our mugs from the battered coffee pot and sat down.

"So, Sadie, how do you like social work school?" Jane began, turning her intense gaze on her housemate. Her eyes were a vivid blue, not unlike those of a Siamese cat.

Sadie's face lit up. "I'm really psyched! I love it already," she said. Her long-lashed brown eyes sparkled. "I'm so impressed that you guys are in medical school," she added. "It must be really tough."

I sipped my coffee. Jane nodded and said, "Yeah, it's pretty weird being so outnumbered by men. And, Kay, you came from an all-women's college, right?" A lock of thick chestnut hair fell over her shoulder as she leaned toward me.

"Yup. Wellesley," I said. "It's pretty surreal, going from no men in class to almost all men. Can't wear my holey chemistry-lab T-shirts around here."

Sadie's dark curls shook as she laughed. "Omigod, talk about culture shock!"

I laughed too. "Oh yeah. We used to see guys pretty much just on weekends, on dates or at mixers. Hanging out with them in class every day? *Big* change." I shook my head.

Jane crossed her arms and nodded. She'd graduated from

a large Midwestern university. "I'll bet. That's one good thing about a coed school—it prepares you to hold your own with the guys."

"It'll take me a while to get the hang of that," I said wryly.

My new friends were a study in contrasts. Jane was slender and fair, clad in blue chambray work-shirts and bell-bottom jeans most of the time. Sadie was about Jane's height, but she was gently rounded and buxom; she often wore brightly embroidered peasant blouses over her jeans. While Jane seemed guarded and watchful, laughter came easily to Sadie. Jane and I had bonded as anatomy lab partners. Sadie and Jane had grown closer while presenting a united front to their housemates Bruce and Will, who were at least as serious about their Jaguars as they were about medicine. Complaining about the guys' car fixation while we drank our coffee, Sadie said, "Bruce and Will and their penis-cars! We can't eat dinner at the kitchen table, because they're always using it to dismantle their engines. Grease and car parts everywhere."

On the nights when I didn't attempt to study in my mother's hospital room, I went to Jane and Sadie's to work for a few hours. We usually settled in Jane's room, sprawled out on the floor or on one of her Scan chairs, which, with the bright Marimekko sheets on the often-unmade bed, offered a stark contrast to the room's dingy walls and shabby dark-blue carpet. At some point, Jane would close her textbook with a decisive *thunk*, signifying that study time was over. We'd take our shoes off and scooch ourselves into a cross-legged circle on the floor. While Jane lit a candle and rolled a joint, Sadie or I would rip open a bag of chips or a package of cookies. A profound, pot-fueled discussion would ensue.

We covered the indignities Jane and I faced in class; the time Bruce told Jane, when Sadie commiserated with her about a difficult biochemistry test, that she should have gone to nursing school; the slovenliness of the guys at 334; and my thwarted attempts to interest Eric in dating me. This was 1973, when Freud ruled, the "talking cure" was still the mainstay of psychiatry, and psychopharmacology wasn't yet a discipline in its own right. Besides being ardent feminists, the three of us were highly introspective and analytical, and we would eventually bring that mix to bear on every conceivable relationship any of us had—with other friends and even with each other, but especially with men.

• • •

By this time, I'd told all the women in my anatomy group that my mother was seriously ill; but Eric, Jane, and Sadie were the only friends who knew just how bad things were. By the beginning of October, I was spending a couple of evenings a week and most weekend days trying to study on the oncology ward, where Mom's condition was inexorably worsening. One evening I took the city bus to visit her. Stepping out of the elevator onto the oncology floor, the lights always seemed a little dimmer, the walls a little grayer. Except for the muted beeps of IV pumps, there was an ominous hush about this part of the hospital. Only once had I seen that quiet disrupted, when a doctor and nurse ran wordlessly with a code cart to one of the rooms.

On this particular night, I found my mother propped up in her bed, which had been adjusted for maximal comfort— the head of the bed raised, the area under her knees elevated. Compared with the last time I'd seen her, her skin was paler, with a new yellow undertone. The circles under her eyes were darker, and she looked smaller against the pillows. A couple of new bruises bloomed on her arms, from blood draws or IV sticks.

"Hi, Mom, how are you feeling?"

"Not too bad, sweetie. Not great, either," she said wryly.

"How's school?"

"A couple of quizzes this week, but nothing too strenuous. We have a histology test coming up that I need to study for." I drew the textbook out of my bag. "There are an awful lot of slides to look at under the microscope, but they tell us it's nothing compared to what pathology will be like next year."

"It must be exciting to look at things under the microscope." She smiled wistfully. "I'm sure you'll do fine on the test."

Over the next few days, our mother became weak enough that my siblings and I had to take turns sitting at her bedside when we visited. She no longer talked much, and she couldn't carry on a conversation with more than one of us at a time. The doctors didn't enter her room as often as they used to. One Saturday morning, they discussed her case outside her door after they'd examined her—which, I would learn during the clinical years of medical school, was an ominous sign.

Mom rallied when her oncology team brought up the possibility of a bone-marrow transplant. Our uncle Walter, her only sibling, flew in from Massachusetts to be tested as a possible donor. The procedure of bone-marrow transplantation, now an established treatment for certain blood cancers and even some other tumors, was in its infancy in 1973. It wasn't available anywhere on the East Coast at that time, not even at Johns Hopkins. Mom would have to be transported to Seattle if she were a candidate. Weak as she was, the prospect of being flown across the country for an experimental procedure didn't deter her in the slightest. She would have done anything to get well.

Unfortunately, Uncle Walt wasn't a match.

4

DRINKING FROM THE RIVER OF SILENCE

On the short walk from my house to Jane and Sadie's, I raised my collar and dug my hands deep into my pockets against the cold October wind. My father had just dropped me off after another evening at my mom's bedside. I was tired, but I wanted some companionship as well as respite from the gloom and sadness of that hospital room. Bruce, our landlord, was hosting a party that night. Perhaps the warmth and noise would cheer me up.

"Here, Kay, have some punch!" Bruce said, as he handed me a plastic cup filled with a bright red concoction. He was uncharacteristically genial and clearly drunk. I took a gulp and promptly regretted it. Jane saw the look on my face and grinned.

"What's the matter, Kay? Too strong for you?"

"Bleah! What's *in* this stuff, anyway?"

"Just 95% ethyl alcohol and Hawaiian punch," she said with a smirk.

"Christ! Like the alcohol you get in the drugstore for cuts and stuff?"

Jane laughed. "Yup. Bruce and Will got some in bulk from a lab. They're really impressed with themselves." I shook my head vigorously and put the cup down on the nearest available surface.

"What's going on? You look down," Jane said. We retreated

to the kitchen, where I filled her in on the last ten days or so of my family's life, starting with the Wednesday night we'd stayed at the hospital until after 3 a.m. I'd sat with Dad and Phil at Mom's bedside while she drifted in and out of consciousness. Dad left the room to call Mary Alyce to tell her he might not be home that night. Then he called Sarah at her Boston dorm, telling her she needed to get home as soon as she could, because the latest scans indicated that the cancer had metastasized to Mom's lungs and kidneys.

After our father returned, the on-call resident took us aside. "Look," he said. "I've been through this with my own father, and I know what it's like." Looking straight at my dad, he added, "I think there's a good chance your wife is going to die tonight. If I were you, I'd plan on staying over." Dad made no sound, but his eyes filled with tears. He nodded in reply. We didn't stay the entire night. Perhaps because he knew I had a test the next day, Dad had dropped me off a couple of hours before dawn. I took the test after three hours' sleep and slogged through anatomy lab that afternoon.

While I toiled through another day of medical school, my sister Sarah flew in from Boston. Dad took her straight from the airport to the hospital, where she found our mother to be tremulous and terribly bloated, yet more alert than she'd been the previous night. Mom acknowledged my sister, but she couldn't talk much.

Sarah had used the weekend wedding of a high school friend to explain her sudden midweek appearance to Mom. Even at this late stage, there was a kind of code of silence, like the Mafia's *omerta*, around our mother's terminal illness. The fact that Mom was clearly dying could not be spoken of. To do so, to break the family conspiracy of denial, would be to admit defeat, to allow death to win. Our mother, even as she faded in and out of consciousness, was as complicit in this conspiracy as any of us. She didn't question Sarah's story.

A couple of evenings later, Mary Alyce and I were alone in the room with Mom when she started having Cheyne-Stokes respirations—a breathing pattern consisting of a few deep, rapid breaths followed by a pause, sometimes a very *long* pause. It's one of the ways in which the body gives notice that death is not far off, even though it could still be days or even a week or two away. When Mom first started breathing this way, I sent Mary Alyce for the nurse, not yet understanding what was happening and not wanting my little sister to be alone with my mother if her breathing should stop altogether.

The following Wednesday, a week after the resident had advised us to spend the night at the hospital, the doctors decided the abnormalities they'd seen on my mother's lung and kidney scans were not metastases after all, but "just" fluid. Even though she was still semiconscious, breathing irregularly, and grotesquely swollen despite their use of strong diuretics, Dad misconstrued the doctors' statement to mean that she was getting better. Seizing on this tiny grain of hope, he called Sarah to tell her that Mom was in remission.

Now, three nights later, on October 20th, I was talking quietly with Jane in the noisy row-house, refraining from any further contact with Bruce's potent brew. Since Sarah's visit, I'd had another week of lectures and quizzes and anatomy lab and Physical Diagnosis, another week of wishing Eric would ask me out, and another Saturday night of holding Mom's hand as I sat at her bedside. She was now completely unresponsive, and her Cheyne-Stokes respirations were continuous. Dad had tried to summon Sarah home again, but he couldn't reach her at her college dorm. Phil accompanied Dad and Mary Alyce to the house in Libertytown that night instead of returning to his quarters in Aberdeen.

"It can't be long now," I told Jane.

"I'm really sorry, Kay," she said as she squeezed my hand.

On Sunday, October 21st, the phone rang in the living room at 334, sometime between 8 and 9 a.m. I put on my yellow bathrobe, a gift from my mother the previous Christmas, and stumbled down two flights of stairs to answer it. Dad was on the other end. He said, simply and with no preamble or inflection, "Mom's dead."

I looked out the window, the telephone receiver still in my hand. It was a beautiful autumn day, cool and crisp, with a cloudless, deep-blue sky. As I numbly started packing for the funeral, I turned the radio on, to Bob Dylan's sadly appropriate "Knockin' on Heaven's Door." I realized I didn't have anything to wear to a funeral, especially my mother's. The closest thing I had to a black dress was a navy skirt—too short, but the best I could do. Before long, Dad, Phil and Mary Alyce pulled up in the blue station wagon, bringing with them the clothes Mom would be buried in—the same aqua knit suit she'd worn a few months earlier at my graduation.

When we went to the hospital so Dad could sign the papers to release her body, the attending oncologist showed us a piece of notebook paper on which our mother had written in pencil, "I wish to donate my body to science." She had not discussed this with anyone—not my father or my brother, and not her oncologist—so it was unclear what her words actually meant. "Do you think she wanted to donate her remains to the State Anatomy Board?" the doctor asked.

I turned on my heel and retreated to the nearest corner.

Resting my forehead against the wall, I broke down completely. I tried not to sob too loudly as I fought off the mental picture of my mother as a cadaver in the gross anatomy lab.

I knew I would never have to see that, even if I failed the course and had to repeat it, since the process of preparing a cadaver took many months. But it was a horribly surreal prospect just the same. Once I'd composed myself and rejoined the others, I gladly endorsed the consensus that an autopsy would be enough to fulfill my mother's wishes.

After leaving the hospital, we stopped at Phil's house in Aberdeen to pick up his clothing for the funeral. While Phil gathered his things, Dad said, with great sadness, "Hell of a way to spend a nice Sunday, isn't it?" When he started sobbing, I patted his shoulder awkwardly for a few minutes before fleeing in tears myself. This was the first time I'd ever heard my father cry. There'd been some silent tears over the course of the last few weeks, but never anything like this.

On our way to Natick, Massachusetts, where my mother was born and would be laid to rest, we stopped at our paternal grandparents' home in Southport, Connecticut, arriving close to dinner time. It was good to spend time in this house that had been a constant and mostly happy part of our childhood. Each of us kids spent at least two weeks here every summer for most of our preschool and elementary school years. Built on a steep incline overlooking Southport Harbor, the house was just one unassuming story from the front. But its two story back was almost all picture windows, with great views of the harbor, the golf course on the other side, and Long Island Sound in the distance.

I put my things in the guest room I would share with Mary Alyce, taking a few minutes to gaze out the window. The grandfather clock in the foyer bonged the hour as I moved slowly down the winding staircase and into the kitchen. Grandma looked up from the stove and pointed with her wooden spoon to the tomatoes and head of lettuce on the table.

"How about you make the salad?" she said.

Suddenly the tears welled up, and I slipped into the powder room to cry for a few minutes before rejoining her in the kitchen. Mom always used to make the salad when we dined at the grandparents' house. It was a special time for her and her mother-in-law to be by themselves for a good visit. When we sat down to eat, Grandma made an announcement.

"We won't be going to the funeral after all," she said. "We want to remember Rae the way she was."

No one said anything. I stared at Grandma in disbelief. How could she and Grandpa abandon us like that? How could they not be there for their son? I could understand their reluctance; Mom's funeral would be an ordeal for all of us. But I was still angry about our grandparents' defection. It didn't occur to me then that older people could be vulnerable, too—that some things were just too much to bear, even for those who'd seen a lot more of life than I had.

Early the next afternoon we arrived at our maternal grandmother's house in Natick. Gram didn't appear to be grieving so much as simply numb. Her gaze was vacant. She looked like she'd misplaced something and didn't know where to start looking for it. My sister Sarah looked shell-shocked. She'd been at Gram's since Friday. After Dad told her Mom was in remission on Wednesday, she'd taken the MTA from Boston to Natick for the weekend. Both Sarah and Gram heard the news of Mom's death from Uncle Walter on Sunday morning. After that midweek phone call from Dad, they'd been totally blindsided. We were not a physically demonstrative family when our mother wasn't around; but that day, each of us greeted Sarah and Gram with long hugs.

On Wednesday morning, we rode to St. Patrick's Church, the Catholic house of worship where my sisters and I had attended Mass whenever we visited Gram as kids. It was a brick Gothic-revival building with a slender spire, not particularly remarkable; but its interior seemed inordinately huge and dark on that day. As soon as we arrived, we viewed Mom's body in the casket. I was appalled at how unlike my mother this corpse looked. It seemed like her face hadn't been put back on quite right after the cranium was opened during the autopsy. Mary Alyce turned away with a muffled sob; to her, Mom looked just as awful as she had in her hospital bed.

After the viewing, we took our places in the front pew. Over the next fifteen minutes or so it became painfully apparent that the only people in attendance were the deceased's husband and children, her mother, her brother and his family—wife and five kids—and one—one!—childhood acquaintance, a homely woman named Claire who had not been so much a friend to Mom as someone who'd followed her around seeking her attention. It broke my heart see so few people bearing witness to our mother's passing.

Our dad had done the best he could with the arrangements, lacking any direction from our mother. He'd figured she would want to be buried near her father in the town where she grew up, even though she hadn't lived there for thirty years. How different would this leave-taking ritual have been had it taken place in Libertytown, where my parents were living when Mom got sick and where she'd taught school for the previous few years? We might be missing out on some valuable support. Months later, I discovered that there were some hurt feelings within that community about being denied an opportunity to say their goodbyes.

Finally, the funeral Mass came to a close. It occurred to me, as I robotically mouthed the prayers that had at one time meant so much to me, that my mother probably would have preferred not to have a Mass said at her funeral. While she had her own idiosyncratic version of spirituality, her church attendance had tapered off even before she got sick, and she'd made no secret of her bitterness about having her life cut short by cancer. I was well aware of this even before I knew about the infamous episode with the hospital chaplain.

When we got to the nearby cemetery, it was another beautiful October afternoon—three days after Mom's death and two days after what would have been her 50th birthday. Not trusting myself to read my mother's requested verse at the gravesite, I handed the priest *The Prophet*, open to the correct page. The poem concludes:

"...Only when you drink from the river of silence shall you indeed sing,

And when you have reached the mountain top, then shall you begin to climb.

And when the earth shall claim your limbs, then shall you truly dance."

Several geese flew over in a V formation just as the casket was lowered. Aunt Mary told her children, "That's Aunt Rae's spirit up there, she's free now." I tracked those geese until I couldn't see them anymore, my eyes stinging with the effort.

We returned to Gram's house after the funeral. The table groaned with food, much of it provided by Unc and Aunt Mary, some by Gram's neighbors, and all of it delicious, no doubt; but none of us ate much. Though food and drink are a mainstay of bereavement gatherings, there was a sense of unreality about the whole day—the viewing, the funeral Mass, the graveside prayers—that made eating and drinking seem somehow beside the point. Our mother, our father's wife, Gram's daughter, and Uncle Walt's big sister, who had shared so many meals with each of us, would never sit at anyone's table again.

• • •

When I returned to Baltimore that Thursday, my life as a medical student resumed its petty pace. I had a lot of catching up to do. I'd missed four days of classes and several quizzes. Every morning I slipped a gold ring of my mother's onto my middle finger, her own grandmother's wedding band. One of the anatomy instructors beamed at me and asked if I'd gotten married while I was away! I said no, I'd been at my mother's funeral. He looked appropriately stricken and offered profuse condolences.

Two weeks after the funeral, Eric surprised me with a cake for my 23rd birthday and rounded up some of our friends to share it with. I was still tired from all the make-up quizzes, and I wasn't exactly in a celebratory mood, but I was deeply touched by his kindness.

During those first weeks after Mom's death, I occasionally saw someone on the street who reminded me of her. The first time it happened, I was walking toward Lexington Market when a substantial woman with salt-and-pepper hair approached. Her build bore a striking resemblance to my mother's before the cancer stripped all those pounds off her frame. I did a double take. As the woman drew closer, I realized she didn't really look like Mom at all, which somehow made me feel worse. Every time this kind of thing happened, I suffered the loss all over again. I wanted so much just to be able to talk with my mother, to tell her about medical school, to tell her how much I missed her.

Our relationship had certainly had its ups and downs. We were both driven, strong-willed individuals, and I'd been a willful child and a moody, covertly rebellious adolescent. Sometimes it was a kind of clash of the Titans. Yet leaving home for college had been more traumatic than liberating. I was insecure and fearful of making mistakes, and I still needed my mother's reassurance. But, as young adults do, I had an equally strong—and painful—need to separate from her, to assert my independence. I'd often felt that my mother was living vicariously through me. Much as I needed her support and approval, I needed even more to have a life that was my own.

And now she was gone. I had a life of my own, all right, but not at all in the way I would have chosen. I felt like I'd been pushed out of an airplane, not knowing whether the parachute would open.

• • •

My mother and I had exchanged letters regularly during my Wellesley years, except for a period of a few months when I didn't speak to her because she had told her first-grade class that "boys are more important than girls"—! I'd been furious. How could my mother belittle me, my sisters, and herself that way? Years later I realized that she'd had that sentiment drilled into her by her tyrannical father, but I didn't have that kind of perspective as a twenty-year-old. She never apologized or acknowledged that she understood my outrage; eventually I let it go.

Mom's letters mostly contained descriptions of the courses she was taking to get her teaching certificate, her apprehension about upcoming parent-teacher conferences, and my youngest sister's high-school activities and burgeoning artistic talent. After her cancer diagnosis, there were descriptions of radiation and chemotherapy, complete with penciled illustrations of where the radiation was directed on her body. When I was applying for financial aid for medical school she wrote, "And on the application write [that] your mother [is] unable to teach due to cancer (that'll scare 'em) and 2 younger sisters to educate, it should help."

These letters were sometimes pretty funny: *"Don't worry if you flunk math, we love you anyway!"*—her response to a panicked missive about my poor performance in my one and only (thank god) semester of calculus. Sometimes they were poignant, as when she wrote to comfort me about a breakup I went through at the beginning of my senior year: "I know this must be hard for you to understand, but it is nonetheless true—that *nothing* hurts as much as having your child hurt. Therefore, I am hurting to the point of heartbreak."

Mom also let it be known in her letters that she was praying for me: "I've gone back to the old habit of saying guardian-angel prayers at night which makes me feel momentarily close to my faraway offspring, whom I love very much." During my senior year, the prayers intensified as I encountered the various hurdles of the medical-school application process, including the MCAT, the medical-school equivalent of the SAT: "Don't worry about the Mcats [sic]. I am praying with great confidence because I know it is part of your mission in life." This was as close as Mom ever came to telling me outright that her own dream for me was that I become a physician.

I'd missed those supportive letters in the last weeks of her life. During that time, I'd experienced a few stark glimpses of the reality that my mother was dying. Though it might have looked like I was faithful to the code of silence because I never spoke the words out loud, I hadn't been able to keep the knowledge from myself. I'd managed to keep mourning at bay by immersing myself in the novelty of city living, the trials, challenges, and occasional joys of medical school, and wistful fantasies about romance with Eric. For a short time after her death, my grief would break through in the middle of a lecture or a lab, or sadness would sneak up on me when I was trying to eat my solitary dinner. But I simply couldn't afford to lose myself in my feelings. I *had* to get through medical school, *had* to become a doctor, even more so now that my mother was gone. It wouldn't be long before my grief would be shoved down deep into my subconscious, and those other aspects of my life—Stricker St., medical school, romance—would come to dominate my thoughts again.

Especially romance.

5

LIFE AFTER DEATH

The cafeteria lunches with Eric, Dr. Hayward, and an assortment of other friends soon became a regular occurrence, something I looked forward to. Dr. Hayward was smart, funny, compassionate, and sensible, and he seemed to relish the company of younger people like us. Because he was warm and approachable, I felt increasingly comfortable revealing my mixed feelings about medical school—excitement, but also anxiety, wondering if I belonged there. Perhaps he was someone I could confide in and look to for advice.

One dreary November afternoon after anatomy lab, I visited the professor in his office, conveniently located in the same building. His door was open; I stuck my head in.

"Dr. Hayward? Do you have a minute?"

"Hey, Kay, come on in. Of course, I have time for you. And, please, call me Preston." His smile was welcoming as he motioned me to a small leather loveseat across from his desk.

"What's up?"

After airing some complaints about medical school, I told him about my mother's recent death.

"Oh, no. That's tragic. She was so young." He shook his head. "It must be hard to concentrate these days. As if medical school isn't hard enough all by itself."

My shoulders relaxed. Apparently, my instincts about Dr.

Hayward were correct.

Haltingly, I told him about my growing frustration with Eric. We'd been joined at the hip since the orientation meeting before classes started, but he wouldn't ask me out. He seemed to be attracted to me, as I was to him; what was the problem? Was it because I was a classmate? One of my college friends, finding herself in a similar situation, had captured that feeling of underappreciated femininity perfectly when she said, "*My* body is being *ignored!*" That was precisely how I felt about Eric.

"I could die of old age waiting for him to ask me out," I said.

Preston laughed and rolled his chair over to the loveseat where I was perched as though poised for flight. Crossing his ankles, hands on his knees, he leaned toward me.

"You know what you need? You need some new input."

"What do you mean?"

"I'm going to make you a list of people you ought to meet, people I know here at the hospital. Call them and ask them to get together for lunch." Preston sat back in his chair and smiled. "You just need to broaden your horizons a little."

"You mean—just call people up out of the blue?" My voice squeaked on the last syllable.

"Sure." He shrugged. "The worst they can do is say no."

"You mean, just call people up when I've never even met them?" I shifted in my seat.

"Aw, come on!" He laughed. "You're a medical student, you can do anything."

I had to laugh, too—though, unlike his laughter, mine was laced with irony. It sure didn't feel like I could "do anything."

His face softened. He leaned toward me again and gently stroked my hair. My eyes widened.

"You're a vital, charming young woman," he said. "Who

wouldn't want to have lunch with you?"

I could feel myself blushing. I looked down, breaking the intense eye contact.

Walking back to his desk, Preston wrote down some names and phone numbers and tore the piece of paper off the pad with a flourish.

"Here you go," he said. "These are people I know pretty well, so you can tell them I put you up to it, if that'll make it easier. I want you to report back to me in a week." When I reached for the piece of paper, he came around the desk and enfolded me in a long hug. "I'm sorry about your mom," he whispered. "And I hope things get better soon." He let go and held me at arm's length. "Now, get out there and make some new friends, girl!"

As I walked home with Preston's list in my pocket, I recalled that hug with a flush of warmth and a smile. I realized I was attracted to him, and the feeling appeared to be mutual.

The next time I saw Eric in class, I told him about my visit with Dr. Hayward in his office, how sympathetic and encouraging he'd been. "He's great to talk to. I'm really glad you introduced me to him," I said. Eric just nodded and smiled, without a hint of jealousy. *Damn. He's really not interested,* I told myself.

A few days later, I was absorbed in lunchtime conversation in the cafeteria with Carol, the only woman on Preston's list of contacts, a medical technician in the hematology lab who was a few years older than me. When Eric sauntered over to our table, I introduced them; when he asked how we'd met, I told him about Preston's list.

"Oh, so Hayward arranged it, then."

I glared at him. *I* was the one who'd dialed the phone each time and heard my heart pounding in my ears while it rang. *I'd* worked to control the tremor in my voice and weathered the surprise (and, in one case, frank displeasure) on the other end. No one had arranged this meeting but *me*!

My obvious irritation didn't stop Eric from pulling up a chair and taking over the conversation. So much for trying to expand my circle of friends independent of him.

The day after Eric crashed my lunch date, I paid Preston another visit. This time I didn't hold back about my friend—the way he'd injected himself into my conversation with Carol, how maddening it was that he spent so much time with me but didn't want to date me. "It really sucks," I said.

"If Eric's not meeting your needs, then maybe you ought to look elsewhere," he said from behind his desk, giving me a long look over his reading glasses. Then he took the glasses off, a gesture that made his gaze more intimate. The color rose from my chest to the roots of my hair as my body responded to that look.

A strong current of physical attraction was flowing between us, but my misgivings held it in check: Preston was a mentor, after all, older than me by almost 20 years. He was recently separated from his wife, not yet divorced. And he was on the medical-school faculty—though, since his emphasis was on research, his role in grading students was negligible.

Preston came around his desk to hug me goodbye, and my heart rate sped up. I wasn't completely surprised when he kissed me on the mouth. It wasn't a hard or lingering kiss; but he managed to convey his absolute willingness to atone for Eric's negligence in the romance department. I felt a flash of exultation. It was so good to be wanted! And I wanted him, too.

Later in November, barely a month after my mother died, Preston and I became lovers. I still visited him in his office a few times a week after anatomy lab, for conversation and a few stolen kisses. Once or twice a week he took me out to dinner and then back to his place, where we would spend the next couple of hours making vigorous, ardent love. He was a virtuoso, playing my body like a fine musical instrument, expanding my sexual repertoire. I returned from each encounter blissfully satiated. One night, when he kissed me goodbye at my door, he chuckled and made a comment about my "well-fucked look." I just grinned at him. I was on top of the world.

One night as we lay entwined after a session of lovemaking, tears sprang to my eyes while he snored softly next to me. When a sniffle escaped me, he opened his eyes and murmured, "What's the matter, baby?"

"This—you and me together like this—it's so beautiful, and it's so—ephemeral." I'd seen with excruciating clarity that we were two naked, vulnerable creatures who'd just experienced a fleeting moment of great beauty and happiness, made all the more poignant by the inexorable fact of death, a fact of which I was all too aware in those weeks after my mother's passing. When I tried to put this into words, I thought I wasn't getting through; but then I noticed a tear rolling down his cheek.

"Oh, you're crying," I said.

"Yeah, it's true, men cry, too." He smiled and kissed my forehead. "I think I know what you're talking about, baby."

My relationship with Preston wasn't just about sex. We had long, wide-ranging conversations about philosophy, gender relations, race relations, social change, and politics. He introduced me to the ideas of the visionary Buckminster Fuller and the pragmatism of Bertrand Russell, whose book, *Marriage and Morals*, was a favorite of his and soon became one of mine as well. Russell was an early women's suffragist; his views on the liberation of women provided a refreshing contrast to what I was experiencing in medical school. Preston shared his own analysis of the problems of our highly technologized society. In his view, main-stream culture had become overly abstract due to our reliance on only two of our five senses—vision and hearing—to the exclusion of taste, smell, and touch. Concepts trumped direct experience, and genuine intimacy between people suffered as a result. I discovered that Preston and I both had outsiders' perspectives when it came to society and its ills: his was that of a Black man in a white man's world, and mine was that of a woman in a man's world.

Preston's perspective on our culture's undervaluing of the sense of touch resonated strongly with me. One of the reasons I saw sex as such an important part of a relationship was simply that I craved warm human touch. Maybe it was my parents' New England background, but I'd grown up in an atmosphere where hugs and kisses were suspect and thus sparingly applied, except perhaps between mothers and their young children. There just wasn't much nonsexual touch in our milieu.

Preston, by contrast, engaged in some degree of affectionate touching with just about everyone. At our lunch meetings, he was as likely to tousle Eric's hair as to chuck Jane's chin or stroke my cheek. At a time when I'd just lost my mother, the one person in my life with whom I'd felt truly free to exchange physical affection, Preston's warmth was a great comfort to me.

In the early days of our love affair, the joy I felt being loved by this man spilled over into the rest of my life. My afternoons on the pediatric ward and even on the medical wards for Physical Diagnosis now gave me a delightful sense of exhilaration in the face of challenge instead of my customary anxiety and feeling of inadequacy. That honeymoon period with Preston made medical school seem like an idealized version of the first weeks of college, where life was supposed to consist entirely of stimulating encounters with people and ideas.

Preston was delighted with this surge of enthusiasm for medicine. When it came to my expanding knowledge and growing confidence, he was always encouraging, saying things like, "I knew you'd ace that test. You're smart, and you're a hard worker." He simply assumed I would do well. This was something else I'd lost with my mother's death but now seemed to have regained. Maybe it really was possible to be a woman *and* a doctor.

• • •

The first Thanksgiving without my mother was a dark blot on an otherwise sunny landscape. The five of us—my father, my siblings, and I—gathered in Libertytown, where my sisters and I put on a passable Thanksgiving dinner. Dad was in a surprisingly good mood; it was the first time he'd been anything but downcast and withdrawn since Mom's death. We all managed to put up a good front.

The next morning, I awoke before the others and entered the kitchen alone to fix myself breakfast. For a moment I forgot my mother was gone. I waited for her voice from my parents' bedroom above the kitchen. It didn't come. When I remembered, I had to grab the edge of the counter for support. Then I sat down and wept. I wanted so much to believe, as I once had, that I'd see her again someday in some kind of afterlife; but mostly I just wanted to see her *now*, to tell her all about medical school and my life in Baltimore. It just wasn't fair.

Those happy weeks were punctuated with moments like that. The sight of a city bus would trigger the memory of riding to Baltimore City Hospital to visit my mother on the oncology ward. A plush bathrobe in a store window would remind me of the one she'd given me the previous Christmas, which had been her last. These sudden moments of grief felt like flashes of lightning, illuminating the sadness I was trying to ignore, revealing the reality of my mother's absence in vivid relief before it disappeared once more into the warm darkness of new love.

Early in December, an undercurrent of unease crept into my relationship with Preston. Was I falling in love too fast? Had I given my heart too quickly? I felt myself recoiling from the intensity of our first weeks together. I continued to meet the people he suggested, and I enjoyed expanding my horizons that way. But sometimes I was put off by his strong opinions about what I needed and how I should act, even while he offered encouragement and support. I was chafing under his mentorship. It appeared I was in a relationship with someone who had at least as much of a need for control as I had. I was afraid of my growing dependency on him, and I was determined not to let my personality be annexed by his.

To further complicate matters, Preston had made no secret—from the earliest days of our relationship—of the fact that he was seeing other women at the same time he was dating me. Newly single and still in the process of getting divorced, he was eager to check out the entire pool of eligible females. This angered and hurt me; naturally, I wanted him all to myself. But much as I did with my grief for my mother, I buried those feelings deeply and managed to put that unwelcome reality out of my mind. When my lover was with me, there was no need to think about him being with someone else.

The 1970s were an awkward decade for relationships between women and men. The Sixties had blown open the institution of marriage. The ubiquity of birth control was now taken for granted, thanks to the Pill; and, after the *Roe v. Wade* decision in 1973, abortion had become legal and accessible. Sexual experimentation was rampant—from serial monogamy to outright promiscuity among single people, and wife-swapping parties for married "swingers."

Patriarchy itself, that unholy and largely unspoken system in which men and their careers, interests, activities, and needs are considered more consequential than women and theirs, was coming under open scrutiny in a way it never had before. Women like my medical-school classmates and me were starting to make major incursions into previously male strongholds.

It was against this background that Preston and I conducted our love affair. While he was a middle-aged man newly released from the confines of an unhappy marriage, I was a member of the Woodstock generation. I'd started taking the Pill before I had sex with my first college boyfriend, with whom I'd been in love—a love that had more to do with the fact that he was my first lover than with the boy himself. When that relationship ended, I'd been deeply disillusioned by my discovery that sexual intimacy wasn't synonymous with true, undying love. For a while I'd castigated myself for not waiting until I was married to have sex, like my mother had taught me. But my own experience in that tumultuous time was showing me that my mother's views about sex and marriage might not make sense anymore.

There'd been several sexual relationships after that, but they'd never matched the intensity of the first one. My college forays into sex had started out as an attempt to find true love, but they'd evolved into a statement of defiance. I deeply resented the double standard—the expectation that *I* should be chaste and passive, waiting patiently for the right man to come along, while my male counterparts could do whatever they wanted with impunity. By being sexually proactive, I was flouting the sexual mores I'd grown up with, because I saw them as unfair and oppressive to women.

Why should men get to have more freedom than women? Why should they hold all the best cards? Much as I loved Preston, I had an inkling that, with his predilection for "multiple interactions," as he put it, he was holding a better poker-hand than I was, and I resented that.

• • •

One Saturday evening in December, I joined Jane and my housemates, Charlie and Jack, for an excursion to one of the neighborhood bars. The medical students among us—Charlie, Jane, and me—were celebrating the end of a particularly arduous week of anatomy and biochemistry quizzes. Jack, the social work student, was along for the ride. We all drank a lot of beer and danced with abandon. Once the initial euphoria of a beer-soaked evening free of studying wore off, Jack and I spent the rest of the time slow-dancing.

Jack had intrigued me from the day I'd moved into the house. There was an enigmatic, Zen-like spiritual quality about him, yet he had a broad, profane sense of humor that I really enjoyed. He was at least five years older than me, and he'd spent time in Indonesia as a Peace Corps volunteer.

When we got back to the house and the others had dispersed, Jack smiled at me and said, "I had a great time tonight." His big brown eyes were magnified further by his glasses' thick lenses.

"Me, too."

"The best part—" he dropped his gaze for a moment— "was slow-dancing with you."

His shyness made me smile, as did his outfit—a short-sleeve paisley polyester shirt, beat-up khakis, and sandals, completely out of place in Baltimore in December. He looked like Jeff Bridges would, decades later, as The Dude in *The Big Lebowski*.

We lingered in the living room, but Tony had the TV turned

up, making conversation difficult. Finally, I said, "You want to come up to my room and talk?"

One thing led to another, and soon we moved from sitting and talking to reclining on my bed, then to making love. We laughed a lot and thoroughly enjoyed ourselves. I'd previously caught glimpses of Jack's wonderful sense of the ridiculous, but it was on full display that evening. (And I loved his Southern drawl, too.)

Preston called me on Sunday night, as he usually did. I took a deep breath before I told him about the previous evening with Jack. I felt that honesty was the best policy, so I plunged right into my story. But I also felt that having sex with Jack had leveled the playing field in my relationship with Preston. There was no hint of jealousy in his response; if anything, the prospect of my making love with another man seemed to turn him on! Maybe this "multiple interactions" game might be okay if I could play it, too.

After that first night, Jack and I met sporadically—usually in my room, rarely in his tiny and disorderly one. We were discreet, and our housemates remained oblivious—or at least politely looked the other way.

My relationship with Preston continued to thrive in parallel with the affair with Jack, who was fully aware of this and had other girlfriends of his own. Though there were still times when I chafed under Preston's mentorship and had some misgivings about our "open relationship," I continued to revel in our love, friendship, and intimacy, our "soul-mate-ship," as I thought of it. He appreciated me as a woman in a way I'd never been appreciated before. He showed me that physical warmth and affection, both within and outside of sex, were something I could not only express, but lay claim to as my human birthright. And, perhaps most important, he made me feel genuinely loved for who I was, not just for what I did.

I took Preston as my date to an intimate holiday party given by my friends Isabel and Michelle, members of my gross anatomy group who shared an apartment and were privy to my relationship with Preston. Everyone else at the party was a classmate, but Preston fit right in. Having a boyfriend accompany me to a party was a welcome novelty for me; I was used to being the odd one out at gatherings of friends. That night, buoyed by our love, I enjoyed socializing with the others even when Preston and I went our separate ways to mingle. Of course, I also enjoyed slow dancing with him, feeling his pelvis pressing against mine while he whispered erotic suggestions in my ear.

Over a cup of punch, Isabel said, "I'm glad you brought Preston. He's an interesting guy. You two are really good together."

We were the animal-magnetism couple that night. He was so fine, and I was proud and happy to be with him.

• • •

A few days before Christmas, I joined my father and siblings at my grandparents' winter home on the Florida Keys. This was only the third time our family had done this—most recently the previous Christmas, when my mother was still alive, frail from chemotherapy and eager for a respite from the cold weather at home. Going back there barely two months after her death proved to be a big mistake. Though my mother's absence was never openly discussed, it was palpable in everything we did together, especially at mealtimes. And Grandpa and Grandma were at their worst, treating all of us like small children. I couldn't believe it when Grandpa excoriated my 28-year-old brother for sailing the small boat beyond the point where he could be seen from the house.

Then one night at dinner, Grandma picked a fight with me about "Women's Lib."

"I think it's ridiculous," she said. "We're the power behind the throne, for heaven's sake! What's there to complain about? All this fuss about 'sexism'!"

I couldn't believe she'd said that. Trying to control my voice, I spluttered, "Grandma, you don't understand!" What I wanted to say was: "Okay, Grandma, let me tell you about sexism. Our professors put pictures of naked women in the middle of their lecture slides. One of them calls the class 'girls' when he's mad at us, and another told one of my classmates she should have gone to nursing school. Would *you* want to be treated like that?" But I was too upset to argue coherently.

"Well," she said with a self-satisfied little smile, "all I know is, I'm *glad* I'm a girl."

I stalked out of the dining room and took a fast and furious walk down the breakwater behind the house. Sobbing with impotent rage, I didn't see my dad until he was next to me. He matched his steps with mine and I finally calmed down.

"Take it easy," he said gently. "You can't let her get to you like that." He looked me in the eye. "And I ought to know," he added ruefully. Though I still couldn't speak, I nodded my head and gave him a watery smile, touched by his unexpected show of solidarity.

Though we weren't aware of it during that not-so-merry Christmas, that would be our last family visit to the Florida Keys. All of us were relieved to return to our respective lives. Dingy, depressing Baltimore, gray and slushy as it was, was an improvement over spending time with the grandparents, even in sunny subtropical Florida. I looked forward to seeing Preston, Jack, and my other friends again. I even looked forward to resuming classes. When I turned the key in the lock of the Stricker St. house, I realized, with a jolt of surprise, that the first semester of medical school was almost over.

6

WHEEL OF FORTUNE

There's a card in the Major Arcana of the tarot known as "Wheel of Fortune." The visual details vary according to which of the many available tarot decks you use. On my Morgan-Greer version, the first thing you see is a giant disembodied hand turning a large wheel. The flailing legs of a man who's just fallen off the wheel form a diagonal at the lower right corner of the card. Comfortably perched at the top is a man wearing a crown. His legs are crossed as though he doesn't have a care in the world, and his left hand raises a gold cup in a toast. His right hand clasps the hand of a similarly crowned woman facing him, whose back is to the viewer. She's looking at the cup, but her other hand is reaching for the skirt of her gown in a vain attempt to pull it free of the falling man's foot, which has pinned the fabric against the wheel. It's obvious that she'll soon go flying off into the void like her predecessor. She seems to be aware of her precarious position, and of the fact that there's nothing she can do about it. In the winter and spring of 1974, I was that woman on the Wheel of Fortune: riding for a fall, losing my tenuous grip on the unanticipated happiness I'd known in the first months after my mother's death.

It started with biophysics. I didn't realize how easy the first semester's courses had been until I hit a wall with this one. While courses like gross anatomy and biochemistry had required oppressive amounts of brute memorization, Catholic school and my Wellesley science courses had prepared me well for that. In fact, I was surprised at how much less academic pressure I'd felt in that first semester of medical school compared with my college years. But anything related to physics was another story; I'd barely passed the undergraduate course. When my gross-anatomy friend Anne helped me with the biophysics quiz I'd failed, I could see that I actually knew most of the answers but had choked when confronted with the test. Besides the humiliation of failure, it was an exercise in sheer frustration.

On the bright side was physiology, the study of how the various organ systems of the body work. I'd loved the subject in college, and my *Guyton's Textbook of Physiology* retained a place of honor on my medical bookshelf. Because I'd done well in the college course, I'd placed into a physiology seminar consisting of discussion sessions and a term paper, a welcome respite from the usual medical-school routine of lectures and multiple-choice tests. Several of my friends were in the seminar, too; and our professor, Dr. Leo Karpeles, proved to be an interesting and sympathetic human being as well as an excellent teacher who supported and guided us instead of stuffing us with facts. The semester also included a neurology course and an introduction to psychiatry, which contained a segment on human sexuality. It was shaping up to be an interesting semester and a challenging one.

Inwardly, though, I was restless. In the midst of studying for first-semester final exams right after that awful Christmas in Florida, I'd started having dreams about my mother, dreams that dogged my sleep every night until I finally dreamed that she'd fully recovered from her cancer and gone home from the hospital, a sort of culminating wish-fulfillment dream. Though I thought and dreamed about her a lot, I didn't feel any sadness or grief, only smoldering anger. Taking their cue from my grandparents, my father and brother had maintained the code of silence that had surrounded my mother's deathbed. Except for one brief discussion with my sisters, there'd been no mention of my mother at Christmas—none. It was as though she'd never existed.

But there was one good thing about that week in Florida: it gave me an opportunity to gain some perspective on my love-life. Upon my return to Baltimore, I questioned the workability of being involved with two men simultaneously, even as I continued to question the legitimacy of monogamy and the institution of marriage. As in most marriages of the time, my mother had either deferred to my father in any matter of consequence or obtained what she wanted through subterfuge and indirection. I wanted a more egalitarian relationship. I thought of myself as a liberated woman and valued my sexual freedom; but my convictions about sexual liberation were about to be put to a rigorous test.

Shortly after classes resumed, Preston told me, over dinner at the Chinese restaurant we frequented, that he was attracted to my best friend Jane and would like to have a sexual relationship with her—not *instead* of his relationship with me, but *in addition* to it. I stared at him, nearly dropping my egg roll into my soup.

I knew he enjoyed Jane's participation in the lunchtime discussions, and he was as affectionate with her as he was with the rest of us, maybe a little more. But—now he wanted to *sleep* with her? Could this declaration have anything to do with his recent revelation that he was starting to feel, as he put it, "a certain amount of dependence" on me? Perhaps he needed to create some distance between us. But I knew he was dating at least one other woman besides me; wasn't that enough? And why did it have to be *my best friend*? I had no idea how Jane might feel about this; but the thought that she might respond favorably made my chest constrict.

To make matters even more complicated, I was aware of feeling attracted to Jane myself. I'd had similar feelings toward a few women when I was at Wellesley, but knowing this only confused me more. I knew for sure that I enjoyed sex with men; did that preclude being a lesbian? Perhaps I was bisexual. I was coming into my sexuality at a time when sexual orientation was pretty much a binary, either/or proposition. The stigma against gays, lesbians, bisexual, and transgender people still ran deep, not only in the population at large, but even among many otherwise open-minded people, including many feminists. I was very uncomfortable with the feelings Preston's revelation was making me confront about Jane. My jealousy went both ways. I didn't want to share my lover with my best friend, but I didn't want to share my best friend with my lover, either. I'd always had an unacknowledged intuition that Preston and I would never marry, but that didn't keep me from wanting him all to myself—his other girlfriends and my other boyfriend notwithstanding. Being so forcefully reminded that I couldn't possess him made me sad and angry.

By the end of the conversation, though, I told Preston that it was okay with me (well, sort of okay, which was as good as it was going to get) if he dated Jane. Besides trying to be liberated, I wanted to be a good sport; I felt guilty about being possessive of Preston. I'd confided in Jane pretty consistently about my relationship with him, so I told her he wanted to date her. Once she'd recovered from the initial shock, she took it in stride when he invited her out to dinner. What surprised me was her casual willingness to go. I didn't have the nerve to ask her the questions I was burning to ask: *Are you attracted to him? Just curious? Are you trying to make me jealous?*

I sat on her desk chair picking at my cuticles while she got ready for their date. She appeared curious yet wary; excited, but anxious. She stopped brushing her hair to ask, "Is this really okay with you? I don't have to go through with it, you know. I can cancel." She gave me a sidelong glance, eyebrows arched.

"Don't worry, I'm fine." I smiled bravely. "You guys have a good time."

Of course, I was anything but "fine." I spent that evening in the throes of jealousy, anxiety, and resentment—and angry with myself for being so insecure. I tried to study but ended up torturing myself with fantasies of what they might be doing at that moment, imagining him stroking her thick chestnut hair and telling her how good she looked, or telling a funny story to put her at ease. Naturally, they would talk about school; he would be sympathetic and encouraging, as he was with me. When I imagined them talking about things he never talked about with me—what would those be?—I hunched over my physiology textbook, arms crossed over my stomach, the words swimming on the page.

Then I pictured her flirting with him—a little hesitantly, a little uncertainly at first, but with growing confidence as she started to feel the power she had over him. Their laughter would grow deeper; their eyes would lock—perhaps he would take her hand. But when he moved a little closer, she would find some way to distance herself from him.

I wished I knew how she did that, because it made men crazy for her. Much as Preston loved my openness and availability, I was pretty sure he couldn't help but fall under the spell of Jane's elusiveness. Where I was there for him body and soul, she would be there and gone, like a butterfly in a field of beebalm.

When I imagined them kissing, embracing (would she let

it go that far?), I had to get up and pace the floor of my room.

How dare my lover ask my best friend out on a date?

How dare she accept? And why the hell had I gone along with it?

I was starting to lose my purchase on the Wheel of Fortune, wondering how much longer I could hang on.

The next day I took a two-hour walk down by the harbor, picking my way carefully among piles of scrap wood, discarded railroad ties, and lengths of metal pipe. It was good to have to focus completely on where I was stepping, with no room in my mind for anything to do with relationships. The acres of railroad tracks and the general air of neglect and abandonment were oddly soothing. I didn't come to any conclusions about my dilemma, but fear and anger loosened their grip. Preston and I went to dinner that night, where he took me to task.

"What did you say to Jane, anyway? You tell me fine, go ahead, and then you make her think it's not okay for us to go out. You're the queen of mixed signals!" It seemed that Jane had used me as an excuse to avoid getting physically closer to him. I felt a quick flash of exultation.

"I told her it was fine," I said. "I didn't mean to give mixed signals, but—" My instant of triumph deflated when I saw his frown. "...but I was so afraid you'd throw me over for her." My voice climbed into a higher register despite my effort to get hold of myself.

"Oh, for Pete's sake!" He sat back and shook his head. His shoulders relaxed, and the anger leached out of him. He reached across the table for my hand. "I told you, nobody can take your place. I'm not going anywhere." He gazed intently at me, rubbing my fingers with his thumb. When we went to bed later, we enjoyed each other's bodies just as we always had. But deep down, I was still angry with him for trying to get me to accept his desire to date my best friend. I pondered an uncomfortable question: how much did I have to do things someone else's way to secure their love?

All this anxiety and conflict was taking a toll. I couldn't sleep well, and it was increasingly difficult to concentrate on my studies. Throughout most of the first semester, my emotions hadn't interfered with my work. With considerable effort, I'd been able to consciously set aside my grief for my mother for hours at a time while reviewing notes for a biochemistry test or looking at microscope slides for a histology quiz. Now that my love affair with Preston was threatened, it was increasingly difficult to compartmentalize my feelings. I'd become prone to fits of restless inertia—underlining sentences in my neurology textbook without really knowing what I'd read, getting up from my desk for yet another glass of water, staring out the window. Too much was being asked of me, in every area of my life. Paradoxically, the only thing that could calm me down was talking with Preston, whether in person or on the phone. The last few months of emotional upheaval were finally catching up with me.

In late January, I had the first of the mutilation dreams that would haunt me throughout my medical training. In this dream, I lay on a cold metal table beneath the bright lights of an operating room while an anesthesia mask descended over my face. When I woke up, there was a big bandage over my lower belly, and I could see that both my feet had been amputated. Eventually they were sewn back on, albeit with big, ugly scars. When I told my friends about this nightmare, Sadie, with her social-work acumen, interpreted it as my femininity being stolen from me, since the abdominal operation was probably a hysterectomy. My ambition was taken from me as well, the amputation of my feet signifying an inability to get anywhere. A spot-on representation of how I felt as a woman in medical school.

Preston and I continued to have long conversations about his ideal of what he called "non-possessive, non-exclusive" relationships. Theoretically, I was all in favor of women having the same degree of sexual freedom as men, but now I questioned whether "non-possessive, non-exclusive" relationships were even possible. If so, was that a good thing? Was sex supposed to be independent of love? It sure didn't feel that way to me, certainly not in my relationship with him.

When I pointed out that I was really *trying* to become less jealous and possessive, he said wistfully, "Just because you don't have any hang-ups about sex, I guess I thought you didn't have any other hang-ups either."

"Wait a minute—are *you* idealizing *me* now?" I laughed, but my elation was short-lived. I knew I wasn't Preston's ideal, a free woman whose love made no demands of exclusiveness or fidelity, and I wasn't sure if that was even what I wanted to be. I was getting tired of living my life as if it were some kind of social experiment. I wanted to be loved just as I was, to hell with *anyone's* ideal.

As February slid into March, the Wheel of Fortune took an upward turn. I was really enjoying physiology, which made medical school easier than it had been for a while. I started studying occasionally with Mike, a guy in the physiology seminar who appeared to genuinely *like* women. He was a tall, gregarious person, with penetrating eyes and an air of casual elegance, who'd been a chef prior to medical school. Mike seemed secure in himself, so being around him made me feel more comfortable in my own skin. He was gay: did that make it easier for him to treat women as equals, because the issue of sexual attraction was taken out of the equation? I was feeling better enough that I took Preston and Jane's second dinner date in stride.

• • •

Spring came early to Baltimore that year, bringing summer temperatures for a few days in early March and afflicting many of us with spring fever. The first Thursday night of the month was especially balmy. Jane would be going out with Preston for a third time later that evening, but in the meantime, we'd shared some potent weed in preparation for an impromptu rock concert at the Student Union, courtesy of a group of our classmates who'd put together their own band.

Under the influence of Jane's weed, we drifted down Lombard Street in a fugue state, not saying much but taking comfort in each other's presence. We were alone, but we were alone together, basking in the late-afternoon sun on our faces and the gentle breeze on our bare forearms. We drifted into the Student Union and drew further into our private worlds as the rock music amplified the pot's effect. I was grateful for the chemical reprieve from my fears about Jane's date. She'd smoked a larger quantity than usual; was she trying to quell her own anxiety about meeting Preston later?

"Time for me to go, I guess," she said from the chair next to mine, which seemed further away than it really was. I came down with a thud that was almost audible.

"Already? Wow, it's almost 7:30, isn't it...Well, have fun," I said. My eyes crinkled as I forced a smile. As I watched Jane amble to the door, I mulled over my mixed feelings about her.

Though our male classmates were drawn to Jane like paparazzi to a celebrity, she was hesitant to move into a relationship with any of them. She seemed to envy my ability to dive right into romantic entanglements, just as I envied her that magnetic quality of hers. Though we supported each other in our feelings about being female in medical school, this mutual envy was an unacknowledged subterranean layer that undermined our solidarity. We were "best friends" on the surface, but I wondered how deep it went. Sometimes it felt like I was in high school again, competing with her for the attention of the popular boys—not that I'd tried to compete in high school, having been consigned to the realm of the "smart girls" whom the popular boys ignored.

Plus, it felt like everyone was always rooting for Jane. She was usually the focus of attention in a group, while I, being quieter and less, well, magnetic, stood in her shadow. When our friends rallied around her after a visit from her college boyfriend ended badly, I caught myself thinking, "Hey, *I'm* the one whose mother just died!" Eric had once observed, "Jane's a more group-oriented person than you are." Perhaps that was it—maybe I was too introverted, not "social" enough. That assessment didn't make the situation any easier.

A few evenings after their third date, when Jane and I were smoking weed without Sadie, Jane admitted that she couldn't handle a sexual relationship with Preston. But there was more.

"I feel like an object," she said, her ice-blue eyes boring into mine. "Like I'm a pawn in a power struggle between you two."

"I—I'm sorry, I had no idea you felt that way." I was genuinely contrite. It occurred to me that Preston and I *had* talked—sometimes argued—about Jane as if she didn't have thoughts, feelings, or needs of her own.

About a week after that discussion, Preston and I met for lunch in the hospital cafeteria. At my request, it was just the two of us. He smiled at me across the table. The smell of institutional fried food and overcooked vegetables took away my appetite. My heart raced as I mentally reviewed what I wanted to say.

"What's up?" he asked pleasantly, his knife and fork clinking against his plate as he ate his ravioli.

"I've been thinking about this thing with you and Jane." My eyes focused on the saltshaker I was twirling. "Turns out I'm really not comfortable with you going out with her." The hum of other people's conversation roared in my ears.

"Really?" His eyebrows shot up. "I've seen her, what, three times now, and this is the first I'm hearing of it?"

I sighed. "I've been *trying* to be okay with it, but it's just not working. I really didn't want to disappoint you, but—"

"Disappoint me?"

"Well, yeah. I know how much it means to you to be free. I just don't think I'm the kind of free spirit you are." Nor, apparently, was I the kind of free spirit he thought I was.

"You know, I'm glad you brought this up." He rested his arms on the table and folded his hands. "Actually, I *am* disappointed. Jane says she doesn't want to get involved with me because she's afraid it would hurt you." His gaze grew more intense. "I thought you were into this open-relationship thing, just like me."

"I thought so too, but it turns out I'm not." I moved forward in my seat, and my shoulders hunched as I gave him my best attempt at a look of defiance.

He eased himself back in his chair and crossed his arms. "So all that stuff about how it was perfectly all right for me to date Jane was actually a load of crap?"

I sat bolt upright. "Hey! I did the best I could to do things the way you want, but now I can see that this is just not my thing."

"Not *your* thing?"

The gauntlet was down. I said, "You think that just because

we're so good together in bed, I'm some kind of all-giving, perfectly-loving sex goddess who will grant your every wish, even letting you fuck my best friend!"

"*Letting* me? Listen to yourself! You don't get to tell me whom I can and cannot fuck! And believe it or not, *I'm* not trying to tell *you* what to do, either! You seem to think I'm some kind of dictator, telling you how to think and feel…"

"Well, if the shoe fits…"

He glared at me without speaking, and I softened my tone. "Preston, you just don't understand. These demands of yours make me feel… I don't know, subservient."

"Subservient? Demands? Girl, you've got it *all* wrong! If anybody's making demands, it's *you*. You're trying to tell me who it's okay to make love with and who it's not, and, believe me, that does not sit well with *any* man!"

"What a bunch of sexist bullshit!"

We glared at each other. My jaw ached. Our voices must have been louder than we realized. People were staring at us.

He eased back slightly and lowered his voice. "Look, I'm sorry, that didn't come out right. It's just that your jealousy and insecurity have been getting to me lately. You know I really care for you."

I just looked at him. It would be days before I could admit to myself that maybe it wasn't normal for a lover to consider it "jealousy" or "insecurity" when you weren't wild about the idea of him having sex with your best friend. One thing was clear: at this point in Preston's life, there was no way one woman would be enough for him, sex-goddess or not.

We stood up. I touched his arm. "I still love you, you know."

He said nothing.

"Would it kill you to say something?"

"You want me to say, 'I love you' back? Well, forget it. I've told you before, I think that word has been so misused that it hardly means anything anymore."

I didn't dignify that with a response. I turned on my heel and stalked off, trying to act like my tears weren't blinding me.

When I got back to my apartment that evening, I was beside myself. I felt as though my heart had been ripped out, cut up in little pieces, and the pieces tossed back in at random. I rocked on the floor, knees to chest, overcome by a terrible sense of loss. I paced my room in circles, trying to outrun my terror at the chasm of loneliness yawning before me. Hatred burned in my belly like ice against bare skin.

Days later, after the worst of my grief had subsided, I realized that Preston and I had been unable to be completely honest with each other because neither of us was completely honest with ourselves. While I'd been able to turn a blind eye to his relationships with other women as long as I didn't know them personally, I could never accept his being involved with my best friend; it was simply too much to ask. Preston vociferously touted his "non-possessive, non-exclusive" relationships, but he appeared to be emotionally involved with me in a way that didn't seem compatible with his own ideal.

As I slowly recovered from our heated exchange in the cafeteria, I took stock of the lessons our rupture had taught me. I'd learned how easy it was to hurt another person, to lash out destructively in my need to protect myself from the knives hiding within intimacy. I'd learned how hate is the other side of love's coin, and fear of exposure is the interface between them. And I'd learned that human communication is never perfect, that total honesty is impossible.

• • •

Like the woman holding the crowned man's hand on the Wheel of Fortune, I was now sliding off, picking up momentum as I felt myself slipping through the fingers of the love and intimacy I claimed to want so much.

7

FREE FALL

I climbed into the back seat of Blake's aging Mercury coupe, admiring its cool sequential turn signals and aura of quaint sportiness. Like me, Blake had gone to college in New England; when I heard he was offering rides to Boston, I signed up right away. Harry, an M.I.T. alum, settled into the passenger seat.

It was the end of March; we had a week off for spring vacation. I didn't have any big plans; I just wanted to catch up on my sleep and spend some time with my sister, my grandmother, and some college friends in the Boston area. To us medical students, it was spring *vacation*—not spring *break*, with its connotations of Caribbean beaches and drunken revelry. A tropical interlude wasn't in the cards for us, even though most of us could have used one, as exhausted and depressed as we were.

"So, Kay, are you enjoying the human sexuality course?" Harry turned and grinned at me from the shotgun seat. He was ebullient, jean-clad, and beetle-browed, with a mop of curly dark hair and a full beard—different in every way from Blake. I'd chatted with Harry in class before, but I'd never really talked with Blake.

I rolled my eyes. "Oh, yeah, I've been loving every minute of it."

"It beats the hell out of gross anatomy, you have to admit," Blake chimed in. "But that's not saying much, is it?" Blake was a quiet guy, good-looking in an absent-minded-professor sort of way: medium height, athletic build, wire-rim glasses, wearing khakis and a button-down shirt—a member of what Harry jokingly called "the Ivy League jock set."

"That lecture about the female orgasm was interesting." Harry waggled his eyebrows at me.

"Yeah, Kay, do you have anything to add?" Blake smiled slyly in the rear-view mirror.

"Not that I'm about to tell you guys," I said airily as I gazed out the window. "There are some things a man just has to find out for himself."

The guys' banter was a welcome distraction from my romantic difficulties. After a period of swapping quips and commentary about the absurdities of medical school, Harry said,

"Hey, Kay, did you know Blake was an English major?"

"Wow! I was almost an English major myself. How'd you meet all the pre-med requirements?"

Blake laughed. "Oh, the usual way—I studied my ass off. I really miss having time to read non-medical stuff."

"Me, too. I've got this stack of novels I want to read, but I just don't have the time."

"We should get together sometime and talk about our favorite writers," he said.

"I'd like that."

My base of operations for this visit was the Cambridge apartment of one of my college friends. Though I'd brought along some homework, I mostly planned to rest, read a novel or two, and visit people. I was really looking forward to being in an academic hub again; the Boston area was alive with students, ideas, and discussions. Medical school presented me with vast quantities of information, but all those facts left me with a hunger for something I couldn't articulate. Creativity didn't seem to have a place there, at least not during the preclinical years, when the main skills you needed were a flair for memorization and a modicum of analytical ability. Plus, there wasn't enough time for the reading and journal-writing that had always helped me make sense of my life.

But much as I enjoyed prowling through non-medical bookstores in Cambridge, I soon became disillusioned with the ivory-tower atmosphere. Living in one of Baltimore's less savory neighborhoods, witnessing people's suffering on the streets and in the hospital, had opened my eyes to the real world beyond the halls of academe. My perspective would never be the same. I struggled to reconcile the world of ideas and the mind with the realities of urban life that I now encountered every day.

One of the things I'd planned to do during my time in Massachusetts was to visit my mother's grave. While screwing up my courage to buy some flowers to take to the cemetery, I was stopped in my tracks by the daffodil bouquets for sale on a Cambridge street-corner, their sunny faces nodding in the brisk March wind. My eyes filled with tears, and I knew I couldn't face that graveyard visit yet. There was something about the flowers that made me connect with the enormity of my loss and longing, the terrible knowledge that, as Thomas Wolfe wrote, "you can't go home again."

My life as my mother's daughter was gone forever.

• • •

When I got back to Baltimore, the phone conversations with Preston resumed, though we seldom saw each other. One evening I called him after finishing a book I'd purchased in Cambridge called *Combat in the Erogenous Zone*, written by Ingrid Bengis, a woman only a few years older than me. It was a wise and poignant early-'70s exposition of the different perspectives of women and men on love and sex. Once I'd finished it, I knew I had to discuss it with Preston. The issues she raised, it seemed to me, were the very issues we'd struggled with.

"*Combat in the Erogenous Zone*?!" He laughed. "Great title. Why this book?"

"It's about the battle of the sexes, by a woman in the trenches. She talks about how hard it is for women and men to really understand each other—how sex for women is not an end in itself the way it is for men. She's tried being liberated, she's tried free love and casual sex, and it all comes down to the same thing: sex without love just isn't worth anything."

"And how do *you* feel about all this?" Preston asked softly.

"She could be *me*! I've tried so hard to be 'liberated,' and it's only making me miserable."

There was a sigh at the other end of the line.

"And another thing—in her experience, the longer two people are sexually involved, the less interested the man becomes, and the more emotionally involved the woman becomes." I pulled the phone receiver away from my cheek to dab at my eyes.

"Is that what you think happened to us?" he asked gently.

"I don't know. I don't know anything anymore." My voice broke. "It's all so confusing, and I'm so lonely."

Another sigh. "Look. I've said this before, and I'll say it again. I'm not going anywhere. I really care about you, you know that. I'm here for you."

I couldn't hold back my tears any longer. "I was doing okay until we had that fight in the cafeteria, and then there was spring vacation, and I started really missing my mom, and now it's all coming down on me…"

"Aw, baby…"

"And now I can't stand myself! I feel like a complete failure and a horrible person."

"Come on, you know that's not true. You're a great person, you're warm and intelligent, you're sexy..."

"Sexy?! Look where *that* got me! And being smart does nothing for me if I'm just going to be lonely for the rest of my life. Maybe if I were less intelligent, all this wouldn't hurt so much."

"Hey, hey! Don't you dare disparage your intelligence! It's a great gift, and you have no right to disrespect it like that." His voice rose.

"Oh, yeah? And why do you care, anyway?"

"Because I *love* you, *that's* why!"

It took a few beats for this to sink in. "What?? *Now* you're telling me this? Why couldn't you have said it before, when I really needed to hear it?"

"Because, missy, not everything I say or do is specifically designed to meet *your* needs."

I pictured him at the other end of the line, drawing himself up to his full height.

"That's for sure!" I couldn't hold back a bark of laughter. Then my voice softened; I was genuinely touched. "But...thanks for saying it, anyway."

He chuckled. "Yeah, you finally dragged it out of me."

"Oh, honey," I said. "I just want it to be like it was before. I miss you so much. I hate this!"

"Yeah, me too. Sometimes I wish we could just start over again."

I thought I heard him sniffle. "Are you crying?"

"Yes, I am. You're not the only one who's lonely." He blew his nose. "It's always sad when two people's needs don't mesh anymore. I've been around the block a few times, so I've known that fact of life for quite a while now. And now you know it, too, baby. I'm sorry." It was good to know that he was having a hard time, too, that it wasn't just me.

Most of our phone conversations during the weeks after our breakup were less about us and more about me. I unloaded on him—all my despondent moods, my lethargy, my difficulty concentrating on my work. It was so hard to accept the fact that I had to start here, now, and make what I could of my messed-up life. I wanted to start all over again and do everything *right* this time, including my relationship with Preston; but that wasn't possible.

I hated feeling so immature and dependent. How could I ever take care of patients if I couldn't even take care of myself? I wanted to be mature, serene, *better*, and I just wanted the pain to stop. Preston listened patiently to my outbursts. He refused to let me get away with saying hateful things about myself. No matter how I tried to manipulate him, he let me know that he accepted me and loved me anyway. No one else had done that for me—ever.

Meanwhile, my relationship with Jane remained fraught with paradox and conflict. And yet, when I was down, she rushed to console me; when she was anxious, I hurried to reassure her. There was a kind of symbiosis between us, an enmeshment that made genuine friendship harder rather than easier. Both of us were staunch feminists who believed that a relationship with a man shouldn't take precedence over a friendship between two women. This kind of loyalty was a matter of principle for both of us. But principle is based on ideas, and ideas often turn out to be emotion's bitch. Much as I loved Jane, I loved Preston more, even after the previous month's rupture. Sisterhood was powerful, but only up to a point.

There were periods of brief respite from my ruminations—time spent with friends outside the claustrophobic circle of my feelings for Jane and Preston and my intensifying struggle with depression. As the days grew longer, Jack and I took occasional walks around the neighborhood in the evening. He listened sympathetically to my angst, giving me the benefit of his own life experience, which was richer than mine. Eric and I had some good conversations when he drove me home after Tuesday evenings at the Campus Inn. My classmate and friend Paul invited me to accompany him to the racetrack one beautiful Saturday afternoon, a first for me. Though I lost my $10 bet, I enjoyed myself more than I had in months.

But despite the support from Preston, Jane, and my other friends, depression and anxiety closed in on me. I *had* to finish medical school, for my mother's sake if not my own; but now I wasn't sure I could do it. My academic efforts were now all but eclipsed by my emotional struggles. Whenever I found myself alone in the house, loneliness morphed into claustrophobic panic. I needed desperately to escape, but I wasn't sure from what, or where to go.

One Monday afternoon when Jane, Sadie, and all my housemates were gone, I paced the living-room floor for an hour or more, wringing my hands and crying, fearful as a cornered animal. Studying was out of the question. I usually turned to Preston when I was upset, so I dialed his number with shaking hands, but he was out of the office. Finally, in a last-ditch attempt to stem the rising tide of panic, I called our landlord, two houses down.

"Hello?" Bruce picked up.

"Oh, thank god there's somebody there! Bruce, I'm scared—I'm freaking out. I'm all by myself here, there's nobody home, I just can't stand it…I—I'm afraid I'm going to hurt myself."

There was a sigh at the other end of the line. "Hold on, I'll be right there."

Within minutes, Bruce and Will were at the door. To their credit, there were no tactless remarks or eyerolls, just brisk efficiency and a reassuring sense that they had the situation under control. Bruce drove me to the University Hospital ER in his pickup truck, where a kindly but tired-looking psychiatry resident listened to my litany of disaster—my mother's death, my failed relationships, the indignities of being a woman in medical school. It felt weird to be talking with a psychiatrist-in-training about depression when I'd just been reading about it in my psychiatry textbook—a strange confluence of medical school and real life.

"It must have been very hard to lose your mother so soon after you started medical school," he said. Then he made me promise that I would not try to kill myself. It was a little strange to actually hear someone say the words "kill yourself" out loud. I hadn't admitted to myself how desperate I was. The resident sent me home with a Librium prescription for anxiety and a referral to a social worker for therapy.

A few days after my meltdown, Preston and I met for lunch for the first time in several weeks. I was having a rare good day, and he was in a good mood. He reached across the table for my hand, and his smile was the kind I remembered from our early days together.

"You look good today, baby. How's it going?"

I told him about the trip to the ER and that I was starting to feel better.

"The medication's already helping me sleep better, and I'm seeing a therapist at the end of the week."

"Glad to hear it. I told you things would get better, didn't I?"

"Yes, you did." I squeezed his hand.

"You just have to give it time. It's hard when you're young; you think you'll be unhappy forever, that things will never get better. But they always do."

At the end of the meal he said, "How about you and Jane come over to my house for dinner tonight? We can share a bottle of wine, listen to some music."

"That sounds great." My eyes widened in surprise.

Jane was as surprised as I was; but the idea of someone else fixing us a meal and plying us with wine sounded good to her, too, mired as we were in quizzes and tests.

After dinner, the three of us snuggled on the sofa with Preston in the middle, enjoying the soft April breeze through the open door to the deck while he read aloud from a book called *How to Be Your Own Best Friend*. Jane and I were both worn down by medical school and in need of nurturing, and he was happy to provide it. When Preston put the book down and turned my face toward him for a kiss, my eyebrows shot up, but I relaxed when Jane reached over to take my hand. Then he turned to kiss her; I noticed, to my surprise, that I didn't feel jealous at all. And when he started stroking each of our necks at the same time, it felt like the most natural thing in the world for us to kiss each other.

Jane and I were silent as she drove us back from Preston's house; we held hands whenever there was a red light. But the bliss of sharing physical affection with these two people I loved soon gave way to a somber what-have-I-done feeling. We'd entered unfamiliar territory, and I wasn't sure how I felt about it. Too much was happening, in too short a time.

For the next few weeks, Jane and I were closer than we'd ever been or would ever be again. Though she'd started dating someone and I remained emotionally involved with Preston, we were able to admit that we loved each other, too, and that there was an erotic component to that love. But mostly we just relaxed into a new level of mutual support and reassurance. I became aware that, while there were some things I could only get from a man, there was a certain kind of tenderness that I could only share with a woman.

• • •

As the end of the school year approached, practical matters claimed more of my attention. Jane, Sadie, and I skimmed apartment listings. None of us had any desire to remain on Stricker Street for another year. The Bolton Hill neighborhood, where some of our friends lived, looked promising. I'd decided to look for a summer job in Baltimore instead of retreating to the family home in Libertytown, so I applied for a summer research position at the Alpha House, a halfway house for women recovering from alcohol abuse.

By the time classes ended, I felt better physically. My appetite improved, and a recent flare-up of eczema was subsiding. With the end of that academic year in sight, I looked forward to a couple of months without quizzes, tests, or pictures of Playboy Bunnies cropping up in lecture slides. Maybe I could regain a foothold on the Wheel of Fortune.

As I'd promised the long-suffering psychiatry resident in the ER, I started therapy with Karen, a social worker, at the end of April. Karen was trim, smiling, and briskly self-assured, with snapping brown eyes and stylish clothing. I was intimidated at first, but she soon put me at ease. She was the wife of a physician, only a few years older than me. Karen didn't waste any time. By our second session, she'd told me that I was turning the anger, even hatred, that I felt toward my mother inward, against myself. This made sense to me. I missed my mother terribly and felt abandoned, cast adrift; yet I hated her for dying, and for my dependency on her.

Worse yet—and this was hard to admit—part of me was actually *glad* she was dead, because now I no longer had to live her dream. I was free to set my own course.

How could I be glad my mother was dead? My guilt after that session only compounded my self-hatred. And—free? Free to do *what*? There was the rub. The downside of finally having my life to myself was that I now had to figure it out on my own, to assume full responsibility for myself, with no one to fall back on and no excuses. For that I would need all the help I could get, in and out of therapy.

Preston and I began seeing each other again, cautiously and sporadically. We went dancing a couple of times, something we both enjoyed. There were some arguments, but the tension always evaporated once we hit the dance floor. Preston's divorce was moving into its final stages, and he told me how painful it was that his contact with his children was now limited to a couple of weekends a month. For the first time, I could see that he, too, was dealing with a lot of upheaval and grief—something that must have been going on for a lot longer than I'd realized.

After one of our dates, we spent the night at his place. As enjoyable as it was to make love with him again, I had a sad little feeling in the corner of my heart the next day, for now I really knew, viscerally rather than just intellectually, that things could never go back to the way they'd been in the first months of our love affair. I still loved him, and I was pretty sure he still loved me, but the honeymoon was over. After that night together, my loneliness returned with renewed force. Our lives had diverged so much that not seeing him at all might be less painful than spending time with him on an irregular basis like we were doing. He just didn't need me the way I needed him, and that lack of reciprocity really hurt.

The honeymoon with Jane was over, too. Opportunities to be alone with her were fewer since she'd started dating Tim, a graduate student; and being alone with her was a mixed blessing. Now that she was part of a couple for the first time since we'd started medical school, my jealousy and envy came to the fore again. I resented having to share Jane with a boyfriend; and I hated being a fifth wheel, the only one of my friends who wasn't part of a couple. Whenever I spent any time with Jane now, Tim was her main topic of conversation. It was clear, from the things she said about him, that our own interlude of closeness was over. Sometimes I sulked and rebuffed her friendly overtures. She usually responded with a sympathetic hug when this happened, attributing my spitefulness to the grief process—which pissed me off, even though it was partly true. I'd come to feel I was just another one of Jane's "hangers-on."

My anxiety crested as the end of the semester bore down on us and final exams loomed. One Sunday I attended an all-woman study group to prepare for the upcoming psychiatry exam. Going over the *Diagnostic and Statistical Manual*, I ran afoul of the section entitled "Pathological Grief."

"Goddammit!" I yelled, throwing the book on the floor. "'Pathological grief?!' Who the hell do these people think they are? Why do *they* get to decide what's 'pathological,' anyway?"

My friends just stared at me. I was fed up with grief. It was already running my life; the last thing I needed was to have to study it for a test.

The physiology seminar concluded with a paper instead of an exam. My friend Mike and I spent several late nights in

Howard Hall working on our papers, drinking coffee, and spurring each other on. I pulled my first all-nighter the night before the project was due and turned in my paper shortly after sunrise. Afterward, I stumbled home along the quiet, dawn-suffused streets of Southwest Baltimore, utterly depleted. A different kind of depression settled over me for a few days, the kind born of feeling hollowed out, totally empty. The first year of medical school was finally over.

My summer job at the Alpha House began in the middle of June. The facility consisted of a couple of adjacent rowhouses and served about fifteen women at a time. The work involved interviewing clients to expand the knowledge base about the social factors involved in women's alcohol abuse. Interviewing was an activity I'd recently discovered—in our human sexuality class, of all places—that I enjoyed and did well. Though some of my interviewees were formidable, even hostile, most of them were good-natured, kind, and touchingly deferential. I listened respectfully and intently to the women's stories; they were sad and funny, about hard times and obstacles overcome. It was easy to relate to their struggles. And it was good to be reminded that other women suffered, too, that I was not alone.

The same week I started my job, I discovered that Dr. Karpeles had given me a grade of Honors in physiology. All my other grades so far had been Pass. Even better, he wrote a glowing evaluation; apparently, he thought highly of me as a person as well as a student. I was happy, proud, and deeply touched.

Unfortunately, those good feelings couldn't withstand the stress of moving out of the Stricker Street house in late June. I fretted about seeing less of Jane and Sadie over the summer. Jane had temporarily moved home with her parents, and Sadie would remain on Stricker St. until her summer classes were over.

I would no longer be able to run over to 330 anytime I felt anxious and needed to talk to someone.

Plus, even after two months of therapy, whatever I did still felt like the wrong thing. I couldn't accept the fact that it had been such a struggle just to get through that year; I thought I should have been able to handle it better. I couldn't give myself credit for what I *had* accomplished—not even that Honors grade in physiology.

When I started working at the Alpha House, I moved for the summer into a lovely townhouse on John Street in Bolton Hill, rented by a group of women from Johns Hopkins Medical School. One was a former Wellesley classmate; I was subletting, holding her place for the summer. The first evening in the house, one of my new roommates, Muffy, told me with a dismissive flick of her hand over a gin and tonic, "I really wanted to be a ballerina, but it didn't work out, so here I am in medical school in a city just crawling with Blacks."

I nearly choked on my own drink. Clearly, Muffy and I would never be friends.

Fortunately, my other roommate, Shayna, an artist about my age, was as different from Muffy as anyone could be. She was wise, gentle, and easy to talk to. During our late-night discussions I learned that Shayna had been hospitalized for depression within the last year, so I felt comfortable sharing my own struggles with her.

Early in July, Preston and I met for dinner at our favorite Chinese restaurant. There wouldn't be any time at his place afterward because he had to meet with his ex-wife to discuss some divorce-related issues. Over mu shi pork and sweet-and-sour chicken, we recapitulated our relationship—the early days of romance and passion, the ongoing mentor/mentee aspect, and the more recent parent/child dimension. And we talked of death—mostly the loss of my mother, but also the end of his marriage and the impermanence of feelings and relationships in general. Our age difference shrank to insignificance.

As he was driving me back to my place Preston said, "You know, I still want you as much as I ever did, even after all that's happened. I just wish life were simpler. I wish your needs and mine weren't so different right now, so we could just enjoy making love and not have to think about anything else."

"Me, too," I said, squeezing his hand. Then he surprised me.

"Actually, I really enjoy our friendship, even when we're not having sex at all." This was a startling admission, coming from this man with whom I'd had such an intense, passionate connection. Yes, there *had* been more to our relationship than sex—so much more. His words turned out to be what I most needed to hear just then; in that moment, I felt genuinely, deeply, loved. As he stopped the car in front of my place, I leaned over and kissed him.

"Thanks, Preston. I love you."

"I love you, too, baby," he said.

Shortly after this I found the courage to write him a letter I'd been mulling over for a few weeks. It took me most of a Sunday afternoon to put my thoughts on paper. On Monday I barged into his office at lunchtime, handing him the letter before I had a chance to lose my nerve. In it was an ultimatum I was pretty sure he would reject: either set aside a certain amount of time for me on a regular basis, or don't spend any time with me at all, at least for a while. Preston smoothed out the pages on his desk and started to read.

"What the hell..." he muttered. When he'd finished, he looked at me over his reading-glasses and shook his head. "I'm sorry," he said. "I can't do this."

Though I was heartbroken, I was not surprised. My anato-my-lab friend Michelle followed me into the ladies' room when she saw me emerge from his office in tears. She gave me a tissue and held me while I cried.

• • •

In the middle of July, another letter delivered some startling news. It was typed on a plain sheet of paper and signed by my sister:

Phil, Kay, Sarah and Mary Alyce White, of Libertytown, announce the engagement of their father, Harlow Hayden White, to Mrs. Patricia Sunderland of Atlanta, Georgia. Mrs. Sunderland is the mother of Toni, John, Cutlar, and Mary.

Mrs. Sunderland is a secretary at Georgia Technical College. Mr. White is employed at Shenandoah Plastics Corporation as the vice-president.

A November wedding is being considered.

Dear Kay,

Surprise!

Love,

Sarah

The note was like a splash of ice water to the face. I knew my father had started seeing Patricia on his business trips to Georgia. Patricia had been divorced for a few years, and Dad was wid-owed; there was nothing wrong with them getting together. But having this happen mere months after my mother's death hurt, so I'd pushed it to the back of my mind.

My father had known Patricia since childhood. Their par-ents had been close friends, and they'd spent time together as children; occasionally Patricia, four years older than Dad, had "baby-sat" him when the two couples went out for the evening. They'd crossed paths again in Europe during WWII, when Dad had been a fighter pilot and Patricia, a dancer and actress, had performed in the USO. There'd been little contact between them once they'd married other people and started their respective families—until those business trips of Dad's. Once I got over the shock of Sarah's letter, I realized I was intrigued by the prospect of acquiring a stepfamily.

Both my ultimatum to Preston and the news of my father's upcoming remarriage got a full airing in therapy. Karen praised me for "taking charge" with Preston, for having the courage to ask forthrightly for what I wanted and to accept the consequences when it wasn't forthcoming. "This is one of the most mature things you've ever done," she declared. She also sounded a cautionary note about the realities of stepfamilies. "It's quite an adjustment, especially having a stepmother—don't expect it to be all sweetness and light."

We also discussed my ongoing guilt and sadness about my own mother. I'd learned from my sister Sarah that our mom had expressed regret during her last months for not having done more with her life, which evoked in me a mix of sadness and determination—not only to get through medical school and establish myself in a career, but to *not* repress conflicts and negative feelings the way my mother had. I couldn't help but make a connection between her habit of sweeping problems under the rug, always putting a good face on things, and the cancer that had caused her premature death.

In August, the same month Richard Nixon resigned from the presidency, I wrapped up my stint at the Alpha House. This involved traveling all over the city for follow-up interviews with the clients in their own homes. The places ranged from dingy apartments in bad neighborhoods to neat brick row-houses with white marble stoops and well-kept lawns. Most of the women were doing well a few weeks after treatment. I was touched by their warm welcomes, the glasses of iced tea and lemonade, and their honesty about their lives. I admired their hard work as they struggled with their addictions and other problems. These women's lives were much harder than mine; hearing about their difficulties put my own suffering in perspective.

Those two months on John St. were a therapeutic and reflective time for me. I was able to think about my love affair with Preston and my friendship with Jane more objectively. With Preston, there'd been a wonderful vitality, a sense of being well-matched, a complementarity that I'd never known with another person. He believed in my intelligence and ability, and his faith in me made me feel that I really could be both a woman and a doctor. This priceless gift helped me change my perception of myself and my potential for the better, even amid all the turmoil and grief of that year.

As for Jane, I could now see that I'd often treated her the way I'd treated my mother—getting angry with her for being unable to make my pain stop, resenting her for my dependency on her. I'd been unfair to both of them.

I spent a lot of time with my family that summer, sailing with my father and brother on weekend afternoons and helping my sisters clean out some of our family's possessions from the Libertytown house to make room for our stepmother and her youngest daughter. Going through the family memorabilia proved to be more painful than I'd anticipated. One afternoon I had to abandon the project and sit outdoors to catch my breath: I was having a full-blown asthma attack while sorting through boxes in the attic, my first such episode since grade school.

For reasons that were never clear, Dad and Patricia changed their wedding date from sometime in November to October 12, not quite a year after Mom's death. I seethed silently about this, and about the fact that Patricia was moving into the Libertytown house. If it had been up to me, my father and stepmother would've started their married life in a new home, one that wasn't fraught with memories of our mother. But the only thing the two women had in common besides their love for my dad was their love of old houses; and the Libertytown house, circa 1811, bore an uncanny resemblance to the venerable fieldstone house in Pennsylvania where Patricia had lived before her divorce.

Of course, all this anger and grief about the dissolution of the family was fodder for therapy. Karen was helpful concerning my dad. She coached me about discussing my feelings about his remarriage with him, and she even offered to have a session or two with both of us—something I didn't pursue, knowing it would have been a bridge too far for my stoic dad. But she was no help at all with my ongoing struggles as a woman in medical school. She told me I was exaggerating the sexism I experienced and implied I might be happier if I stopped resisting the traditional model of womanhood I'd grown up with.

I couldn't believe it! I'd expected more from a woman therapist. I'd been aware from early in therapy that I held some things back from her, fearing she'd judge me. Plus, I envied Karen. She was married and had a young child, while I aspired to marriage and children but didn't know if they'd ever happen for me. And there was a hint of smugness about her that I'd never liked. Though I held these things against her, I knew I was slowly getting better with her help, so I opted to put up and shut up. Fortunately, the doctor doesn't have to be perfect for the medicine to work.

One night I approached my father cautiously while he was reading the *Baltimore Sun* and listening to Mahler's First

Symphony on the stereo.

"Dad," I said haltingly, "can we talk?"

He put down his paper. "What's on your mind?"

I cleared my throat. "I'm having a hard time with you getting married again," I said. "Don't get me wrong, I want you to be happy, and I'm glad you don't have to be alone anymore, but…I feel like we're being pushed aside, especially the girls and me. It's like this place isn't home anymore."

Dad shook his head and gestured for me to sit next to him on the sofa. "No, no. You're my children," he said earnestly. "You'll always be part of my life, and you'll always be welcome here." He looked me in the eye and gave my hand an awkward pat. I knew I'd pushed his ability to talk about feelings to the limit.

I felt a little better, but I was far from reassured. For some reason I stopped short of telling him how hard it had been to clear out our stuff to make way for Patricia and her daughter, how I hadn't felt ready to banish my mother from this place. Difficult as it was to accept, I would simply have to adjust to the new reality.

As August segued into early September, my friends and I turned our thoughts toward the coming academic year. After combing the listings for places in the Bolton Hill area, Jane, Sadie, and I signed a one-year lease on a large five-bedroom house on W. Mount Royal Avenue near the Maryland Institute College of Art (MICA). Such a grand house would be a financial stretch for us, but we could swing it if we found two more roommates. Meanwhile, my family and I had established Mary Alyce in a Preston St. apartment in time for the start of her classes at MICA. She and I would live within walking distance of each other, a comfort to both of us.

The second year of medical school would start the week after

Labor Day. It was hard to believe so much had happened in just one year, amid all those tests and quizzes and studying: the death of my mother, the most significant love affair I'd ever had, a suicidal depression that I was still recovering from. What would the next year bring? Considering what I'd just been through, I allowed myself some trepidation.

But after that restorative summer, I was ready to clamber back onto the Wheel of Fortune. Ready or not, it was time for the giant hand to give the wheel another turn.

8

THE 24-HOUR
ENCOUNTER GROUP

When Jane, Sadie, and I walked into the house at 1416 W. Mount Royal Avenue on that late August afternoon, the smell was perfume to our nostrils: fresh paint and varnish with an undertone of sawdust, a far cry from our former digs on S. Stricker Street. Built in 1880, the nearly 3600-square-foot brick townhouse had just been restored to its former glory as a single-family home after years of exile as a warren of apartments. We roamed the expanse of newly refinished hardwood flooring and freshly painted cream-colored walls, wide-eyed with wonder.

"Wow!" Sadie was the first to speak. "This is fantastic!"

"It's so clean, I could weep," Jane said.

"Look at these high ceilings. The windows. The light!" I was gobsmacked.

After we signed the lease earlier in the month, Sadie found two women from the School of Social Work to fill out the roster of five we would need to afford the rent. Penny was a student from Sadie's class. Kirsten, a married student from the incoming class, lived some distance from downtown Baltimore and needed a place to stay on weeknights. For now, though, it was just the three of us, so we got to pick the best rooms.

Since Jane did much of the legwork finding the house, she

got the biggest room—the third-floor front room with its beautiful triptych window. Sadie chose the second-floor front room, which had a bay window overlooking the street. I was delighted to claim the second-floor rear bedroom, at the end of a narrow hallway. Besides a bay window looking out over a little park behind the house, the room had its own bathroom.

When I first moved in, the space felt perfect. The high ceiling and the alcove of three large windows provided good air circulation and plenty of light. By late fall, though, it was obvious the radiator didn't work. Despite several calls to the landlord, I had to go without heat for the entire winter. I fought the cold by using my fully unzipped sleeping bag as a comforter, to supplement the blankets on the bed.

I decorated my space with curtains I'd made from brightly patterned single-bed sheets, which were just the right length for the windows. Then I splurged on a set of floral print sheets for the double-bed mattress and box spring I'd bought from Shayna at the end of our summer on John Street, which now rested on the floor. I'd come from a home where mattresses were on bedsteads, bed sheets were always white and ironed, and you didn't sleep in a double bed until you were married, so this was living on the edge. The braided rug I'd brought from the Libertytown house was my only concession to the bedroom-furnishing standards I'd grown up with. The old maple desk with its rope-ladder fire escape went in front of the bay window; concrete-block-and-board bookshelves filled the opposite wall. The bathroom fixtures were vintage in appearance but brand-new and contemporary in function. After the cramped and unsanitary shower stall of the Stricker St. house, I reveled in the glory of being able to soak in a bathtub.

Being separated from the rest of the house by that corridor

was no hardship. I spent some time in Sadie's similarly appointed room and some time in Jane's. All four or, rarely, five of us would hang out together from time to time in the spacious, bay-windowed living room, sitting on the secondhand sofa or sprawled in a beanbag chair. In those first few months we often ate together in the dining room, with its gleaming oak floor and thrift-shop table, chairs, and sideboard. The kitchen was large and filled with light. Its back door opened directly onto a driveway off the alley. The appliances were all new and there was lots of counter space. The view from the sink, like that from my bedroom window above it, was of a small brick terrace separating our back alley from that of Rutter St., the next street over. When you washed the dishes, you could look out over the little park and watch your neighbors across the alley doing the same thing, providing an urban sense of camaraderie among strangers.

I settled happily into the lovely old townhouse on Mt. Royal Avenue. Cooking and eating together, sharing responsibility for keeping the place up—the homelike atmosphere ran deeper than the fact that it was a beautiful house. Perhaps living in a household of women would provide a sense of refuge and sanctuary from the constant feeling of being an interloper in medical school because of my gender. Plus, being part of a genuine community might counteract the feeling of exile from my family home that had been so painful over the summer. For the first several weeks of the fall of 1974, the Mt. Royal Ave. house did feel like a second home.

Penny proved to be a welcome addition to the group. She was lively and funny and had energy to burn. Her boyfriend was from Rhode Island, where I'd spent part of my childhood. I found myself lapsing back into my "Ruh Dilan" accent—which has a lot in common with those of Boston and New York

City—whenever he came to visit. Penny was also an exercise enthusiast. In the evenings, we would jog as a group over to the shabby-genteel neighborhood of Eutaw Place, our breath fall-frosty under the streetlights.

Kirsten, our married weekdays-only roommate, quickly assumed a mother role and shepherded us into a formal rotating division of chores that we loosely adhered to for most of the year. She took a dim view of our lengthy pot-infused confabs, in which we dissected our relationships with everyone, especially men. One of her visitors once said to her, in our hearing, "Man, this place is like a 24-hour encounter group!" shaking his head in disbelief as he left. Jane, Sadie, Penny, and I just looked at each other and laughed.

As I was settling into my new home, I checked out the curriculum for the upcoming year. The second year of medical school would be more challenging than the first. The main courses were microbiology, pathology, and pharmacology. Many of us had been exposed in college to one or more of the first-year courses, like biochemistry and physiology; and many biology majors like me had taken a comparative anatomy course in college, which gave us a decent foundation for gross anatomy and embryology. But in the second year, the only course that might have shown up in a college curriculum was microbiology, the study of bacteria, viruses, and fungi. The college version was a lot less detailed than the medical-school course that would take up much of the second year's first semester.

Pathology occupied the entire second year of medical school and was the backbone of our preclinical studies. While gross anatomy is the study of where things are in the body and physiology is the study of how they work, pathology teaches us how it all goes wrong. In pathology lab, we looked through a microscope at the disruption of cells, tissues and organs that happens when diseases wreak havoc. We learned the normal laboratory values for such things as glucose levels and white blood cell counts, and how they fluctuate and change with factors like age and gender. We studied how the various constituents of blood, bone marrow, and other bodily fluids are affected by disease. And we found out how X-rays and other imaging studies reveal abnormalities within the body.

Looking ahead to the second semester, I saw that pharmacology would take the place of microbiology. Pharmacology teaches us how to use drugs to treat disease; it requires much memorization of chemical structures and even some mathematical formulas. And the stakes are high: giving a patient the wrong drug or using the wrong dose can have dire consequences. To make matters worse, the professor in charge of teaching the course had a reputation for being both very demanding and an egomaniac—never a desirable combination. Unlike most of our courses, people had been known to fail pharmacology.

At the beginning of the school year, my summer position at the Alpha House morphed into another modestly paying job related to the care of people with alcoholism: I worked as an alcoholism counselor at University Hospital's emergency department, adding an extracurricular activity to my already-busy schedule. One evening a week, from 6 to 11 p.m., I sat behind the desk of a small office in the back of the ER. When people came in with minor alcohol-related injuries or mishaps, they had the option of speaking with the counselor about AA groups and other resources—once they were, theoretically, sober enough. Some folks were genuinely interested in seeking help; others just wanted someone to talk to. As with the women at the Alpha House, I spent a lot of time listening to stories—but, unlike the situation in the women's halfway house, the stories I heard in the ER were delivered with widely varying degrees of sobriety, candor, and civility. Even so, having a window on these people's difficult lives put my own problems in perspective. When things were quiet, I got some studying done, shot the breeze with the cop on duty, or chatted with one of my friends on the phone.

One early-October afternoon, I took my place in the lecture hall before the start of pathology class. The unspoken seating protocol established in the first year was disrupted when Blake, from the previous spring's road trip to New England, sat down next to me—a pleasant surprise. After we'd chatted about our studies for a while, I said, "My dad's getting married next week." This fact had been foremost in my thoughts for the past several days.

"That's great," he said, beaming. "I'm actually the product of my dad's second marriage." His enthusiasm cheered me and relieved some of my anxiety about the upcoming nuptials and the whole business of acquiring a stepfamily.

But I still resented the fact that my mother hadn't even been dead for a year. By the time the big day came, my sullenness made it hard to look my father in the eye. I didn't hear him tell me I "looked nice" until one of my sisters nudged me after the third time he'd said it.

The wedding itself was a small, tasteful ceremony attended by family and a few friends in Bucks County, Pennsylvania, where Patricia's children had grown up. Two of them, Antonia and John, catered the reception in Philadelphia, in their apartment on Rittenhouse Square. Antonia's madeleines would have made Marcel Proust's mouth water, and John's stuffed mushrooms were equally memorable. I was awestruck by my new stepsiblings' culinary expertise and general sophistication, so I was honored when they invited me to hang out with them after the festivities ended. Once the pressure of food preparation was off, my new siblings both seemed upbeat about the marriage.

Our parents' wedding pictures reveal a handsome middle-aged couple: Patricia at 57 was slender and beautiful in a way my mother had never been, and Dad looked dashing in his gray wedding suit, with his thick black eyebrows and distinguished graying sideburns. The look they shared was that of much younger newlyweds whose passion for each other was there for the world to see, a look that inspired both admiration and envy in me. I felt a mixture of happiness for my dad and sadness for my mother. Whatever negative feelings I might have had about their timing, I had to admit that my father and Patricia made a lovely couple.

A few weeks later, I celebrated my 24th birthday with my roommates around our dining-room table. They'd fixed a wonderful dinner, complete with a chocolate birthday cake and plenty of wine. I sat at the head of the table, relishing the cheerful sounds of talk and laughter, the passing of bowls of food, and the clinking of cutlery and glassware.

"This is lovely, you guys," I said. "Thank you *so* much."

"Hey, any excuse for a party," Penny said, laughing. "No, really, happy birthday."

"And many happy returns," Sadie said, raising her glass. The others joined her in a toast. I beamed at them all.

"I've been feeling kind of homeless lately," I said, "what with moving my stuff out of my dad's house and his wedding and all. But now I feel like I have a new home, and I really appreciate all of you for making that possible." The glasses clinked again. I felt uncharacteristically good about myself and my life—loved rather than abandoned.

"More wine, Kay?" Jane smiled at me, the bottle poised over my glass. I smiled and nodded.

"Thanks," I said. "And thanks for that beautiful corn plant—I'm going to keep it right here in the dining room, where we can all admire it. I think it will look really nice by the window." I lowered my voice. "Thanks for the card, too—it really meant a lot."

Inside a simple birthday card with a cheerful flower on the front, Jane had written a note which concluded: "*The kind of support (security, love or whatever) that I feel from having had all these experiences together this past year & still having you around is one of the things that's holding me together right now. I hope I don't hide that feeling; and I hope that if I do, you'll let me know. Happy birthday & have a great year. You've got my love and support*".

Jane squeezed my shoulder. "I meant every word," she said. Then she turned to her new boyfriend Morris and offered him more wine.

Blake dropped by after dinner, making my day complete, and we shared the rest of the cake and wine. After we talked until almost midnight, he abandoned his original plan to go home and study. We spent another hour in my room, smoking weed, exchanging stories, laughing, and sitting very close together on the floor.

Having been celibate for the past few months, I tried not to singe him with the heat of my desire.

"I guess it's time for me to go—or something…." he said with a laugh.

I couldn't hold back a giggle at his lack of subtlety. Much as I wanted to jump his bones then and there, I also wanted to project an aura, however illusory, of being hard to get and thus of greater value. So I made do with a few meaningful kisses and the assurance that he would take a rain check.

A few nights later, Blake and I had a dinner-and-study date at my place. About a week after that, he invited me for dinner at his apartment on a Friday night. No studying this time. After a delicious meal and an abortive game of chess—it turned out I'd completely forgotten how to play since my last attempt back in high school—we adjourned to his waterbed where he read poetry aloud. I lay back on the pillow and blissfully closed my eyes when he switched to the last sentence of *The Great Gatsby*, one of my favorites in the English language— "*So we beat on, boats against the current, borne back ceaselessly into the past.*"

Before long we were kissing and touching, those long months of celibacy receding into the distance. At a critical moment, Blake pulled a couple of condoms out of a box next to the bed and asked, with a little smirk, "What's your color preference—red or green?" I just gave him a look. Whatever happened to romance? This was turning into too much of a calculated seduction for my taste. After we finished making love he said, "Which poem was it?"

"What?"

"You know what I mean—which poem broke down your resistance?" He smiled slyly. I didn't say anything. Was I just another conquest to him? My ambivalence about having rushed into sex turned to outright anguish. A tear trickled down the side of my face as I stared stoically at the ceiling.

Blake propped himself up on an elbow. "Hey, what's the matter?" His voice was gentle, the flippancy gone.

I shook my head. "This was a big mistake."

"Aw, come on, now," he said, stroking my arm. "I thought it was great. I—well, I have kind of a hard time getting close to people; I don't usually just go to bed with somebody. It was nice to have something in my life be spontaneous for a change. We don't get much of that in medical school, right?" He laughed softly.

Though I was skeptical, I had to smile. Blake was revealing a tenderness I hadn't seen in him before, and his unexpected openness made me feel better.

The next morning, he bounded out of bed as soon as the sun was up, full of the physical, high-spirited joy that men—and, ideally, women—feel when they've had satisfying sex after a dry spell. I wished I could have shared his euphoria instead of feeling angry with myself for capitulating to my own desire so quickly. In my journal, I summed up my performance that evening as follows: an A for foreplay; a B for the actual sex—as with college courses, I was accustomed to A's, but my ambivalence had taken a toll; a C for sense of humor, since I felt I'd overreacted to Blake's silliness with the condom; a D for putting up a good front; and either an A for honesty or an F for self-deception, depending on how you looked at it.

• • •

While I was becoming more involved with Blake, the happy-family atmosphere at 1416 was beginning to fray. Jane's whirlwind romance with our classmate Morris had progressed to the point where he essentially lived in her room, so she didn't socialize with the rest of us the way she used to. Morris was a well-meaning guy, kinder and more considerate than some of our classmates; but he was often oblivious to the subtleties of human interaction, at least with anyone but Jane. Besides Morris practically being a 6th member of the household, Sadie's and Penny's boyfriends habitually stayed over for the weekend. The four of them were always happy to include me on excursions or when passing a joint; but I missed having a boyfriend of my own. After that night in his waterbed, my relationship with Blake was a halting, fits-and-starts affair. I felt like a high-school sophomore sitting by the phone, waiting for a boy to call—a situation I'd hated the first time around and didn't like any better now. Keeping busy with my studies and working in the ER once a week helped me maintain some perspective, but I was starting to feel like a fifth wheel and an outsider in my second home.

Late in November, my focus shifted once again to family. My brother Phil's wedding to Zella—a vivacious, intelligent army nurse with red hair and porcelain skin—took place six weeks after Dad and Patricia's, and I was a bridesmaid. Phil chose Cutlar, the eldest of our stepsiblings, as his best man. It was a joyful occasion which brought our families closer together, but it was also stressful. Having been confronted with yet another wedding so soon after my dad's, I felt more isolated and abandoned than ever. Everywhere I turned, people were pairing off.

One Sunday afternoon in early December, a few weeks after our night together, I dropped in on Blake unannounced. We'd had some brief conversations at school, usually initiated by me. Since these hadn't led to any more evenings together and I was tired of waiting for him to call, I decided to take the initiative. My chronic malaise and depression were in temporary remission that day, after an enjoyable brunch with some good friends. After a few false starts and a lot of walking around Blake's Bolton Hill neighborhood, I finally rang his doorbell. He seemed glad to see me. He was defrosting the refrigerator, and his kitchen counter was littered with mysterious foil-wrapped chunks covered with ice crystals. We chatted while he worked, then practiced looking at each other's retinas with his ophthalmoscope.

"Wow!" I said when Blake shone the bright light into my right eye. "I see this pattern that looks like blood vessels radiating out from the optic nerve *in my own eye*—it's really cool!"

"Whaaat?? You're making that up. I didn't see anything like that."

I knew what I'd seen, but his laughter was infectious, so I didn't challenge him. When he started fixing dinner I made as if to leave, but he insisted I stay and eat with him. As we were cleaning up, I asked him something I'd been wondering about for a while.

"Have I been imposing myself on you? Like, by dropping in on you today?"

"Of course not. I like being surprised; I like spending time with you. And I even kind of like being pursued." He gave me a sly smile. "I've felt a rapport with you since that trip to Boston last year.

"But you need to understand something. I'm not up for getting into a heavy relationship right now. Just so we're clear. I don't want you to be disappointed."

Emboldened by Blake's honesty, I pushed my advantage.

"You give off a lot of mixed signals, you know," I said, as I dried and stacked the plates. "Sometimes you really seem to enjoy talking with me, and sometimes when we're having a conversation after class you just up and leave. How come?"

"I don't know. I feel kind of weird when we're at school." He rinsed a glass and focused his gaze on the window in front of him. "I guess it's hard for me to mix business and pleasure." He shrugged, nearly dislodging the dishtowel from his shoulder.

I looked at him out of the corner of my eye while I dried the other glass and Linda Ronstadt belted out "When Will I Be Loved?" on the stereo.

Then he added, "Well, I do like women who aren't submissive, and I like women with good minds."

I smiled. This was encouraging.

"But I don't know," he said. "Maybe I'm threatened on an unconscious level by women who are smart and assertive."

I raised my eyebrows. This little nugget sounded like something right out of the "24-hour encounter group" and a clever dodge on his part, enabling him to have it both ways. Still, I was impressed by the fact that Blake was able to give both gender equality and the unconscious some respect. This was something I'd rarely encountered with men, especially the men I'd met in medical school; it was part of what made me want him.

When I left for my place, he kissed me goodbye and squeezed my butt—talk about mixed signals. I pondered my options as I walked home. My desire for sex, reawakened by our night together a few weeks earlier, was even stronger after that ass-grabbing farewell. But I didn't want to sabotage the possibility, however remote, of a "real" relationship. Things had been so much simpler last year with Preston, when "sexual relationship" and "real relationship" had not been disparate entities.

Back at the house on Mt. Royal Avenue, I couldn't concentrate on my studies for more than a few minutes at a time. I'd recently read Erica Jong's novel, *Fear of Flying*, in which the heroine fantasizes about a no-strings-attached sexual encounter which she dubs a "zipless fuck." I hadn't been able to get the book out of my mind, and it certainly colored my deliberations that evening. I considered my options: pursue a relationship with Blake, which may or may not become "real" at some point; pick up a guy for a one-night stand (I was that desperate); or—could I be "just friends" with Blake *and* sleep with him, as long as I didn't get too emotionally involved? Voila—problem solved! The practice of "friends with benefits" existed long before the phrase was coined.

Galvanized by this stroke of inspiration, I picked up the

phone before I could get cold feet and dialed Blake's number, even though it was after 11 p.m.

"Hello?" He didn't sound like he'd been sleeping, fortunately.

"Hi, Blake. I've been thinking, and…" I laughed nervously. "…well, I know you don't want to get into a heavy relationship right now, but—how do you feel about casual sex?"

Now it was Blake's turn to laugh nervously. "Well, I—I like it! You know, I felt kind of bad after that time you spent the night, like maybe you felt used or something."

"Well, I did, a little, but that's my problem, not yours. And I think we understand each other a lot better now. So…I'm game if you are."

"My god! Are you *propositioning* me?" He radiated pure incredulity and disbelief. *He really didn't see this coming?* I asked myself. I imagined him shaking his head at the other end of the line, like a swimmer trying to get water out of his ear. "Wait a minute, I really can't handle this right now."

He paused for a beat. I kept my mouth shut. Then he changed the subject.

"Remember that thing you told me about seeing blood vessels when I was looking at your retina? Well, I looked it up and it turns out it's a real physiologic phenomenon. It's called phosphenes."

I raised a fist in a silent victory salute while Blake took a breath.

"Your place or mine?" he said.

I sprinted most of the five blocks to Blake's apartment. When he opened the door, he noticed I was slightly out of breath and asked if I'd been running. "A little," I admitted. He shook his head.

That night proved to be a corrective for the first one we'd

spent together. I gave the experience an unqualified A+. After sex, we cuddled throughout the night, which was probably a violation of the "friends with benefits" code; but my feelings about our second night together, unlike the first, were completely positive. I felt vigorous, healthy, integrated, whole. I felt good about the talks we'd had and the friendship and mutual attraction that flowed between us. Plus, I'd made a choice and taken decisive action. It was one of the few things I'd done in many months that was completely by and for myself, that I could own.

• • •

When I wasn't pursuing Blake, I was studying frantically for microbiology and pathology quizzes and tests; only a third of the first semester remained. My evenings in the ER provided some respite from the drudgery of my studies and the growing tension at 1416. Things were changing at the Mt. Royal Avenue house. Though Jane and I still talked occasionally, she was struggling with her studies and increasingly inaccessible, so I found myself turning more often to Sadie and Penny for commiseration and counsel. We all noticed that Jane was more withdrawn, spending most of her time outside the classroom cocooned with Morris.

The night before the last day of classes for the semester, I went to a holiday party with my classmates. We'd had our last test until final exams, which were scheduled after the New Year, so it was time to let off steam—and let off steam we did.

Blake had pretty much ignored me since that second night together, so my good feelings about it had long since dissipated. I drank at the party in a way I hadn't since college, mixing beer with hard liquor indiscriminately. And it was paying off. I was having a great time dancing and flirting with classmates and friends—until Blake showed up.

"Dammit," I said under my breath. His appearance put an

immediate damper on my inebriated fun. I sensed, rightly or wrongly, that Blake, alias "Mr. Cool," didn't really like my openness and lack of inhibition—not just while dancing drunk at a party, but also in the stultifying atmosphere of the lecture hall. (It didn't occur to me at the time that this very openness and lack of "cool" might be why he'd been attracted to me in the first place, that Blake might wish he were a little less inhibited himself.) After fuming for a while, I swallowed my pride and sauntered over to him. We ended up spending the rest of the evening together, talking and, eventually, dancing—Blake would only dance to Motown music, and only after he'd had enough to drink, so I had to wait a while.

Naturally, I carried the conversation. "I think of you as the master of ambiguity," I told him with a drunken flourish. "I just wish it weren't so much *work*, being with you—never really knowing where I stand. It's like trying to nail Jell-O to a tree."

Blake laughed. "What do you want from me? I told you I'm not looking to get heavily involved with anyone right now." He held my gaze with a little smile and a lift of his eyebrows. When the party was over, we rode home with Mitchell, a friend and classmate who lived near both of us and often gave us rides to school. We sat in the back seat, and Blake held my hand for most of the ride. When he said goodnight and climbed out, I marveled at the way we moved in and out of each other's lives—so close one minute, light-years away the next, like planets with crisscrossing orbits.

When I got home, I was still drunk, but too wired to sleep. In this unfortunate state, I became obsessed with the idea of spending the night with Blake—not to have sex, just to share his bed and his body-warmth. The boozy euphoria of the party had worn off, and I was coming down hard. It took a good five minutes of throwing pebbles at the screen, then a knock at the window, to alert him to my presence; I didn't dare ring the door-bell for fear of awakening his roommate. I heard a knock from the other side of the window. When I looked up and saw his room alight, I had a momentary spasm of fear, much like a child caught in a prank. Blake let me in and gestured for me to sit next to him on his bed.

"I don't want to make love with you, I don't want to talk to you, I just want to lie next to you, do you understand?" I said.

"Wait a minute. I get what you're saying, but I think we do need to talk. Are you okay? It's not like you to be this—dramatic."

"I'm just so tired of being lonely, and now I've fucked every-thing up with you." I started to cry in spite of myself.

After a while he said, "Look, Kay, you don't really want a heavy relationship now any more than I do. You're chasing after a fantasy, an illusion." I pictured myself as a female Don Quixote, tilting at windmills. "This is more like a crush or an infatuation, not really love." His voice was gentle; he wiped away one of my tears with a finger. Much as it hurt to admit it, I knew he was right.

We lay beside each other and talked some more, fully clothed except for our jeans. Soon he drifted off to sleep, but I stayed awake. Finally, I was starting to get it. Blake wasn't the only one who was ambivalent or elusive. For all my noise to the contrary, I was as good at keeping love at bay as he was. I wasn't sure which I was more afraid of, loneliness or genuine intimacy. We were like two magnets aligned with the north poles facing each other, very close yet permanently kept apart by an invisible force field.

The next morning was wretched. Badly hung over, I dragged myself home before dawn, lay briefly in the haven of my own bed, showered, dressed, and rode to school with Mitchell and, unfortunately, Blake. No handholding in the back seat this time. I must have drawn the short straw, to get stuck with discharging my responsibility to the class note-taking service for the 8:30 a.m. pathology lecture the day after the holiday party. It certainly wasn't my finest hour as a note-taker. I was glad to get out of town later that day.

• • •

This was the first Christmas we'd spent at the house in Libertytown in three years. At that Christmas of 1971, my mother's cancer hadn't even been diagnosed yet. The changes at the house since Patricia had moved in were jarring. The colonial-style living room sofa had been replaced by a striped couch with a canopy that was uncomfortable to sit on. There was a different dining room table and a corner hutch with unfamiliar decorative pieces, including a delicate porcelain spider web complete with a small black porcelain spider—not my mother's taste at all, or mine. Patricia had appropriated some of our mother's things and consigned others to oblivion. I felt a sort of "lose-lose" resentment about this: how dare you take my mother's things? But also—what, my mother's things aren't good enough for you? Fortunately, my difficult feelings about Patricia becoming mistress of the house were offset by my father's good spirits. He was warm and welcoming to all of us, and by the end of the vacation I felt closer to him than I had in a while.

Unlike dealing with our stepmother, interacting with our stepsiblings was an exciting adventure. We were all truly interested in getting to know each other, and each of us put our best foot forward. It was like discovering a set of long-lost cousins. I was particularly drawn to John and Antonia, since they were closest to me in age—John slightly older, Antonia slightly younger; the three of us had already started to become friends at our parents' and my brother's weddings.

After the better-than-expected holiday break, I was surprised at how glad I was to get back to my life in Baltimore. I had the house to myself for a couple of days, a rare treat. Jane and Morris were the first to join me; I noticed how quickly my tension level rose when I was once again exposed to their exclusive preoccupation with each other. Soon the others trickled back, and my sister Sarah joined us from Libertytown for a small New Year's Eve party at 1416. I decided to dress up for the occasion. Except for weddings, I'd done very little dressing up since my dates with Preston the previous year. I coaxed my long, thick hair into tight curls by wearing it in tiny braids for a couple of days beforehand, which made it look like Carole King's on the *Tapestry* album. I added a long skirt, a lacy black blouse, and some eye makeup, lipstick, and rouge. Having shed my customary jeans and shirts, I felt feminine and sexy for a change. We rang in 1975 sitting on beanbag chairs and the living room floor, passing a joint while the Doobie Brothers' "Black Water" played on the stereo.

"Why did you feel you had to wear makeup and a skirt?" Jane regarded me with the cool detachment of a psychoanalyst as she took a hit off the joint.

I stared at her, confused. Was Jane, my friend with whom I'd shared so many of the slings and arrows of sexism in medical school, now implying that I was selling out the sisterhood by dressing up? I would have gone to the mat for her whenever she felt her femininity was being attacked; and—now she was attacking mine?

"It's New Year's Eve. I felt like getting dressed up. Is there something wrong with that?" My voice rose, along with the color in my cheeks. Sadie and Penny exchanged looks. Sarah's eyebrows shot up. Morris played with a piece of lint on the rug.

As my high color receded and my heart rate normalized, it occurred to me that I hadn't seen Jane in a skirt or makeup in all the time I'd known her. Was she envious of my ability to look traditionally feminine when I felt like it?

• • •

January, the first month of the new year, meant preparing for final exams, always a difficult time at best. Blake's and my orbits overlapped early in the month when we studied together at his apartment a few times. One of our study-dates ended in his bed, which turned out to have been a bad idea; all my feelings of vulnerability and emotional greediness crowded back in, and I could now see that this "friends with benefits" thing wasn't going to work for me.

As exam-tension rose and Blake (predictably) withdrew, I wrote him off. I could see that my pursuit of him had been consistent with my idea of how a "liberated" woman ought to behave: proactive, fearless about taking the initiative, and anything but passive. But in fact, I felt very insecure about acting this way with him, especially in the face of his obvious ambivalence about my pursuit. I was deeply discouraged to find myself back in an old unfulfilling pattern of forced passivity. The remarkable thing about my time with Blake was the fact that we'd managed to experience some genuine closeness and friendship despite all the murky water that had flowed under the bridge of our relationship.

On the second week of January, there was another birthday in the Mt. Royal Avenue house: Jane's. Working closely with Morris, I headed up the celebratory preparations. Even though it was the first week of exams, I made a special chicken dish and baked a birthday cake. Morris supplied the wine. Penny and Sadie joined us around the dining room table, and we raised our glasses and offered birthday felicitations. But the sense of family that had meant so much to me at my own birthday party wasn't there this time. For one thing, Kirsten had decamped; she'd finished moving out before the semester was over. Being slightly older than the rest of us and married, our "24-hour encounter group" bull-sessions must have been too much for her.

Then there was Jane herself. She was distracted, not really engaged with the rest of us even as we joined in this celebration in her honor. When Morris thanked me later for my role in the proceedings, she awoke from her trance long enough to say offhandedly, "Oh yeah—thanks."

I was hurt. I'd hoped that the evening would restore her to us, at least for a few hours, but that hadn't happened. I knew she was struggling with school and other issues, and I could certainly empathize with her. I really wanted to help, but she always seemed to push me away. She always went to her boyfriend for support instead of coming to me, or any of us women. In her birthday note to me, Jane had asked that I let her know if she was hiding her affectionate feelings for me. Sadly, I wouldn't have known where to start.

The last exam of the first semester was the microbiology final. Those of us who'd done well on the two previous tests didn't have to worry about our grade this time, because the lowest of our three scores would be dropped; but we were still required to take the exam. Someone came up with a plan for making a mockery of this typical medical-school Catch-22: anyone who didn't need a good grade on the test would drink a couple of beers before the exam. Anti-authoritarian as I was, especially that year, I was an eager participant in this scheme. A group of us got together right before the test and downed a plastic cup or two from a keg obtained for the purpose. I entered the classroom with a pleasant buzz. As I stared at the multiple-choice questions before me, I could feel my thought processes slowing to a crawl. It turns out alcohol really *does* impair performance on tasks requiring mental agility. Though my grade on the test suffered as expected, something good came from the experience: I would never be tempted to drink on the job.

Once that final exam was over, I high-tailed it to New York City to visit a college friend for the weekend. One weekend was all the break we would get before second semester started—the last semester of the preclinical years. One more semester, and then we'd be out of the classroom and onto the hospital wards.

9

THE HANGED MAN

It was the third week of January 1975, and there was still much to learn before we were thrust into our third-year role of make-believe doctors. We faced another semester of pathology and the looming threat that was pharmacology. The preceding weekend hadn't been nearly enough time between semesters. Everyone at 1416 Mt. Royal Avenue seemed depressed and withdrawn; it wasn't just me. We may have been suffering in part from a national malady—the situation in Vietnam was deteriorating rapidly, and the price of gasoline was rising precipitously. While I didn't have a car to feed, images of long gas lines and Vietnam footage on TV exacerbated my low spirits.

Plus, studying in my heat-challenged bedroom wasn't working. With stiff fingers, I struggled to underline key points in my pharmacology textbook; it was so cold I could practically see my breath. I started spending most of my evenings at the University of Baltimore Law School library, a short walk from the house. I'd never been fearful of walking alone in the city at night, even in the Southwest Baltimore neighborhood I'd lived in the previous year. Sometimes I'd get a leer or a threatening glance from a passing male, but I returned these with a frank don't-fuck-with-me look and always managed to get home safely.

One afternoon at the end of January, I slogged through grimy slush on my way home after classes. The previous day's snow was melting. The combination of car exhaust and cold, damp air made my airways constrict. On a sudden whim, I ducked into the Greyhound bus station and approached the ticket counter.

"Um, how much is a one-way ticket to Chicago?"

"One way?" The clerk gave me a sideways look. "That would be $29.99. You buyin' a ticket?"

"No, no, just checking. Thanks." I gave him a sheepish grin and slunk off. Chicago?! What was I thinking? Sure, I was desperate to escape, but… Chicago in January? It had to be colder there than in Baltimore. I should have asked about someplace warm, like Miami or L.A., but Chicago was the first place that came to mind. *Anywhere but here,* I told myself.

There's a card in the tarot deck called The Hanged Man, which shows a young man whose left ankle is suspended by a rope from a crossbar between two tree trunks stripped of their branches. He holds himself in perfect equipoise. If you turn the card upside down, he could be dancing a jig: his right leg is bent at a precise right angle behind his left, and both hands are behind his back at the level of his waist. His face is expressionless. He doesn't look the least bit distressed by his predicament, even though he's clearly stuck. There are a few interpretations of this card, chief among them that it represents surrender of the self to the universe and trust in its wisdom. Another version suggests that what you want and what is happening seem to be going in different directions at the same speed, so surrender is the wisest course. At that point in medical school, what I wanted and what I was experiencing were certainly going in opposite directions. But, surrender and trust in the universe? That wasn't happening. And, unlike the Hanged Man, I *was* distressed by my situation.

Though I plowed through those winter days encased in a shell of brightly-smiling indifference, I was not just depressed,

I was *bored*—bored with the same old issues and problems, the loneliness and feelings of exclusion. Bored with talking about these problems in therapy; bored with myself. And bored with medical school's dismal grind of memorization.

The basic science studies of the first two years had given me a bad case of myopia. Despite the clinical exposure of Physical Diagnosis class and the Pediatric Tracking program, I couldn't grasp the larger picture, the actual practice of medicine waiting at the end of all the quizzes and tests, the lecture notes and textbooks underlined in yellow marker, the anatomy specimens and microscope slides. There were so many other things I wanted to do with my life besides what I was doing at that moment, and I was afraid I would never get to do any of them.

Even my job as an alcoholism counselor was losing its appeal. My clients were disillusioned by previous encounters with the system, tired of the same old recommendations that hadn't worked—recommendations that were offered by people who didn't understand what their lives were really like. Sometimes, when confronted with a particularly obnoxious client, I would be appalled by my own arrogance when I caught myself thinking, *Hey, wait a minute, I'm trying to* help *you here! You're supposed to thank me, not boss me around.* Even as a second-year medical student, I knew I wouldn't be much help to people if the main point of my effort was to receive praise and gratitude.

My chief avenues of resistance to everything I hated about medical school—the repetition and memorization and, especially, the sexism—were writing in my journal and reading *The Diary of Anais Nin.* This woman sought to live a multiplicity of lives in one, to extend her life by broadening it, chiefly through a series of love affairs—a tactic I, naturally, found intriguing. Though providing a temporary escape, neither the writing nor the reading did anything to ameliorate my self-absorption and isolation; if anything, they only made them worse. The best time of day came at the end when, after a few hours at the law library, I dropped my textbooks on the floor of my freezing room, smoked part of a joint, and slowly eased myself under the covers of my cold bed, making vigorous snow-angel motions with my arms and legs to warm up the sheets. Dreaming had become my principal creative outlet. In that shadowy realm, I could be like Anais Nin—writing in a cafe in Paris, sleeping all day and taking part in alcohol-fueled literary discussions all night, traveling to exotic locales, and taking up with fascinating lovers.

While I was dragging myself through the semester's first weeks, the cast of characters at 1416 was changing. Early in February, Paula, an art student, moved into Kirsten's former room. She was a couple of years younger than the rest of us— cute, blonde, and cheerful, with a quirky sense of humor. Best of all, the drama of the "24-hour encounter group" just rolled off her back. Her sunny temperament was just what the rest of us needed during this gloomy time. Sadie broke up with her boyfriend Gabe that same month, and she and I became closer now that we were both single. Sometimes on weekends we checked out the man situation together at No Fish Today, a nearby bar. Jane continued to hunker down with Morris, and my friendly overtures to her tapered off, since they were usually rebuffed. When she started asking for help with pharmacology, usually the night before a test, I did my best; but I gave up trying when it became apparent that she either hadn't retained anything she'd learned or simply hadn't studied. When she failed a test I hadn't helped her to study for, I felt a mixture of guilt and schadenfreude.

Toward the end of February, something interesting happened: Blake started coming around again. At first, he would chat with me for a while after class. Then he asked me to study with him at his place a couple of times—which I did warily, avoiding any physical contact. I managed to maintain a certain inner distance as well, taking his overtures with a grain of salt. I felt a mix of attraction and hostility. Previously I'd had trouble maintaining eye contact with him; now I could look him in the eye with ease, and he sometimes had to look away. We were like dogs who'd switched roles, and I was now the alpha. Now that *he* was pursuing *me*, the balance of power had shifted.

One afternoon, he invited me to join him for a beer.

"My dad's dying," he began.

"Oh, no, I'm sorry to hear that."

"Don't worry, it's not imminent. But he's had Parkinson's disease since I was in high school, and now he's wheelchair-bound and the medications aren't working anymore."

"That must be tough."

He shrugged. "Well, he *is* in his 70s, it's not like he's a young guy. But…I feel like I've always had to worry about him and look out for him.

"The part that really sucks," he added, "is that I'm afraid that when he *does* die, I might not even feel anything."

"Why do you say that?"

"Because of medical school. It's worn me down so much, I feel like—I don't know, some kind of robot."

"I know what you mean." I nodded. "But, believe me, you'll feel something. When my mother died last year—man, I was all over the place! Even though she'd been sick for a while, it was such a shock when it actually happened. It took a while to sink in, and when it did…well, I couldn't let myself think about it or feel it for very long, or I'd be crushed. Then I'd be euphoric for a while, then I'd crash again…I'm still trying to get it together, and

I know I've got a long way to go."

He looked at me with a respect I hadn't seen before.

"Here's something you might want to keep in mind," I said. "I don't really believe in heaven or a life after death; but I do believe my mother still lives on in some way. I don't think our loved ones who die are ever really gone while we're here to remember them."

"Thanks. That helps." He smiled.

We moved on to other things, dancing around any direct reference to our earlier intimacy. Blake acknowledged that he'd been using the demands of medical school to avoid examining his own life and feeling his emotions. Whereas I couldn't seem to avoid examining my life or experiencing my emotions even if I wanted to, medical school notwithstanding. When he got up to leave, I reached over to touch his hand, but he disappeared before I could make contact.

When Easter break came at the end of March, I spent a few days in Libertytown with my father and stepmother. Walking past the general store and the freshly painted little post office, the Civil War-era tin-roofed houses, it felt like a ghost town, despite all the crocuses, forsythia, and other harbingers of spring. The place harbored not only my mother's ghost, but also the ghost of a "me" who was no more, her daughter.

A tipping point had occurred that I wasn't aware of until that day: I now belonged in Baltimore more than I belonged here, where my mother had spent the last years of her life. When I opened the door of the fieldstone house where my father now lived with his new wife, I realized it wasn't my home anymore. I was glad it was the last day of vacation.

Back in the city, spring arrived, despite pathology, pharmacology, and all the rest. On a particularly lovely April afternoon,

Blake's and my orbits crossed again. He'd called me out of the blue to ask if he could come over to take a break from studying. I watched him from my desk chair as he lay on the bed, hands clasped behind his head. The sunshine poured in from the large bay window, illuminating his face and accentuating the gold highlights in his hair. He was wearing a pale-yellow shirt, which enhanced the sense of a room filled with sunlight.

"I almost called you last night," he said.

"Oh?"

"Yeah. I wanted to spend the night with you."

My eyebrows rose.

"But then I figured I just had a bad case of spring fever." He laughed.

"Spring fever, huh? I'm flattered."

"Sorry, that didn't come out right. I really enjoyed the times we slept together, but...I guess what I really want is for us to be friends."

"That would be nice," I said with a shrug, wondering where he was going with this. As he spoke, I could see that Blake was just like me in some important ways: he was a romantic, bewildered about where to put sex in his life, and he struggled with the push-pull of fear and desire just as I did. The difference: he was way more scared to open up than I was.

"Here I am," he said, "24 years old, and Ms. Right still hasn't walked into my life yet."

I resisted the temptation to ask, "So what am I, chopped liver?" But I had to admit, I couldn't really think of Blake as "Mr. Right," either. Before long, he slyly slipped in a proposition: "Could we try that having-sex-as-friends thing again?"

"Ha! You really do have spring fever, don't you? I think we'd better not," I said, smiling even as I shook my head. I was tempted by his knowing grin and his inviting pose on my bed; but, especially after this frank discussion, I knew it was a bad idea. It was almost comfortable for both of us to hold the possibility of love at bay, to tease each other with our ambivalence. If we'd given in to our mutual desire that day, we both would have felt cheated, that there should have been more to it. Sex by itself simply wasn't enough. I shouldn't have been surprised or hurt when our orbits diverged again after that conversation, but I was.

A few weekends later, I decided to forget about men and do nothing but study from Friday evening until bedtime on Sunday. It was a good time for a marathon study weekend. Monday's pathology test would be on the kidney, perhaps the most complex organ in the body aside from the brain. It's not just a simple matter of filtering the blood and excreting waste; the kidney has to "know" when and where, along its lengthy and convoluted tubing, to excrete sodium, for example, and when and where to reabsorb it.

Knowing what to hold on to and what to let go—not unlike my own life.

My single-minded effort paid off beyond my expectations: I got a perfect score on that test, the only perfect grade I got in medical school. Someone took a picture of me checking my answers against those posted on the bulletin board, and the picture ended up in the yearbook. I'm wearing a windbreaker, and my hair is pulled back in a kerchief. Even though my face is in profile, it's not hard to see the look of dawning elation.

After that triumph, I toyed with the idea of dedicating the few remaining weekends of the preclinical years entirely to study. One of the biggest problems I had with medical school was the experience of being mediocre—not exceptional, not outstanding, not distinguished in any way. This had never happened to me before. After that pathology test, it was painfully clear how large a role my own resistance to the requirements of medical school had played in this. But I couldn't bring myself to put aside everything else in my life—such as it was—for the sake of a few perfect scores on tests, not even for a mere few weeks. All those hundred-percents in grade school and high school, even the A's and honors in college, had not made me feel any more secure or given me genuine self-confidence, so there was no reason to think that a spate of perfect scores in medical school would now. And the creative person within me rebelled at the constraints that such a regimen, however temporary, would put on my spirit.

The following week, fresh from my pathology-test coup, I dropped in on Preston in his office one afternoon after class—the first time I'd seen him since the previous summer. It was a sunny day, spring was well-established, and I was in a good mood. I'd been thinking about him a lot, partly because things with Blake were so frustrating, but partly because I'd figured out a few things about my relationship with Preston and felt a strong need to talk with him again. When I stepped into his office, he was on the phone. His eyes grew wide, and a big smile spread over his face. He motioned for me to sit down. "My daughter," he mouthed.

"Yes, honey," he said into the receiver. "I'll pick you up from drama club. Yes, your mom knows. It was her idea." He rolled his eyes at me. "I love you, too, baby, I'll see you tonight. Bye."

Then he walked around his desk, said, "Well, look who came to visit!" and wrapped me in a long, tight bear hug. As we rocked back and forth, I said into his neck, "God, I've missed this. I've missed *you*!"

"Me, too." He stood back, grinning, and looked me over. "You look fantastic! I haven't seen you in ages. What you been up to?"

I told him about the perfect score on the kidney test, and that, all things considered, I was feeling pretty good about myself.

"That's great. Did you notice anything when you said that?"

"What do you mean?"

"You just flat-out told me you were feeling good about yourself. No equivocation, no making me drag it out of you." He chuckled. "I think you must've grown up a lot this year," he added softly.

I filled him in on my dad's remarriage and my instant step-family, the "24-hour encounter group" on Mt. Royal Avenue, and my on-again, off-again relationship with Blake.

"I didn't realize until just now how starved for hugs I was, how much I've been craving affection," I said. "Being held while you're having sex doesn't really count as a hug, especially when that's the only time it happens." He cocked an amused eyebrow at me.

"So, how've you been?" I asked.

"I'm really glad I got to see you today, because I'm leaving for the Netherlands on sabbatical in a few weeks."

"How exciting! You'll be gone for a year?"

"Yeah. Should be interesting. I've never been there before."

"That's really cool. I'm glad we got to talk before you leave."

We reminisced about the carefree early days of our relationship and reflected on the friendship that had grown out of it despite last spring's turmoil and pain. We even shared some of the old passion when we kissed goodbye, and he joked about the effect I always had on him. My face flushed as we shared one last hug. Walking back to Mt. Royal Avenue in the bright April sunshine, I realized that my relationship with Preston was a kind of gold standard. Despite all his foolishness about "multiple interactions" and my own panoply of issues, we'd experienced a rich connection that I was deeply grateful for—one of affection, mutual respect and regard, and deep caring. As I approached the front steps of my house, I wondered if I would ever know such intimacy again.

Early May brought television images of the fall of Saigon. My sister Sarah graduated from Simmons College in the middle of the month, and I flew to Boston for the ceremony. Like my brother's wedding six months earlier, the event proved to be more stressful than I'd anticipated. We all missed Mom, of course; this was the first college graduation without her. And relations between my paternal grandmother and my stepmother were not as cordial as they'd been before Patricia had the temerity to marry Dad. I was glad to get away from the family drama and back to my room in the house on Mt. Royal Avenue.

One Friday morning, Jane approached me in the kitchen as I was having an early lunch. She confided that she would be driving to her parents' beach house on the Eastern Shore for some time alone, away from everyone, even Morris—time to think; and she'd appreciate it if I didn't tell anyone where she'd gone. I was surprised. We'd barely spoken to each other for weeks. I was touched that she'd entrusted me with her secret, but I was also uncomfortable. Inventing plausible cover stories was not my strong suit, and it didn't occur to me to ask when to expect her back. Sadie and Penny bought my vague explanation of Jane's absence, but Morris was frantic at the prospect of her having taken off for parts unknown. What if something bad happened? Might Jane even try to hurt herself? His visions of disaster finally wore me down, and I told him where she was. He promptly took off on his motorcycle to rescue his damsel in distress, whether she wanted to be rescued or not.

Several hours later, Jane's blue Datsun sedan pulled into the driveway that opened onto the alley behind the house. I swallowed hard and met her at the kitchen door.

"You're back already."

"Well, yeah, since you sicced Morris on me." Her ice-blue eyes flashed a fury I'd never seen there before.

"I'm sorry, Jane, I tried to keep him from going after you, but—"

"Dammit, Kay, I *trusted* you! I told you about going to the beach in confidence, so I could have some time to myself to think. I thought you *understood* that!"

"Of *course* I understood!" Now I was getting angry, too. "But Morris was really scared something bad would happen to you, and I couldn't—"

"Having Morris come after me was the *last* fucking thing I need right now!" She glared at me as she stalked past and stomped up the stairs to her room.

When my heart finally stopped pounding and my gut unclenched, I had a minor epiphany: if this was what having a boyfriend in medical school had done for Jane, then maybe I was better off without one. Her tongue-lashing evoked some remorse—I *was* genuinely sorry I'd made her life more difficult. I was also upset about the fact that I'd blown a major opportunity to regain some of the closeness she and I had lost over the course of that difficult second year of medical school. But I was angry, too—angry that she'd put me in such an untenable position to begin with, angry at the way she'd lashed out at me when the situation went sideways.

The month of May also brought final exams. The less strenuous courses came first: Social and Preventive Medicine, Psychiatry. Then there was the three-hour Pharmacology exam, right before the first day of the Memorial Day weekend. Some of us would decompress afterward by spending the holiday weekend white-water rafting in West Virginia, an activity that was new to me. I'd been pleased when my Physical Diagnosis partner Rob invited me to ride to the campsite with him and his fiancée—until I found out that Blake would be rafting, too. I enjoyed Rob and Denise's company and spent some time with them in the evening, but otherwise I pretty much kept to myself. The knowledge that Blake was there had put a damper on my high spirits, much as it had at the holiday party a few months earlier. Sleeping alone under the stars proved to be a balm for my bruised soul and the high point of the weekend.

The next morning dawned clear and bright. The guy from the raft rental company gave us instructions and we donned our lifejackets, grabbed our paddles, and climbed aboard. The raft ride itself was exhilarating—the weather was perfect, the water was cold and refreshing, the rapids were neither too tame nor too wild. After running the rapids to a quiet part of the river, it was playtime: people started pulling each other into the water and capsizing each other's rafts. When Blake came nosing around, I gleefully attacked him with water from the bailer. He grabbed my hand and started to pull me into the river, but I fought back. I crouched in the bottom of the raft, resisting his superior physical strength, cursing colorfully, and feeling an exhilarated enjoyment of the contest. Then Blake just…let go of my hand and swam away. Once he was at some distance, he called out: "I know reluctance when I see it!"

And that was that. I'd been high on the struggle, intoxicated by a mixture of love and hate and pride and desire; and then he just—stopped. He dropped my hand and swam away. There couldn't have been a more perfect metaphor for our relationship.

Later that afternoon Blake and I talked very civilly, as if

nothing had happened—a complete about-face from the glares and grimaces of our combat. I couldn't bring myself to ask him why he hadn't tried harder, why he'd given up so easily. When I told my housemates the story after I got back, they told me I'd "won," I hadn't let a man "overpower" me. I rolled my eyes. *For god's sake*, I thought, *it's not like he was trying to rape me!* It was a pyrrhic victory, to say the least, and I was quietly devastated.

My failed relationship with Blake marked a turning point in my choice of men as prospective life-partners. The medical-school situation of being surrounded by men yet having so little access to them as romantic partners was very frustrating. Though a handful of my male classmates would marry women from the class, before or after graduation, most of the guys shied away from involvement with any of us. They preferred to date nursing students, social work students, physical-therapy or radiology-tech students, even art students from MICA.

It seemed that the movement toward gender equality still had a long way to go in this regard: even though many—not all—male medical students could accept having women as classmates, most of them were just not ready to see their female colleagues as potential dates and thus as desirable women. Blake had seemed special to me because of our shared literary interests; somehow, I'd thought that might make a difference (and he'd certainly been attracted to me). But I finally figured out that, if I couldn't establish a relationship with someone like Blake, with whom I had something significant in common besides medical school, then I probably ought to look for love outside of medicine.

Though we'd finished our second-year course work before Memorial Day, the academic year wouldn't be officially over until we took Part 1 of the National Board of Medical Examiners' Test, aka the National Boards, in early June. Part 1, then a two-day affair, was taken at the end of the preclinical years. We would take Part 2 about fifteen months later, during our fourth year; and Part 3 would be administered at the end of the first year of residency, the internship year. Passing the National Boards was a prerequisite for being licensed to practice medicine anywhere in the United States. The first part of the Boards, the basic sciences section, was also critical for getting into a good residency program. It was widely regarded as the hardest test an aspiring physician would ever take. When Morris asked me the day before the exam if I was nervous about taking it, I barely managed to refrain from retorting "Is the Pope Catholic?" Like most of my classmates, I was a nervous wreck.

After completing the test, I celebrated by heading back to New England for a brief round of visits with family and friends. On my return to Baltimore a week later, I attended the first of two weddings of medical-school classmates that summer. Counting those of my father and brother, this brought the grand total of weddings I'd attended in the past year to four, breaking my previous record of three during the summer between my junior and senior years of college. Would it ever be my turn? This June wedding rubbed salt in the wound of Preston's departure on sabbatical, which happened around the same time. We enjoyed dinner together one last time the night before he left, and I missed him already.

I was not the only member of the "24-hour encounter group" who was grieving lost love. One July evening, Jane was in the kitchen—without Morris, for once—and I was reading in the living room when Sadie came in. Hearing her breath catch in a sob, I followed her into the kitchen. Jane looked up, startled, from her mug of tea when Sadie plopped down in the chair next to her and burst into tears.

"Sadie, what happened?"

"I went to see Gabe."

Sadie and Gabe had been broken up for five months now. I'd dropped in on ex-boyfriends a few months after the breakup myself, so Sadie's behavior was not foreign to me. Jane was hunched over her tea, looking intently at her; I took the seat at the other end of the table and reached for Sadie's hand. She dabbed at her eyes with her other hand and shook her head.

"I don't know what came over me. I missed him so much, even though I was the one who broke it off. I wanted to talk it over with him, to see if I could figure out what really happened."

"And did you?" Jane asked.

"Yeah. I just felt so hemmed in last winter, I didn't know what else to do but break up with him."

"Aw, Sadie, I'm sorry," I said.

Jane nodded and took Sadie's other hand. "I think I know where you're coming from. You want to have that closeness, maybe even be taken care of, but you really want to be free to be yourself, too. It's so hard."

"Yeah, I get that," I chimed in.

And, to my surprise, I really did. I'd been incredulous when they broke up in February. Gabe was such a nice guy (and so good-looking!); why on earth would Sadie break up with him? I would have killed to have a boyfriend like that—or *a* boyfriend, period, especially after my experience with Blake. But that conflict between wanting to be taken care of and wanting to be your own person? I totally got that. (Why did women have so much trouble with this when men didn't seem to at all?) Hadn't that been the crux of my dilemma with Blake? Hadn't it always been, with Preston and all the others before him? Yes, I could definitely relate.

"Thanks, you guys," Sadie said. Then she laughed a little shakily. "Well, here we are again, just like the old days on Stricker Street."

"Except I was the one freaking out back then," I said wryly. But I knew something special was happening: Jane, Sadie, and I were like sisters again, if only for an afternoon—trying to bear each other up over the treacherous, fear-ridden ground we were traveling. Each of us moved around in her own private fog much of the time, but occasionally we reached out our hands to one another for comfort and support. If I was having trouble assuming responsibility for my own life, I was certainly not alone. And perhaps I wasn't the only one to feel that my home was no longer with my family, that we friends were making a home with each other.

• • •

At the beginning of July, I started a summer clinical fellowship, dividing my time between the pediatric outpatient clinic and the intensive care nursery, hoping to prepare myself for clinical rotations in the fall. In the outpatient clinic, I was confronted for the first time with the realities of trying to provide medical care to children, especially toddlers and preschoolers. Their noisy unwillingness to submit to unpleasant procedures required a lot of patience, which did not come naturally to me. The patients I'd seen through the Pediatric Tracking Program hadn't prepared me for this.

The intensive care nursery presented me with a much bigger challenge—my first experience of the death of a newborn infant. Baby R. was a term baby who'd suffered severe asphyxia at birth. Over the next two days, it became clear that he was brain-dead. When his heart rate dropped, the pediatric residents started to revive him, then remembered that there was a "Do Not

Resuscitate" order on his chart. It was hard to watch the physicians struggle with their desire to do everything that could possibly be done instead of letting the infant die peacefully. But it was even harder to watch the baby himself, his skin like alabaster due to the poor circulation of impending death, taking the labored breaths of his last hours of life. I walked home that afternoon in a daze, oblivious to the sights and sounds of the streets.

Late that summer, Sadie told us she would be moving out of the Mt. Royal Ave. house. After a road trip with her new boyfriend, she'd spend some time at her parents' home in New Jersey. Jane was moving out, too. To my distress, she'd failed pharmacology and would not be graduating with our class. Paula had moved out earlier in the summer, and another art student had taken her place shortly before Sadie's announcement. We would not be renewing our lease at the end of August after all.

I was crushed. I loved that house. Granted, it wasn't as nice as when we'd first moved in. A year of student life had taken a toll, even though we'd all done at least a modicum of housework. The hardwood floors needed to be cleaned and polished; the walls bore marks and scars. Cockroaches had established a beachhead in the kitchen when the weather warmed up in the spring.

But it wasn't just the house. I also loved the intentional-community ideal that it had represented for me. At least for a while, these people had been a second family at a time when my own family of origin had broken up and was still in the process of reconstituting itself in ways that were often difficult for me to accept. My failure so far to establish the kind of love-relationship that might lead to a new family of my own made all this more painful. And, self-preoccupied as I was, I couldn't help but wonder: did Sadie's leaving have anything to do with the tension between Jane and me? Was this my fault, too?

Or maybe Sadie was going through something like my own struggle: wanting to be a free agent, a full-fledged, responsible adult, yet scared to death at the same time. Scared of the responsibility, scared of the possibility of failure, suspended immobile like the Hanging Man.

I hadn't yet figured out that mistakes were inevitable and actually necessary for growth. But, ready or not, it was time to move on—to a new living situation, and to the next phase of medical school. My anticipation was tempered by longing for what had and hadn't been, and by the sadness of my dawning understanding that, whenever we move forward, something is always left behind.

• • •

The room I'd once been so happy to make my own, where I'd studied and thought and read and written, where I'd laughed and cried and despaired and sometimes rejoiced, looked forlorn now. There were boxes on the floor, books in piles, clothes on hangers tossed on the bare mattress; the pillowcases were stuffed with bed sheets and other dirty laundry. Saddest of all, the windows were bare now; those cheery homemade curtains were gone. I'd spent the previous day painting the Bolton Street apartment I'd be sharing with my classmate and friend Isabel. Another friend would soon arrive with a pickup truck to help me schlep all my belongings the few blocks west to my new home. On that final evening at 1416, I got to watch one last sunset out the bay window of my room, the sky a flaming rose-pink over the little park behind the grand old house.

Across the alley, a woman about my age stood before her kitchen window, washing vegetables for her family's dinner. For a moment, I wished I could trade places with her.

10

REAL MEDICINE

Labor Day came early in 1975, on September 1ˢᵗ. It was the month of Lynette "Squeaky" Fromme's failed assassination attempt of President Gerald Ford, NASA's launch of the Viking 1 space probe to Mars, and the canonization of Mother Elizabeth Ann Seton, a Marylander who was the first American Roman Catholic saint. It was also the start of my first clinical rotation—5-1/2 weeks of obstetrics and gynecology, aka OB-GYN. On the morning of September 2, I woke up full of nervous anticipation. While I sipped coffee in my medical student's white jacket, I recalled our second-year Physical Diagnosis lectures with Dr. Woodward.

T.E. Woodward, chairman of the Department of Medicine, was one of the fathers of the subspecialty of infectious diseases. While in the army during World War II, he did groundbreaking work on the control of typhus and typhoid fever, which wrought havoc on soldiers and civilians in the North African theater. After the war, his clinical research demonstrated the efficacy of a newly discovered antibiotic, chloromycetin (aka chloramphenicol) as a cure for typhus, typhoid fever, and several other infectious diseases. He'd received numerous awards for his research and been nominated for a Nobel Prize, but his first love was teaching.

We medical students sat spellbound in P.D. class while Dr. Woodward interviewed a patient to show us how it was done.

He had a remarkable way of getting the person to tell their story with a minimum of prodding. His questions were few and to the point. More than anything, it was his respectful attentiveness, his complete absorption in the patient's story, that elicited the information needed to make a diagnosis. After the patient had been wheeled off the stage, Dr. Woodward would look at us over his half-moon glasses. "If you just listen to the patient, boys and girls, he'll tell you what's wrong with him." Once, after we'd discussed an interview with an alcoholic who'd stopped drinking when he noticed he was turning yellow, Dr. W. gave us that stern look over his glasses and said, with his usual reedy drawl, "God is good, boys and girls. He doesn't let the liver shrivel up from cirrhosis right away. No, he gives you a warning with alcoholic hepatitis, like he's doing with the gentleman we just spoke with. Let's hope this man can continue to abstain from alcohol. It doesn't have to kill him."

And now it was time for us to start doing real, actual hands-on medicine. My classmates and I would carry Dr. Woodward's sage advice and bedside manner with us as we took to the wards. Would any of us ever be that kind of consummate clinician?

I arrived at University Hospital a few minutes early, clutching my OB-GYN textbook to my chest like a life-preserver. I took the elevator to the gynecology (GYN) floor, where women were treated for everything from pelvic inflammatory disease—a painful sexually-transmitted infection of the uterus and fallopian tubes requiring IV antibiotics—to the kinds of ailments that cause women to have hysterectomies: uterine fibroids, heavy menstrual bleeding as menopause approaches, and cancers of the uterus or ovaries. With my fellow third-year students, or MS-IIIs, I would be assigned to a first-year OB-GYN resident, with whom I would see patients and for whom I would run errands. Three mornings a week, our team would perform surgery in the OR. We MS-IIIs would observe, answer the questions put to us by attending physicians and residents, and occasionally hold retractors while they did the actual surgery. I couldn't wait to get started. Real medicine at last!

It was one of my first afternoons on the gynecology ward. We were standing around a table in a small examining room, preparing to examine a young Black woman with pelvic pain. There were several of us: a third-year resident named Ted, a couple of first-year residents, and three MS IIIs besides me, the only female. All of us were white. The patient's feet were in the stirrups, barely; she was clutching the sheet that still covered the lower part of her body, and her knees were touching. Her face registered fear and embarrassment.

"Come on, honey, you're going to have to move down the table a lot more than that," Ted said. "Scooch down all the way, till your bottom hangs off the table a little bit, that's right. Now I'm going to push the sheet up so we can examine you."

The young woman's thighs trembled as her lower body was exposed.

"Miss Williams," Ted said, "I've got some student doctors here, and some other residents, and we're all going to examine you, okay?" He spoke gently to her as if to a scared animal. She nodded. Then he turned to us.

"First, we check the vulva for any lesions or other abnormalities." His gloved finger pointed to her external genitals; then he gently poked and prodded for a minute. His exam was brief, but not cursory. The other residents followed suit, then the other MS-IIIs. When it was my turn, I looked carefully, then palpated the labia as I'd seen the others do; but my exam was as brief as I could make it, as though I were touching a hot stove. I couldn't get past the strangeness of being expected to touch another woman's most intimate body parts, as if this were just another part of learning to become a doctor—which, of course, it was. Plus, having been on that kind of examining table myself, it felt weird to be on the other side of it, especially when Ms. Williams and I were the only women in the room.

"Did you see or feel anything unusual?" Ted asked.

Some of us shrugged, some shook our heads.

"Good," he said with a smile, "because there wasn't anything. No lesions, no masses, no chancres of syphilis." He turned back to the patient.

"Okay, you're going to feel something inside you now." The resident rubbed the metal speculum with his gloved hands to warm it up, dipped it in water, and started to slide it into her vagina. The patient made a stifled sound.

"I'm sorry, honey. I'll slow it down. There. Is that okay?" She nodded.

"Okay, fellas," he said, looking straight at me, the only non-fella in the room except the patient. "You'll have plenty of chances to learn how to insert a speculum properly in the clinic, so I won't have you do that right now. But I want all of you to take a look." I flinched as I recalled the times I'd felt a speculum inside my own body.

Ted adjusted the examination light so we could see up the vaginal walls to the cervix. One by one, we looked—some searchingly, some with a quick glance. Our patient's thighs started trembling again.

"You see that greenish-yellow stuff coming out of the cervix? That's a purulent discharge."

The other residents nodded knowingly while we MS-IIIs looked at each other with raised eyebrows. We knew "purulent" meant "pus"; this couldn't be good.

"Next is the bimanual exam," Ted said. He gently withdrew the speculum, and the young woman gave a small sigh of relief. Then he covered two fingers of his gloved left hand with K-Y jelly and inserted them into her vagina.

"Yow!!"

"Oh, I'm sorry, honey, I forgot to tell you the jelly would be cold." He shook his head as if to say, "All the things we have to tell them instead of just doing the exam—" which made me even more uncomfortable than I already was. Then he pushed gently with his right hand against her belly, starting just above her pubic bone. When he checked the left side of her lower abdomen, she started moaning. When he got to the right side, she screamed.

"I think we have the source of that purulent discharge," Ted said as he withdrew his fingers and pulled off his gloves. He looked into the young woman's eyes. "Look, I'm sorry I hurt you," he said. "You have an infection in your reproductive organs."

"My what?"

"Your uterus, your tubes, your ovaries. We need to give you IV antibiotics for several days to clear it up, okay?"

She nodded, a single tear coursing down her cheek.

Ted turned to us. "I would have let you guys do a bimanual exam, too, but you can see that Miss Williams has had enough for today." He gave the woman's thigh a sympathetic pat. "I can tell you that, besides the tenderness, I felt a mass on the right. What would that mean?"

One of the junior residents answered, "T.O.A.—tubo-ovarian abscess."

"That's right. Not just your standard pelvic inflammatory disease, but something worse. What happens if she doesn't respond to antibiotics?"

"We'd have to operate to remove the abscessed tube and ovary, once it's cooled down," answered the other junior resident.

The young woman's eyes widened. "Operate?" she said. Without further comment, Ted helped her off the examining table and into a wheelchair; a nurse came and wheeled her back to her room. Once she was gone, one of the first-year residents turned to the MS IIIs.

"What do you call it when a patient screams like that during a bimanual exam?"

We looked bewildered.

"A positive chandelier sign. It's like they hit the ceiling." He snickered. I turned away as an angry flush spread over my face. Between the awkwardness of the group pelvic exam, the senior resident calling the patient "honey" the whole time, and the poor woman's agony when he palpated the tubo-ovarian abscess, the junior resident's oafish "chandelier sign" comment was too much. OB-GYN was interesting, in theory; but now I didn't know if I would be able to tolerate this rotation. It deeply disturbed me to witness women being treated this way. I resolved to do better with my own patients.

As a newly minted MS III, I couldn't articulate at the time what was wrong with the way our patient had been treated. With the benefit of a few decades' worth of hindsight, however, I can cite a few things. First, Ms. Williams should have had an explanation of what was going to happen before she ever got on the examining table—including the fact that several people would be examining her because this was how student doctors learned medicine. Second, Ted should have explained to Ms. Williams what his findings meant while he was conducting the exam, in terms a non-medical person could understand: "There's some pus coming out of your womb" and "You have an infection in your tubes." Plus, he should have explained what he meant by operating: "If the antibiotics don't cure the infection, then we might have to do an operation to take out the tube on that side." Third, he shouldn't have called her "honey." Unfortunately, this may have had as much to do with race as gender. At University Hospital, most of the doctors and medical students were white, and most of our patients were Black. We witnessed a lot of paternalism and racism during our training, much of it probably unconscious.

It would still be a few years before female chaperones would be required whenever doctors did pelvic exams. A female nurse—a woman who wasn't tasked with learning how to do an exam as I was—would have held Ms. Williams' hand and offered her support. I can see in retrospect that that gynecology resident, misogynistic and paternalistic though he may have been, was simply a product of his conditioning. He was clueless, not evil; and, sadly, he was not at all exceptional.

There was a lot of idiosyncratic terminology in the world of OB-GYN besides "chandelier sign," I would soon discover. "The patient is saddled and on the floor," for instance, meant that a woman in labor had been given a saddle block—a type of local anesthesia no longer used in obstetrics—and was in a labor room on the obstetrical ward (the floor) rather than one of the delivery rooms, as delivery wasn't expected imminently. One of the residents depicted this on a blackboard with a crude rendering of a pregnant woman on all fours with a saddle on her back. He grinned, and a couple of other residents applauded. I glowered at them from a safe distance. *Not funny, jerks!* I thought.

As MS-IIIs, we took night call with one of the residents a few times during the rotation. We wore scrub attire since we would need to be ready at a moment's notice to run to the delivery room or the operating room. The regulation hospital-issue scrubs for obstetrics were pale pink; the men wore pink tops and pants, and I, like the nurses, wore a pink dress. Many of the OB-GYN attending physicians wore white loafers, often patent leather, which was stereotypical footwear for men in that specialty at the time. A typical evening in the Labor and Delivery suite involved a lot of sitting around, waiting for Mrs. Smith's labor to progress, or for Mrs. Jones to be prepped for her C-section.

Our attending physician that night was a big guy with a Spanish accent who sat back in a desk chair with his white-loaf-ered feet elegantly crossed at the ankles and propped up on the counter where the residents wrote their notes, arms folded across his ample pink-shirted chest, shooting the breeze with the residents, some of whom affected white shoes like his. (A poor choice, it seemed to me; the paper shoe covers we wore at a delivery or in the OR couldn't be relied upon to keep all the blood off our footwear.) As the MS-III on call that night, I sat apart from the others with my OB-GYN textbook, trying to cover a chapter or two while surreptitiously watching all these pink-clothed men as if I were an anthropologist observing some exotic culture on a remote Pacific island.

How does a male physician make the choice of dedicating himself exclusively to the care of women? Though some of them undoubtedly loved delivering babies and genuinely cared about their female patients, a lot of them didn't talk as if they harbored a great affection for the gender. Was it money? Since this was partially a surgical specialty, its practitioners were paid better than pediatricians or psychiatrists or family practitioners, though not as well as surgeons. How could a man adequately empathize with a woman's pain in labor? A similar question could be asked of a woman physician who became a urologist, perhaps; but at that time, women were just starting to break into OB-GYN, and they were extremely rare in urology.

My last night on call for that rotation started uneventfully. Joe, my resident that night, was rotating through OB from the Family Practice program. He was a kindly, down-to-earth guy who wore brown oxfords instead of white loafers. We looked in on Mrs. Rivers, a large, cheerful woman in early labor at term with her fourth baby. Then we headed to our respective call rooms to crack the books and catch a few Z's. I hadn't been asleep for long when Joe paged me. Mrs. Rivers was ready to have her baby.

I joined him in the delivery room, still a bit groggy. The big overhead light was way too bright, and there was a high-intensity lamp aimed at Mrs. Rivers' vulva. She'd had local anesthesia, but that didn't do much for labor pains when delivery was imminent. She was alternately shouting and cursing through gritted teeth. Joe sat on a stool in front of her bulging perineum, pointing at the newly visible head of the baby with its copious black hair, slick with amniotic fluid. He turned to me with a big smile.

"She's crowning. You want to catch this one?"

"Sure!" My adrenaline kicked into high gear and all grogginess fled.

"You're gonna love this. I'll talk you through it, step by step." Joe's enthusiasm matched my own. True to his word, he guided me patiently through the process: first, making an episiotomy—a cut in the space between the vagina and the rectum to ease delivery of the head, which soon popped out like a cork from a champagne bottle. Then, gently easing one shoulder out, then the other, and grasping the head and the buttocks firmly while the rest of the baby slipped out like a seal on a water-slide.

Finally, clamping the umbilical cord in two places an inch apart and cutting between the clamps. The baby howled. The fresh, earthy tang of amniotic fluid filled my nostrils as the baby's cries filled my ears, and I felt a rush of pride: I had delivered Mrs. Rivers' baby!

Then Joe brought me back to earth again. "Now we wait for the placenta. And then you get to sew up the episiotomy!"

I met his cheerleader's excitement with a deflated sigh. I knew it could take fifteen minutes or more for the placenta to emerge, and my adrenaline had run out; I just wanted to go back to bed. He shrugged. "Hey, it's part of the deal," he said.

We sat in silence for a few minutes until the uterus contracted strongly, expelling the placenta. Then Joe waved me aside and injected Mrs. Rivers with some more local anesthetic. After that he got up and motioned for me to sit back down on the stool, handing me a curved needle with suturing thread on a hemostat and offering a reassuring smile. "Here you go. Don't worry, you'll do fine."

Oh no! I had never sutured anything that didn't involve fabric before, and a woman's perineum didn't seem like the ideal place to start. It took *forever;* fortunately, Mrs. R. was well-anesthetized and bonding happily with her new son. But Joe's patience was flagging, and I was exhausted. We were both relieved when I tied off the last stitch. Since I was unlikely to see Mrs. Rivers after her hospital discharge, I could only hope that my amateur workmanship would heal uneventfully.

• • •

While I was doing my first clinical rotation, I was also settling into a new home: the 3rd floor front apartment at 1210 Bolton St. Technically, it was a one-bedroom apartment. The bedroom was the province of my roommate Isabel, one of my anatomy lab partners and a close friend ever since; and, usually, her fiancé Michael, another classmate whom I'd known since our first year. Michael rented the tiny one-bedroom apartment on the second floor, but he spent most of his time at our place. We'd converted the living room into my bedroom, and I'd made the space my own, purchasing a royal-blue plush bedspread for the mattress and box-spring on the floor and bringing an old television set from my father's house in Libertytown—the first time I'd ever had a TV in my bedroom. The room was sunny in the late afternoon, with three west-facing windows overlooking the street.

Once again I inhabited the front room on the third floor of a Baltimore rowhouse, just like the first year of medical school; but Bolton Street was a far cry from S. Stricker St. It was a quiet avenue of well-kept brick townhomes with lots of trees, a little oasis a few blocks southwest of my previous home on Mt. Royal Avenue. One Saturday afternoon, I sat by one of the windows. The late-afternoon sun highlighted the yellow leaves and warmed the bricks of the houses on our side of the street. A breeze rippled through the plants on the windowsill. As I immersed myself in an ordinary weekend afternoon of outdoor sounds—children shouting, the noise of metal hitting bricks in some mysterious ritual of backyard maintenance, the waxing and waning of traffic, the calling of birds and insects—I felt a quiet joy. Despite all the craziness and struggle and suffering I was witnessing and experiencing as a medical student, life was still a thing to be celebrated. Moments like these were real medicine for me.

The OB-GYN rotation ended on a Friday in October with a written exam which I aced. I'd studied hard; and there'd been an opportunity on the essay part of the test to display my knowledge about pre-eclampsia, the pregnancy complication which had been the subject of my physiology paper a year and a half earlier. The evaluation I received was mixed. While I passed the course without difficulty, a discrepancy was noted between my superior book-knowledge and my hesitancy and lack of self-assurance when it came to my work on the ward and in the clinic. I felt better about the evaluation when one of the residents told me I should consider going into OB-GYN.

After a weekend off, I started the 5-1/2-week pediatrics rotation. The Pediatric Tracking Program made this transition a lot easier than the start of OB-GYN. Several of my classmates from the tracking program were on the rotation with me, which was comforting; and the 5th floor, where most of the Pediatrics Department resided, was reassuringly familiar. For the first few days, we MS-IIIs ran errands for our residents and observed and assisted with procedures like drawing blood and starting IVs. We also attended the daily Core Conferences at lunchtime, where residents learned about basic pediatric topics from specific cases on the wards and current journal articles.

I was awed by the scope of what a pediatric resident was expected to know. In the preclinical years, I'd been intimidated by the sheer volume of material we needed to learn. But on the wards, it was a question, not just of information, but of judgment, of discernment, of knowing what to do and what *not* to do. I was beginning to appreciate what an awesome responsibility it was to be a doctor, to hold a patient's—especially a child's—life in your hands. As the time approached when I would take charge of my own patients, the prospect of that responsibility weighed heavily.

After the first week, we MS-IIIs started taking a more active role in patient care, interviewing the child (if they were old enough) and the parents to obtain the medical history, then performing the child's physical exam. We discussed our findings and impressions with our assigned resident, and together we came up with a differential diagnosis—a list of possibilities in order of likelihood—and a plan of action.

What tests needed to be done? What treatments would we implement? When we worked in the outpatient department, feedback came quickly. The child would get better and go home, receive a follow-up appointment to the outpatient clinic, or be admitted to the hospital. Working on the wards with the sicker children, we had a longer time to see how well our treatment plan had or hadn't worked. The work was challenging, exciting, interesting, and exacting.

A few days before my 25th birthday, after eighteen months in treatment, I terminated therapy with Karen. Our work had been invaluable in helping me regain my footing during that awful spring of 1974; I felt stronger and more stable. Though I knew I had more work to do, I felt I'd gone as far as I could with her. We'd talked about terminating for several sessions before the final one; but our last hour together was highly emotional for me. To my surprise, Karen's eyes filled with tears, too. I thanked her when the session was over, but I couldn't bring myself to hug her or even to shake her hand for fear I would break down completely. Once I got back to my apartment, I let the tears flow freely—tears of loss, but also tears of gratitude.

As fall progressed, I immersed myself in the study of pediatrics. About halfway through the rotation, the MS-IIIs had a special meeting with Dr. Murray Kappelman, the Associate Dean of Students at the medical school and a member of the pediatric faculty who'd spent a lot of time teaching us on the rotation. We were meeting to discuss our personal experiences with death and dying. Elisabeth Kubler-Ross's landmark book on the subject had been published in 1969, six years previously, and the stages of grief had worked their way into the vernacular.

It was strange to have this discussion in a pediatric setting, where the patients seldom confronted us with the issue. But talking of death and dying at some point in our clinical training was consistent with the University's approach to difficult subjects, starting with that first exposure to the cadaver; and the Department of Pediatrics was particularly attuned to psychological issues.

So, there we were, sitting in a circle in the 5th floor conference room, looking (and feeling) uncomfortable—five guys, Dr. Kappelman, and me. Most of my classmates sat slouched in their chairs, arms crossed. I had a hard time keeping still. If there'd been an arm on my chair, I would have been drumming my fingers on it. I'd talked with several of my classmates, including some in this group, about my mother's death; but the prospect of this discussion still sent me into adrenaline overdrive. Dr. Kappelman began.

"My mother died last week," he said softly. We all sucked in our breath.

"My father died many years ago," he continued. "There's something about losing the second parent; you feel like you're losing the first all over again."

We were given a little time to let this sink in before going around the room with our own experiences. Louis had recently lost a friend to suicide. Terry had lost three family members in rapid succession. Gary had lost his grandfather within the last couple of months. Bob's grandmother, whom he loved very much, had died within the last few weeks; he wept openly. When I started to talk about my experience, my mouth was dry and my heart was pounding. Hard as I tried, I couldn't keep from crying. Most of the guys looked at their feet; but Art, who knew my story better than the others, reached over and rubbed my shoulder.

For some reason, this was different from most of the talking I'd done about my mother's death. It was not a catharsis, but a most intimate sharing, which made it more difficult. Louis closed the meeting with a beautiful poem by Elizabeth Barrett Browning. I went up to Dr. Kappelman and offered my condolences and a kiss on the cheek. As we gathered our things to leave, Terry said, "Anybody feel like a beer at the Campus Inn?"

"Oh, yeah! We need to reaffirm life," Louis said. Bob and I joined them. It was still early afternoon, but the four of us split a pitcher of beer.

When the Bee Gee's "Nights on Broadway" came on the jukebox and Louis asked me to dance, I jumped up and took his outstretched hand, and we danced out all our grief and sorrow. It felt good to move my body. Dancing was one of the best ways I could think of to express the beauty of this life that could be over at any moment. Things might be difficult right now, but listening to others' experiences of death reminded me how ineffably precious life is; and it was good to laugh. When Louis attempted to teach me the Hustle with mixed success, he said, "It's like medical school, Kay, you've gotta move your ass."

All things considered, the pediatrics rotation was an emotional roller-coaster ride. I'd harbored a secret hope that all my ambivalence about pursuing a career in medicine would magically disappear with the transition to the clinical years, but so far that hadn't happened. Now that my efforts were dedicated to the area in which I planned to specialize, the stakes were higher. I hadn't felt as much self-imposed pressure to perform on the OB-GYN rotation. Even in pediatrics, a specialty known for its humanistic emphasis, there was an element of competitiveness, of "roundsmanship"—being the first to give the right answer to a question by the attending physician or resident, like a *Jeopardy* contestant slamming her hand on the button.

I had mixed feelings about this competitive aspect. It made me feel insecure and inadequate, but it also forced me to confront my own fiercely competitive instincts. In the course of a morning, I could go from excitement and exhilaration at all we were learning, to anxiety—how will I ever master all this?—to anger at my inadequacies, real and imagined. I failed to hit the vein of the crying 7-year-old who needed blood drawn, and the resident had to do it. I answered the attending's question about juvenile diabetes correctly, but in a fading whisper after one of my classmates beat me to it.

I don't remember much about the pediatrics final exam except that I was called upon to discuss a patient I'd taken care of during the rotation. I picked a child with Down syndrome, the most complex patient I'd cared for. I hadn't realized just *how* complicated a condition like Down syndrome was until that exam, but I managed to answer the examiner's questions with some degree of intelligence and equanimity.

Several weeks later, my evaluation showed that my efforts had paid off: I received Honors in pediatrics. There were a lot of complimentary words on that piece of paper—things like, "…did an admirable job… her industry and interest were at an extremely high level… very willing to work hard… found by all to be a charming, earnest, and thoughtful young woman… Her dedication to Pediatrics strongly suggests that she will be an excellent physician." Hallelujah! I was surprised and delighted by all the positive feedback; but the part that stood out was similar to what I'd read on my OB-GYN evaluation: "…she should be encouraged to speak up more often." Heartened by all the kind words, I resolved to work harder on my "roundsmanship."

My 5-1/2-week psychiatry rotation at University Hospital began right after the pediatrics rotation, on Monday of Thanksgiving week. I spent that Sunday night talking with Isabel and Michael about what to expect from this area of medicine. They were both planning to become psychiatrists, and Michael had completed his psych rotation already. My friends were a study in contrasts. Michael's bushy black beard and intense gaze gave him a leonine look; Isabel was a fair, blue-eyed redhead, more reserved than her fiancé. Michael had fixed us ratatouille with a salad and crusty bread for dinner. Isabel put the kettle on for peppermint tea, a leisurely ritual they'd introduced me to, which I'd come to love. She took a drag on her after-dinner cigarette, looking at me contemplatively, while we waited for the water to boil.

"So, what's the psych rotation really like?" I asked Michael.

"Pretty much like all the others. They assign you to a resident, you follow them around, learn how to interview patients, and then you get your own patient and the resident supervises you. The big difference is, there are no physical exams or procedures. It's basically all talk."

"Do you think having been in therapy will make it easier?"

Michael shrugged. "I suppose it could." Isabel, who was in therapy at the time herself, winked at me as she stubbed out her cigarette. "If being in therapy gives us a leg up, you and I should ace it," she said. We all laughed. Those evening meals with my friends were another form of medicine for me.

The psychiatry resident to whom I was assigned was a guy who resembled a black-bearded Santa Claus, complete with a red nose and a belly that shook when he laughed. Despite his girth, Nick often sat with one shoeless foot and leg under him; a couple of times he even crossed his legs in a full lotus on the seat of his chair. I marveled at his flexibility and felt oddly attracted to him, even though he laughed at inappropriate times and most of his arcane references to the psychiatric literature left me baffled.

After the first two weeks, Nick assigned me a patient of my own. Leah was ten or fifteen years older than me—a slender brunette with a lot of nervous energy and a scary-intense way of looking at whoever she was talking to. I wondered if Nick had assigned her to me just so he wouldn't have to interact with her much himself. Leah was highly intelligent and manipulative; I really had to be on my toes when interviewing her, trying to figure out what was going on with her and how we could help.

I often felt threatened by her, even angry; it took a lot of self-restraint to put aside my own feelings and maintain clear professional boundaries. Leah's policy was: the best defense is a good offense. Blowing cigarette smoke at the ceiling and giving me a sideways look, she would say things like, "You're one of those do-gooder types, aren't you? You think you'll be able to find some magic formula to fix me when all these other people can't? Hah!" Her prickliness and sarcasm forced me to confront my own defenses: trying to be nice, ingratiating myself in order to avoid confrontation, withdrawing in the face of a possible power struggle. Working with her was a crash course in learning how to be assertive without being aggressive, to be firm yet compassionate, to stand up for myself without becoming a bitch.

But it wasn't hard to see the distress beneath Leah's pugnacious exterior. She paced the floor continuously, chain-smoking the whole time. She seemed trapped, afraid, and anxious, encased in an awful isolation. Hadn't I felt that way myself at times? As I watched her walk back and forth, I thought, *There but for the grace of god go I*. Working with Leah was nerve-wracking, sometimes exasperating as hell, but exhilarating at the same time.

The ten-day Christmas vacation came halfway through the psychiatry rotation. It was good to get a break from the intensity of working with Leah. The holidays provided some respite from the hectic pace of the past three months—a time when I could read and write and think to my heart's content. But Christmas with the family in Libertytown was not without its own stresses. When my brother Phil stopped by for a night, my stepmother told my sister Mary Alyce and me to make up the sofa bed for him. *For god's sake*, I thought, *why can't he make up his own damn bed?!* I couldn't bring myself to express my annoyance directly to my stepmother, but my sister picked up on it and offered to make the bed by herself, an offer I gratefully accepted. To my embarrassment, my brother joined her, good-natured and seemingly oblivious to my hard feelings, which made me feel like a jerk. As my irritation dissipated, it dawned on me that it wasn't my brother I resented, it was his *privilege*. That privilege had nothing to do with being better, or smarter, or even older than me; it was simply because he was *male*. Thanks largely to my own mother's gender-based favoritism, I'd been fighting this since my earliest days. And now my stepmother was picking up where my mother had left off.

After the holiday break, the new year began with a couple more weeks of weird Nick and challenging Leah. Then the psychiatry rotation was over, and I could cross another semester off—five down, three to go. I steeled myself for what was coming next: internal medicine, the most important rotation of the third year of medical school.

11

THE VA SPA, OR, TIME STAGGERS ON

The nine-week internal medicine rotation, the backbone of the clinical years of medical school, took me away from the now-familiar hallways of University Hospital—a source of considerable anxiety. I'd picked the V.A. Hospital for this rotation because medical students were supposedly able to do more hands-on patient care there than at University. Fortunately, I would share the daily half-hour commute with Michael, who, like me, was also doing internal medicine at the V.A, but unlike me, had a car.

On the cold late-January morning of our first day, Michael threaded his way through rush-hour traffic to our destination, crawling up Greenmount Avenue and across 33rd Street to The Alameda at its intersection with Loch Raven Blvd., while I fidgeted in the passenger seat. I was excited about starting the internal medicine rotation and part of me felt ready to tackle it, but I was scared, too.

"Look at it this way," Michael said. "It's only nine weeks out of your whole life. How bad can it be?"

"But it's my first time away from University. I won't know where anything is. What if I get in trouble for being late? What if I'm the only woman on my service?"

Michael shook his head. "God, you sound just like Isabel!

You'll get through this just like you've gotten through everything else. Don't worry so much."

Somehow, I was not reassured by the prospect of getting through the internal medicine rotation "just like I'd gotten through everything else." Though my evaluations for OB-GYN and psychiatry had been pretty good and I'd received honors in pediatrics, these were considered the "easy" rotations of the third year. My strategy had been to get the less challenging rotations under my belt first so that I'd be better prepared for internal medicine and surgery. Now, at the start of the second semester, it was time to face the music.

Michael pulled into the parking lot. We found our assignments, which were on different floors, and wished each other luck. Michael reassured me one last time, "You'll be fine."

The old Loch Raven V.A. Hospital opened in 1952 as a research and treatment facility for veterans with tuberculosis. By the mid-1960s, TB hospitals were being phased out, thanks to the advent of isoniazid (INH) and subsequent anti-tuberculosis drugs. The Loch Raven V.A. then became a general hospital for veterans until a larger facility opened at the corner of Baltimore and Greene Streets, just north of University Hospital, in 1993. Hundreds of University of Maryland medical students in the second half of the 20th century got their first exposure to the rigors of internal medicine at the Loch Raven V.A. Hospital, affectionately known to generations of students, interns, and residents as the "VA Spa" (pronounced "vah spa").

The irony of this moniker hit me full force when I first stepped into the building. It felt like walking into a mausoleum. While my sense-memories of that place are conflated with those of several old buildings I worked in over the course of my career, the VA Spa was the first. There was a tenebrous gloom about its hallways which the harsh fluorescent lighting couldn't dispel. The floor was brown concrete in some places and cracked, worn linoleum in others. The walls were painted depressing shades of gray, yellowish tan, or brownish olive green. The PA system emitted a nearly continuous blare of pages of varying sound quality. (Some of the more memorable ones included the calls for "Dr. Doctor" and "Dr. Butcher.") As for the smell—well, all hospitals have that scent of antiseptic attempting to mask the sour odors of bodily secretions and excretions, of illness and death; but in the VA Spa, like other old hospitals I've worked in, there was also an underlying aroma of *old building*—a soupcon of mold here, a pinch of dry rot there. Some old hospitals have a kind of quaint, decrepit charm about them; the V.A. hospital on Loch Raven Boulevard was not one of them. My visceral response to the place was one of revulsion.

I made my way to 2B, the ward, or service, to which I'd been assigned. Fortunately, I was on time, but I did note that everyone else there was male. I shook hands with the senior admitting resident, or SAR—a pleasant guy with a thick mustache and curly brown hair named Irving, whose smile put me at ease. The SAR was the medical chief of operations who ran the service on a day-to-day basis, supervising everyone below him. Irving was in his third and final year of residency, though a SAR could be a second-year resident, especially in May or June, the last months of the residents' year. Irving supervised three junior residents and three third-year medical students, or MS IIIs. At the VA Spa, the term "junior resident" covered first- or second-year residents in internal medicine and family practice as well as 4th year medical students (MS- IVs) who were there to gain more experience before starting residency.

Once we MS IIIs had been introduced to all the junior

residents, it was time to start the day. Work rounds, the first event, began at 8:00 a.m. sharp: the junior resident would present his "hits," or admissions, from the night before—the patients he'd admitted to the ward from the emergency room or a doctor's office. The format went like this: "Mr. Jones is a 67-year-old white male who presented to the E.R. with chest pain of 2 hours' duration"—followed by Mr. Jones' relevant medical history, the findings on physical examination, lab results, and the results of other tests such as a chest X-ray or electrocardiogram (ECG). I sat motionless and wide-eyed as one of the junior residents rattled off a spiel for each of *five* admissions. (*When*, I asked myself, *did the poor guy get any sleep?*) Each presentation of a case was followed by the presenter's ideas about the diagnosis and appropriate treatment. The senior resident and the other junior residents would ask questions and make suggestions, and a plan for the day would emerge.

After presenting the new patients, it was time to discuss those who'd been on the ward for a while. Each resident would give a quick summary of how each of their charges fared overnight, together with today's vital signs, any changes on physical exam, and the results of any relevant tests, culminating in a plan for the day: "I'll increase Mr. Brown's insulin, and if he doesn't start drinking more fluids, I'll start an IV on him." As we were finishing with the last patient, the chief resident stuck his head in the door.

"Hey, Irv, how's it going?" he asked. "How many hits didja get last night?"

"Old Buck here set a record for the month so far—five."

"Poor bastard!" The chief resident grinned at Buck, who was slumped in his chair. "Anything I need to know about?" he asked.

"Nah, same-old same-old."

"Okay. Keep up the good work, guys!" And with a wave of his hand, he was gone.

The chief resident was the SAR's immediate superior—someone who'd risen above their peers sufficiently to be selected for a fourth year of residency, in which they would assume teaching and administrative responsibilities for the entire residency program. This honor was usually shared by two people, since the administrative responsibilities alone, notably scheduling, were very demanding. Being a chief resident was a good thing for an aspiring academic physician to have on his or her CV.

At this point we had about an hour and a half before attending rounds. Irving swept all the MS IIIs with his gaze.

"Okay, kids. For today, you guys are going to shadow your resident. Tomorrow, they get to make you do stuff. Got it?"

We must have looked like deer in the headlights because he broke into a grin.

"Aw, c'mon, guys, it's not *that* bad! Before you know it, you'll be running morning rounds yourselves. You, Lee—go with Chet here."

He assigned each of us to one of the junior residents. Mine was Patrick, an MS IV who wasted no time, whisking me to the bedside of an uncomfortable-looking elderly man with a distended belly. After introducing me to the patient, Patrick said loudly, "We're going to put a tube in your stomach, Mr. Brooks. It'll go in through your nose." Mr. Brooks drew back sharply. "Whaaat?"

"Don't worry, we'll put something on it so it won't hurt," Patrick said, opening a packet of K-Y Jelly and sticking the end of the tube into it. Mr. Brooks looked skeptical.

Patrick proceeded to thread the tube carefully through the man's left nostril, his other gloved hand resting gently against the patient's right cheek. Mr. Brooks' grimacing and coughing gave way to a sigh of relief as the tube entered his stomach, releasing air and fluid into the large syringe attached to the other end. Then Patrick looked up at me with a grin.

"Next time, you get to do this while I watch, right?"

I attempted a casual smile in return, but I was horrified. I'd assisted with procedures on the OB-GYN and pediatric rotations and even drawn patients' blood a few times under close supervision; but it was clear that a lot more would be expected of me, procedure-wise, on the internal medicine rotation.

After this harrowing start to the workday, I spent some time reading the charts of Patrick's patients, since I'd be acting as his dogsbody for the next few weeks. Promptly at 11:00, our attending showed up to round with us. Besides being answerable to the chief resident, the senior admitting resident was also accountable to an attending physician who was a full-time member of the medical school faculty or a practicing physician on the clinical faculty. The attending made rounds with the service several times a week. These rounds generally consisted of an MS III—today, mercifully, it was a junior resident—presenting a patient to the attending, one with a particularly interesting or relevant diagnosis as determined by the SAR.

The student followed the format Buck had used when presenting his admissions on morning rounds, but in more detail and with more emphasis on discussion. On a medical ward, these discussions were more Socratic in nature than the ones I'd encountered on the OB-GYN and pediatric wards. They basically consisted of grilling the medical student, who was supposed to have been prepared for this ordeal by having presented the patient to the senior resident on morning rounds. Sometimes a resident had to step in to clarify some aspect of the patient's problem or supply a critical piece of information the student had forgotten to mention. While this happened to most of us at one time or another as MS IIIs, it was always a source of embarrassment.

I spent much of that first day's attending rounds rolling my eyes inwardly at the atmosphere of medical geekiness in which I found myself. The specialty of internal medicine was the province of the *crème de la crème* of obsessive-compulsive physicians, and physicians are a pretty obsessive-compulsive lot. On an internal medicine service as on no other, references to journal articles footnoted every utterance; and exhaustive lists of every possibility, however remote, had to be considered in formulating the differential diagnosis of a patient's illness. During our pre-clinical years, our physical diagnosis instructors had taught us an old internal-medicine proverb: "When you hear hoofbeats, think horses, not zebras"—or, rule out the more common diagnoses before going after the rarities. But when attending rounds were conducted on an internal medicine service, horses and zebras got equal time. While I had no problem with the internists' expectation of attention to detail, the enumeration of *all* the horses and *all* the zebras, plus the discussion of obscure points from the latest journal articles, went on for*ever.*

By 1:00 my stomach was growling. Our attending finally took his leave, and we were free to take about 30 minutes for lunch. The cafeteria fare at the VA Spa was even worse than that at University Hospital. Lunch that first day consisted of gristly Salisbury steak; I had to scrape off the glutinous gravy before I could eat it. Anything truly edible was prepackaged—cookies, crackers, chips, ice cream sandwiches—none of which was conducive to good nutrition or weight control (it was a good thing we had to walk so much). Eventually, many of us would either bring food from home or get our meals from vending machines, often a bit of both. Medical students and residents often joked that the five food groups for our kind were caffeine, sugar, fat, salt, and nicotine. I never became a smoker, but I had to cop to the other four, especially caffeine and sugar.

In the middle of the afternoon, we MS IIIs were dispatched to perform one of our most onerous tasks: collecting the lab results for our patients. These were carbon copies on small slips of paper, since computers in the 1970s were not yet at a point where they could be found on most hospital wards—not at University of Maryland Hospital, and certainly not at the VA Spa. The patients' blood had been drawn in the early morning; the lab slips revealing the results were ready around 2:00 or 2:30, when there was a feeding frenzy of medical students jockeying for position at the inexplicably small table where the slips were unceremoniously dumped by one of the lab techs. Efficiency in completing this task required quick reflexes and sharp elbows, but it raised an MS III's standing in the eyes of their superiors and added considerably to their street cred with their peers. Woe be unto the hapless MS III who was last to report back to his or her service with the day's lab slips.

In general, the lot of the lowly MS III was to perform the most menial of the tasks of medical management, commonly known as "scut." Besides gathering lab slips, we were to drop off requisitions for various tests, and to retrieve X-rays from the radiology suite, ECGs from cardiology, and patients' charts from Medical Records. To the extent of our ability, we would also perform various procedures on the patients, including drawing blood, starting IVs, obtaining urine specimens and testing them in the ward's small satellite lab, and placing tubes in orifices. The most unpleasant of these were those nasty nasogastric tubes, as well as urinary catheters for patients whose intake and output needed close monitoring. There were other procedures as well, which MS IIIs might be allowed to assist with or even to do with supervision on occasion, but most of these were above our pay grade. They included spinal taps to look for meningitis and other neurological problems; endotracheal intubation—placing a breathing tube in the windpipe so the patient could be hooked up to a ventilator; and inserting deep indwelling lines—CVP lines—into the vein closest to the heart for monitoring cardiac function in the critically ill.

The rule for procedures was, "See one, do one, teach one." As with Patrick and me on that first day, a medical student would first observe a resident doing a procedure while the resident explained what was happening; then, the next time an opportunity arose, the MS III would do the procedure, first with supervision by the resident and then on their own. Eventually, the student would teach the procedure to someone else; but few of us would be proficient enough for that before our fourth year.

When MS III's weren't doing scut work or procedures or writing up a history and physical exam, we were expected to be studying. Each of us lugged our own weighty copy of *Harrison's Principles of Internal Medicine* to the hospital every day, hoping to sandwich a chapter or two in between our other responsibilities. We were also expected to make use of the library, especially the journals—*New England Journal of Medicine, The Lancet, Journal of the American Medical Association,* and others. Sometimes the senior resident would pass out photocopies of current articles for our edification. Any reading we couldn't finish on the ward needed to be done when we got home at night. I found it nearly impossible to do any reading on the ward and difficult to get much done at home after the usual 10-hour day.

Though that first day at the VA Spa was pretty benign, it didn't take long for my confidence and enthusiasm to wane. Part of this had to do with my personal life rather than medicine: I was lonely. I missed the sense of family I'd enjoyed at 1416 Mt. Royal Avenue. Sometimes I missed my therapy sessions with Karen. And I longed for a boyfriend. Friendly and inclusive as Isabel and Michael were, being a part of their household only reinforced my singleness. In the evenings, they would make wedding plans and I would excuse myself to take a walk around Bolton Hill. Strolling past the noble old townhomes, looking in their large front windows, I marveled at the beautiful interiors and sometimes caught a glimpse of the occupants' domestic bliss. Would such happiness ever be mine, or would I always be on the outside looking in?

Plus, there was the unwelcome reality that most of the practice of medicine does, in fact, consist of caring for old, sick, and dying people. I'd been shielded from this truth during my previous rotations. Serious illness and death were thankfully rare in obstetrics—though not in gynecology, as I would soon discover on my surgery rotation. Life-threatening illness in children was heart-wrenching when it occurred, but most childhood illnesses were acute, not chronic; and kids, resilient little beings that they were, usually recovered completely. Psychiatry represented an entirely different realm of human suffering from the other medical specialties: there were no IVs, respiratory equipment, bedpans, catheters, or the like on a psychiatry ward.

Internal medicine was where it got real in a most corporeal way. Most of these people were old and debilitated. They'd already been admitted to the hospital many times, with voluminous charts to prove it; and many would die of whatever was currently ailing them—if not during this hospitalization, then during a later one. It was depressing, and nowhere was it more so than at that dingy old V.A. hospital. Besides the uninspiring physical environment, there was a serious shortage of nursing staff—all women at that time—which must have added to the patients' misery.

In fact, I was one of very few women in that entire place. Besides the paucity of nurses, there were few female medical students or residents—none of them on my service—and even fewer female attending physicians. Also, there were no female patients, since very few veterans at that time were women.

One of the nurses, Mrs. Peacock, had it in for me. She didn't have much use for the male students either, but her antipathy toward me was of a different order. When one of my male classmates informed her that Mr. Jones' IV fluid bag was nearly empty, he might get a little sigh of annoyance, followed by a resigned, "Okay, I'll take care of it as soon as I can."

If I said the same thing, I'd get a glare or an eyeroll and something like, "Well, what do you expect me to do about it? I've only got two hands!"

When I asked Mrs. P. to show me how to give an intramuscular injection, she was incredulous: how could I not already know this? (Did she think this information came with having ovaries?) She used an orange to show me what to do—the standard nursing-school instructional technique at the time—with exaggerated deliberation, as though I were of subnormal intelligence; and she acted like she was being terribly imposed upon the whole time.

Then there were the men. The guys from my class weren't generally a problem. Though none of my closest friends from the preclinical years were on 2B with me, the guys in the group and I were well enough acquainted from our years as a captive audience in Howard Hall to know what to expect from one another. Roughly the same was true of the fourth-year students who rotated through our service.

The residents were a mixed lot. Some were deeply good-hearted, especially Irving, who remained our senior resident for the first two weeks. He planned to go into oncology as a subspecialty and demonstrated a wonderful bedside manner, especially with the cancer patients, that I never forgot. Jim, a first-year family practice resident, was not only generally kind and caring, but he cried openly when one of his patients died unexpectedly during a procedure.

Other residents were hard-boiled, like Bert, who rode a motorcycle to work without a helmet because he preferred out-right death to paralysis in the event of a bad accident. Bert was the junior resident with whom I participated in the care of Mr. Dotson, a good-natured, middle-aged Black man who was a mail-carrier with a houseful of teenage kids.

"How are you, Mr. Dotson?" Bert asked, running his fingers expertly over the man's neck as he spoke.

"I've just been getting more and more tired, doc, and it's starting to worry me, especially when I can't catch my breath."

"And when do you notice you can't catch your breath?"

"Sometimes when I'm walking my route, especially when I have to climb stairs. But lately it's been waking me up out of a sound sleep. It's really scary, waking up 'cause you feel like you can't breathe." Mr. Dotson's already-prominent brown eyes opened even wider when he said this.

After a few more questions, it was my turn to examine Mr. Dotson. Bert had spent longer than usual listening to the man's lungs with his stethoscope. When I applied my own to his chest, I found out why—there were abnormal crackling sounds on the right side. The most alarming finding, however, was the hard, quarter-sized lymph node above his right collarbone, a harbinger of malignancy. Mr. Dotson's chest X-ray confirmed our suspicion: a large tumor in his right lung, with a couple of lymph nodes in his chest pressing on his windpipe. The next day, Mr. Dotson went to the operating room for removal of the cancerous tissue.

Later that afternoon, Bert pulled me aside while I was completing the items on my scut list. He looked me in the eye and told me that Mr. Dotson had died on the operating table, that these things happened sometimes.

"Oh, no!" I started to cry.

"Yeah, it's really a bummer. But, judging by the size of those mediastinal lymph nodes, he probably wouldn't have lived very long after the surgery anyway."

I wiped the tears away only to have them return. I just couldn't believe it.

Bert's brow furrowed. He placed a hand on my shoulder.

"Hey, you need to get hold of yourself. You can't fall apart every time somebody dies. You can't afford to get so attached to your patients. It doesn't help them, and it doesn't help you."

I turned away. How was I supposed to be compassionate and caring without getting "too attached" to my patients? Where was the line that I'd apparently just crossed? If you weren't attached to your patients, at least to some degree, then how could you really take care of them, anyway? Though there'd been a few teachable moments about death earlier in medical school, the only formal discussion we'd had about the topic had been the meeting with Dr. Kappelman during my pediatrics rotation a few months earlier; and that discussion had been about our personal experiences rather than the deaths we would encounter on the wards and in our medical practice. While I'd recently met death up close and personal in my own life, this was the first time I'd experienced the death of a patient I was taking care of, and I hadn't been ready for it.

By far the most insufferable of the residents I encountered at the VA Spa was George, the senior resident for most of the time I was there. Unlike many men who choose internal medicine as their specialty, George was exceptionally good-looking, with a charming demeanor to match. But, like his less physically attractive counterparts, he quoted endlessly and at great length from the *New England Journal of Medicine* on rounds and expected us to do the same. Knowledgeable as he was, he would have been an excellent teacher if it hadn't been for his air of smug self-satisfaction. His attitude toward me, one of his less confident and therefore "weaker" students, was one of mild condescension and forbearance. He responded to my tentativeness on daily rounds and my reluctance to volunteer answers to questions with amused indulgence or mild exasperation. How I envied those of my classmates—especially the women, few as they were—who had the self-assurance to volunteer answers even if they might be wrong. I wished I had the self-confidence to give as good as I got, even if it meant being labeled a "ball-buster!"

While several of my male superiors at the VA Spa made me feel defensive and unwelcome to varying degrees, the patients were the ones whose sexism was the most blatant. Attempting to honor the male residents' dress code of white uniform shirts, pants, and jackets, I'd purchased a couple of pairs of men's white jeans to wear with my student's white jacket. I'd considered wearing a skirt, as I'd done on previous rotations; but my few skirts were in dark colors rather than white, and they were short—too short for the VA Spa. Even wearing pants, I received plenty of comments and leering looks from patients, especially the younger ones. I was being ogled at work the way I often was on the street, and I was angry about the sheer intrusiveness of these looks and comments. Who were these men to pass judgment on me, to make assumptions about me, a stranger to them, simply because of biological traits in which I'd had no say?

I'd been acutely sensitive to sexism from the first day of medical school, and I'd developed a heightened awareness of racism during the OB-GYN rotation; but my time at the VA Spa took my consciousness of all forms of discrimination to the next level. I'd never before had such a clear understanding of how both racism and sexism turn their targets into objects. People assumed they were entitled to judge a person entirely based on how they looked, without knowing anything else about them. Naturally, being objectified as a woman the way I was at the VA Spa added another layer of difficulty to the challenges of learning to practice medicine, and I didn't suffer it gladly; but it also gave me, a privileged white woman, a better understanding of the obstacles our Black patients faced every day.

One of the more insidious aspects of sexism, or any "-ism", is the feeling of exclusion, of not being able to gain admission to the club. I felt this keenly throughout my rotation at the V.A. hospital. A major contributor to this was the fact that my patients generally assumed I was a nurse.

"Nurse!" called an emaciated old guy from the bed next to the patient I'd just finished examining. I sighed as I looked over at him, knowing what was coming.

"Nurse," he repeated. "I've been on this bedpan for twenty minutes, and nobody's come to take it away. And my butt hurts."

"Um, I'm not a nurse, but here, let me give you a hand."

I'm sure male students and residents occasionally helped with these things, too, but they weren't tacitly *expected* to do them, as I was. All this nursing-care activity added up over the course of a day and cut into my study time, so I paid a price in terms of "roundsmanship" and thus potential admission to the boys' club. To add insult to injury, one of the residents actually chided me for spending time helping the patients instead of studying! Speechless in the face of this criticism and still too intimidated to speak up for myself, I felt a hot spasm of indignation: were we here just to impress each other with our arcane knowledge, or to actually *take care* of patients?

About halfway through the rotation, I assumed care of my first primary patient, Mr. Smith. I oversaw his diagnosis and treatment as if I were an intern, answering only to George, the senior resident. Mr. Smith was a white man in his late thirties with severe hypertension. Besides starting medication expeditiously to avoid a heart attack or stroke, a cause for his high blood pressure needed to be sought—though there usually wasn't a discernable one—and the state of the heart, kidneys, and other organs affected by the condition needed to be evaluated. In the course of the workup, a potential urological problem turned up—an unwelcome development for both of us, given that Mr. Smith was none too pleased about having a "woman doctor" in the first place. My heart sank when I saw those red blood cells in his urine under the microscope. While they could be related to his high blood pressure and not dangerous *per se*, the possibility of something grave like bladder cancer had to be ruled out.

So I trundled Mr. Smith down to the urology suite where he was made to assume the "lithotomy position:" flat on his back with his feet in stirrups—that posture so well known to women when we undergo our annual pelvic exams but reserved in men for non-routine urologic procedures. Once Mr. Smith was properly positioned, the urologist inserted a scope into the bladder through his penis. Thankfully, there was no cancer or other evidence of pathology. But the procedure was traumatic for both of us: he'd cried out when the scope went in, despite its generous coating of local anesthetic; and he'd squeezed my hand so hard that it hurt for a while afterward.

After I'd worked up Mr. Smith's hypertension, it was time to discuss his case with George. I looked over the notes I'd taken and exhaled sharply. I hadn't realized how complex a common, garden-variety condition like high blood pressure was until I encountered Mr. Smith. And now, when it was time to put it all together, I was exhausted. I presented the patient to George, and we talked about the diagnostic and therapeutic possibilities; I wrote orders as we discussed them, and George signed them. As the process was nearing completion, I glanced at my watch. "Do you have somewhere you need to be?" he asked, with a knowing smile. It was 8 p.m. by this time, about two hours later than I usually left, on a Friday night. I'd taken the edge off my hunger with a bag of potato chips a couple hours ago, but the stomach pangs were back.

George didn't seem at all concerned about the time; perhaps he was on call that night. I told him, guilelessly and without rancor or irony, that a friend of mine was having a party and I'd hoped to be able to attend at least part of it. He shook his head and then treated me to a lecture about dedication to the practice of medicine. By the time I'd wolfed down a sandwich and changed my clothes back at my apartment, the party was almost over when I arrived.

The following week, George's superciliousness gave way to full-blown wrath—admittedly, not without cause. I'd been tasked by a junior resident with drawing blood from Freddie, a young man in the ICU who'd acquired endocarditis, an infection of the heart valves, from injecting heroin. Because Freddie's veins were shot, and because his cardiac function needed invasive monitoring, he had a central venous pressure (CVP) line in his chest instead of a simple IV in an arm. My choices for drawing Freddie's blood were to use an artery in the wrist, a painful procedure; or to use the CVP line. I'd watched Irving draw blood from Freddie's CVP line a few times, doing the procedure offhandedly while he quizzed us or gave us a mini-lecture; it looked pretty straightforward.

It wasn't. When I drew Freddie's blood from the CVP line, it clotted in the tubing. Panicked, I ran from the room. George was furious, not least of all when I told him I'd only been following his predecessor's example.

"You never, *ever* draw blood from a CVP line!" he hissed. Sensing George's fury, my classmates glanced up from their textbooks long enough to give me looks of alarm or, in one case, mute sympathy. Once my dressing-down was over and George had stalked out of the room, the sympathetic guy told me he thought I'd been treated unfairly, which made me feel a little better. After that incident, George's attitude toward me was one of cold civility, and he ignored me whenever possible.

Two years later, as a pediatric intern in the Intensive Care Nursery, I would remember George's excoriation and shake my head as I drew blood from a premature baby's umbilical artery catheter, the newborn equivalent of a CVP line and a lifeline for these smallest of patients. In the 1970s, umbilical catheters were used routinely for blood sampling as well as blood-pressure monitoring and IV fluid administration. We had to draw blood through these catheters several times a day; but if we proceeded slowly and gently and were meticulous about sterile technique, complications like the clotting of Freddie's CVP line rarely occurred. And we *never* got yelled at for what was then standard practice.

My father had an expression which fit those nine weeks well: "Time staggers on." After the CVP debacle, there were good days and bad days, but, thankfully, no more major gaffes. I became a little more proficient and a little more efficient at working up patients; and I came to enjoy caring for my primary patients after Mr. Smith. Finally, I was getting a handle on internal medicine— even though it was still hard to find time to cover the basics in *Harrison's,* much less the latest clinical pearls from the *New England Journal.* Patients continued to mistake me for a nurse; they also continued to sicken and occasionally die. Every time a death occurred, I would dream that night about Mr. Dotson.

A couple weeks before the end of the rotation, it was time for a new senior resident. I'm pretty sure I wasn't the only one to mutter "Hallelujah!" under their breath. As I watched George's back retreat after he bade us goodbye on his last day, I thought of the phrase some of the residents used when a particularly obnoxious patient was discharged: "A.M.F.—adios, motherfucker!"

Our new leader, Alan, was a down-to-earth, no-nonsense family practice resident—a refreshing change from Sanctimonious George. Family practice residents had a reputation for being more practical and less fixated on arcane minutiae than their internal medicine colleagues.

On my last day at the V.A., Alan beckoned me into an empty office and asked me to take a seat across the desk from him. I was dimly aware of the overhead pages and the voices of a couple of classmates laughing and joking in the hallway.

He got right to the point.

"Look," he said. "You need to improve, and you need to

develop more self-confidence if you're going to make it as a physician. The only way to do that is through practice. I strongly suggest you do an externship." This meant spending the summer doing the work of an intern at a community hospital, for a nominal stipend. Application forms for externships at Union Memorial Hospital had just become available, he told me. I picked one up before I left.

My official internal medicine evaluation was submitted by the elderly endocrinologist who'd rounded with us as our attending. It consisted of a single sentence: "She could have worked harder."

The obvious lack of thought, or of any idea who I was, other than a "she"—much less how hard I *had* worked, though perhaps not always at the right things—deeply hurt and infuriated me. Alan's opinion of me may not have been any higher than our attending's; but at least he'd paid enough attention to have some concept of my actual weaknesses, and he'd combined his critique of my performance with a specific, practical suggestion for how I could improve. That was the greatest kindness I received from any of my superiors during the clinical years of medical school.

Alan might have no memory of me, but I will never forget him.

12

DÉJÀ VU

The alarm buzzed, waking me from a dream about my mother in which she was just about to tell me something terribly important. Cursing at the rude awakening, I hit the alarm button with more force than necessary. It was still dark outside. I'd slept until near-dawn during the internal medicine rotation; but on this 4-1/2-week general surgery rotation, I had to arrive a full hour earlier, with no guarantee that the day would end any sooner— not that it really mattered, since my life that semester consisted almost entirely of working and studying.

Donning white jeans and a knit top under my medical student's jacket, I tossed my purse and general surgery textbook onto the passenger seat of my dad's powder-blue VW Beetle, loaned to me for the remainder of medical school. The sky shifted from indigo to mauve to pink as I drove across town in the cold late-March morning, taking Eastern Avenue to Baltimore City Hospital, now known as Johns Hopkins Bayview Medical Center. I shivered a little as I approached the old yellow-brick edifice where my mother had died 2-1/2 years earlier. I asked myself why on earth I'd chosen to do my surgery rotation in this awful place, as though returning to the scene of a crime. But I had to face down my demons and prove to myself that my mother's death no longer held me in thrall.

The rising sun blazed onto ward 3B as I entered its hallway

from the cafeteria after a quick breakfast, morning cup of coffee in hand—a bitter, concentrated brew with the texture of used motor oil. First, I needed to find out what had transpired with my patients overnight. Had anyone died? This had happened once so far in my first six days on the ward. I also checked to see if anyone had been moved to the ICU, which was almost a nightly occurrence. Once I'd scanned the census for changes, I started checking the vital signs and lab data on the ten patients I followed with my resident, Evan Jacobs. There were also wounds to look at and dressings to change before the team rounded at 7:30, but I made sure to touch base with Evan before I did anything. He was not one to applaud initiative on the part of a third-year student. I'd been severely chewed out a few days earlier after taking it upon myself to change a dressing without him, thus depriving him of the opportunity to look at the wound himself.

It seemed you couldn't win—you'd better not do anything without consulting your resident, yet you were supposed to be first to pipe up with a diagnosis and a plan of treatment on rounds; and if you weren't, you'd be regarded as passive or "weak."

Asking questions on rounds was another minefield. Only the people who were already regarded as "strong" students—which, on a surgical service, automatically excluded women—could afford to ask a question without incurring knowing smirks, even frank ridicule. I'd witnessed one of my female classmates being subjected to such treatment in the first days of the rotation. My cheeks had burned with anger and in sympathy with her humiliation.

Being grilled by the chief resident in the OR was another rite of passage. It wasn't enough that we had to stand holding retractors for hours at a time, ignoring things like hunger and the need to pee; we also had to know the anatomic intricacies of, say, the branches of the celiac artery or the biliary tree, and be able to promptly regurgitate these on demand.

Evan had been on call the previous night and looked like he hadn't slept at all. His black hair was disheveled. His face was paler than usual, and his too-close-together dark eyes were snapping with impatience. "Here," he said, thrusting a handful of charts at me. "You see these, and I'll do the rest."

"Don't you want to see the wounds yourself?" I asked timidly.

"Nope. Frankly, I don't give a fuck today. They were all okay last night. That bowel obstruction from yesterday and the new admission kept me up all night." Evan frowned as though the patients had prevented him from sleeping on purpose, just to make his life difficult—a feeling I was starting to understand a lot better since the start of the general surgery rotation.

My first four patients were stable. But when I walked into Room 342 and pulled the privacy curtain around my fifth patient's bed, I discovered that Mrs. Rawlins—a large, maternal African American grandmother in her early 60s—was in a lot of pain.

"This tube in my nose really hurts, and my belly is killing me," she moaned.

"I'm sorry, Mrs. Rawlins. I need to examine you and check your dressing. Can you bear with me for a minute?" I listened to her abdomen with my stethoscope for bowel sounds, the rumbling and pinging sounds that indicated the resumption of normal intestinal activity after surgery. There were none. Her abdomen was more distended than it had been yesterday, and she groaned and sobbed a little as I pressed gently on it. When I gingerly lifted the dressing from her belly, I found a large, angry-looking vertical scar—red, hard, and with greenish pus between a couple of the stitches. *Shit*, I thought. *A wound infection AND an intestinal obstruction. Evan's really going to love this.*

"Mrs. Rawlins," I said, turning my attention back to my patient, "I think we need to get an X-ray and do some blood tests. I need to talk with Dr. Jacobs first."

Mrs. Rawlins looked up at me with tears in her eyes. "Can you just get the nurse to give me my pain medicine now?"

"Of course. I'll tell her right away."

In the meantime, a few patients in nearby rooms had begun a Greek chorus of moaning and crying. The mournful noise followed me down the hallway as I continued my rounds. It was all I could do not to put my hands over my ears to drown out the sounds of pain. These women were gynecology patients. All of them had had surgery to remove cancers of the reproductive system, and several had undergone a procedure called "total exenteration" in which not only the uterus and ovaries were removed, but also the bladder and part of the colon. The surgeons pronounced the "en" in "exenteration" as though it were a French word, so it sounded like "total exoneration"—a most cruel irony.

Mrs. Rawlins' bowel obstruction was evidence that the cancer had attacked her small intestine and was probably no longer amenable to surgical treatment. Her wound was healing poorly and now looked infected, which meant she wouldn't be a candidate for radiation or chemotherapy either. She would likely die in that bed, crying for pain medication, and there wasn't anything I could do about it except be as kind and gentle with her as I could, helpless in the face of her suffering. This was the part of being a doctor our professors and attendings hadn't taught us how to deal with.

I'd already seen this kind of thing once in my brief time on 3B, and I was crushed to see it happening again, especially to

Mrs. Rawlins, with whom I'd bonded when I did her admission history and physical the night before her surgery. Just a few days earlier, she'd been a warm and vivacious woman who showed off pictures of her newest grandbaby to anyone who would look at them.

Filled with sad thoughts about Mrs. Rawlins, I was distracted on work rounds, when Evan and I met with the others on the 3B team—Rick Davis, the senior resident; Josh Stein, the other junior resident; Nurse Powell, the head nurse; and the other MS IIIs—to discuss the patients and the plan for the day. Evan glared at me when I gave Dr. Davis a wrong answer about postoperative pneumonia. By the time rounds were over, the pain-chorus had ratcheted up even further. I just couldn't stand it anymore. I had to get some air.

I took the stairs two at a time and slipped out the fire door on the hospital's southwest corner, then hunkered down just outside the exit and let myself cry for a few minutes. I'd had no idea it would be *this* hard. Would it have been any easier if I'd been assigned to a ward where the patients weren't all women? My mother's lymphoma had been a different kind of cancer from these patients', and her pain had been bone pain in her legs, not the pain of feeling like your gut was going to explode. I'd never heard the kind of helpless moaning from her that I heard from these women—thank god—but the hopelessness of Mom's plight had been no different than Mrs. Rawlins'.

I dabbed my eyes and blew my nose. When I looked up, a skinny Black kid who looked about fifteen stood in front of me, holding out a joint.

"You want some?" he asked shyly. I recoiled at first, but then my heart melted at this simple, if illegal, act of human sympathy and kindness. "No, thanks. I have to go back to work." I smiled at the boy. "But it was really nice of you to offer. Have a good day."

"You, too." Then he mumbled, looking at his feet as he spoke, "Hope you feel better."

Oddly enough, I *did* feel better. The memory of the young man's kindness helped me get through the rest of the day, and the sheer incongruity of it made me smile even amid all the *tsuris*—the wailing women, Evan's glowering, and Dr. Davis's casual contempt.

The residents at City Hospital were from Johns Hopkins, the academic Mecca, rather than the University of Maryland, which graduated most of the state's primary care doctors. The Hopkins folk appeared to view University MS IIIs as gum, or worse, on the bottom of their shoes. Since I was from the University of Maryland *and* female, I was doubly *persona non grata,* or so it felt to me.

These residents from one of the most prestigious surgical training programs in the country seemed to relish the typical surgery schedule of taking call every other night; but even they, exalted as they were, paid a price for their dedication. Evan's sarcasm and hostility were always more pronounced the day after his night on call. Residents showed their exhaustion in other ways, too—flippant answers to questions, sagging shoulders, dozing off on rounds, sometimes a burst of inappropriate laughter. None of this was surprising, since the luckless "post-call" resident would not be allowed to go home any earlier than his peers, whether he'd gotten any sleep the night before or not. I wondered how much of this *machismo* had to do with being in the Hopkins program and how much was attributable to the field of surgery itself.

One day I actually scored some points with my Hopkins

superiors. A little girl had presented with a lump in her neck. After the residents and MS IIIs examined her, Dr. Davis turned his gaze to me.

"So, doctor," he drawled, "what might the lump in this child's neck be?"

"It looks like scrofula to me," I replied tentatively, though I was pretty sure I was right. Scrofula, an infected lymph node in the neck due to a bacillus related to tuberculosis, was something I'd seen on my pediatric rotation several months earlier.

Dr. Davis looked mildly surprised. "And what's the treatment for scrofula?"

"Well, since the bacteria aren't very sensitive to anti-tuberculous drugs, most authorities think surgical excision is the mainstay of treatment."

"Very good!" Dr. Davis said, even as he did a comical little double take. Then, to my surprise, he smiled at me. "Yeah, I guess you'd know about scrofula, since you're interested in the kiddies—it's one of those *pediatric* things, isn't it?" His tone of voice was only mock-scornful, and he actually winked at me. I felt a flush of satisfaction, of victory, even. It carried me through the rest of the week.

One Sunday about halfway through the rotation, I was assigned to work alongside the resident on call. Mark Mason was a burly former college football player with straight brown hair and a chronically worried look. Despite his size, he moved faster than most of the more slender, wiry guys I'd worked with. Since it was a weekend day, he had to respond to requests for consults from all over the hospital. These usually involved the placement of an IV cut-down in an arm or leg, or a CVP line like Freddie's at the VA Spa—lines that would last longer than the usual small catheter or needle in a hand or arm. After Dr. Mason and I had rounded on the patients, a whirlwind process that left me slightly short of breath, he received a phone call.

"6A? A CVP line?" Dr. Mason rolled his eyes at me. "Okay, get six units of platelets to the bedside STAT and we'll be right there." He shook his head as he hung up the phone. "Today's our lucky day," he said wryly. "We get to put a CVP line in a leukemic who's crashing. Her platelet count is practically in the single digits." The normal platelet count was at least 100,000.

My gut clenched. Here we go, I thought. 6A was one of the Hematology-Oncology wards—possibly the very one where my mother had died. When I'd signed up for general surgery at Baltimore City, it had made a strange sort of sense to me, forcing myself to confront the loss of my mother by returning to the hospital where her death had taken place. Now it was about to get real.

And placing an indwelling line in the vena cava, the largest vein in the body, was a risky procedure in a patient with a low platelet count. Even if we transfused platelets to help with blood clotting as soon as the line went in, there was a chance the patient wouldn't survive the procedure—though she definitely wouldn't survive without any access to her circulatory system for medication and fluids. It was a rock-and-a-hard-place situation and bound to be a bloody mess.

My heart pounded as I tried not to lose sight of Dr. Mason sprinting up the stairs, and it didn't slow down when we got to 6A. What would we find there? *Please, god, don't let this woman look anything like Mom*, I prayed.

When we jogged into the room, I heaved a sigh of relief. The woman on the bed was diminutive and appeared to be in her 80s, looking nothing like my mother. There was, however, a lot of blood in evidence. A nurse was alternately removing blood from the poor woman's stomach and replacing it with iced saline, all through a large-bore tube emerging from one nostril, while the other nostril bled freely. Dr. Mason cursed under his breath.

"She's circling the drain, for god's sake," he muttered to me. "Why can't they just let her go in peace?"

I'd asked myself the same question when my mother had occupied a bed on the oncology unit. It had been clear that the experimental chemotherapy wasn't working, and I'd been acutely aware of the way in which the medical team stayed outside Mom's room to discuss her case during those last several days of her life—the very thing the 3B team was now doing with many of our patients. It both angered me and broke my heart to see how I'd become part of the "other side" myself. I felt strongly that this defensive stance of evasion and denial of death was wrong, but I also felt powerless to do anything about it. This wasn't how I wanted to be a doctor.

With a sigh and a shake of his head, Mark scrubbed his hands and arms, donned sterile gloves, and got to work. Similarly scrubbed and gloved, I handed him the instruments and tubing and tried to maintain my composure. Breathing deeply and slowly, I fought the urge to flee, the little voice in my head chanting, *Get. Out. Now.* I hoped with the fervor of a prisoner before a parole board that I would never again have to return to the oncology ward at Baltimore City once my general surgery sentence was up.

The woman survived the procedure, at least while we were there; I never found out what happened to her after that. I moved in a numb haze through the rest of the day, assisting Dr. Mason with a few more central lines. Fortunately, there were no more bloodbaths; the rest of the patients had reasonable platelet counts. Mark let me suture a wound in a school-age boy who required three stitches in his leg for a dog bite.

When I finally got back to my apartment that evening, my roommates were out. I poured myself a drink, put my feet up, and burst into tears. Grief, apparently, wasn't some tumor you could just cut out and be rid of. The sights, sounds, and smells of 6A had slammed into me, taking me right back to the time when I'd been on the oncology ward as a family member rather than an MS III on a clinical rotation. The surreal quality of that day's experience made me think of Dorothy in the *Wizard of Oz,* in the scene where she's sucked up into a tornado and then set down with a bang in an utterly alien and frightening landscape.

It didn't make things any easier that my paternal grandfather had died just as I was starting the general surgery rotation. Phone conversations with my father had clued me in to the fact that something had been amiss since Christmas; but Grandma's descriptions of the problem had been vague. Grandpa's mortal fear of hospitals had delayed medical intervention and probably shortened his life. He'd died peacefully not long after his cancer diagnosis. I hadn't been able to attend the funeral, but some of that evening's tears were for him.

Stress began to take a physical toll on me. After my first week at Baltimore City, the MS IIIs began to take night call, which rendered us part of the zombie nation of post-call sufferers the next day. But there were two crucial differences between residents and students: the residents, being more accustomed to sleep deprivation, had developed various compensatory mechanisms which we students had yet to work out for ourselves. On the plus side, we were allowed to leave at 3:30 p.m. on our post-call day, provided our work was done.

One evening while checking a new patient's lab work, I tested my own urine sample. Voiding had been excruciating for most of the day. My lower belly hurt, and frequent trips to the restroom had revealed some non-menstrual blood in my urine. When I carried the plastic cup into the small satellite lab to look at the sample under a microscope, a resident from another ward saw the bloody specimen and gave a long whistle.

"Damn, that's some serious hematuria! Whose urine is *that*?!"

I glared at him. "Mine," I said. The guy gave me a horrified look, finished what he was doing, and got the hell out of there. *Boy*, I told myself, *I might not be the world's best medical student, but I can sure clear a room in a hurry.* I spun the bloody urine in the centrifuge and looked at a drop of it under the microscope. No casts, fortunately—no evidence that the problem was at the level of the kidney, where it would be a sign of serious illness. (Like many medical students, I was prone to assume the most life-threatening diagnosis for any symptom of illness in myself.) It was only a bladder infection, albeit the worst one I'd ever had, thanks to stress—nothing a course of antibiotics wouldn't fix. Once I was on the medication, I still felt lousy for several days. When the weekend rolled around, I didn't drag myself to my assignment in the Baltimore City ER—which, unfortunately, meant that I missed the best opportunity I'd have for learning how to suture minor lacerations, a skill it would have been good to master before pediatric residency.

• • •

A week later, on a Friday night, loneliness caught up with me. I walked to No Fish Today, the bar I'd frequented with Sadie the previous year. I hadn't had a date, much less a relationship, in over three months. Many of my friends were married or at least involved with someone, and my roommates Isabel and Michael were totally absorbed in their wedding plans. I was bone-tired of the drudgery and emotional hardship of the surgery rotation and the lack of camaraderie, to put it mildly, among that group of Hopkins men. Plus, I was discouraged because I was falling behind academically. It was even harder to find time to read the most basic chapters of the surgery textbook than it had been to keep up with my internal-medicine reading.

On this lovely spring evening, I was full of inchoate longing: not just for love or some facsimile of it—physical intimacy, cuddling, just being touched; but for something else as well. I flashed back to summers in high school, when I visited my grade-school best friend in Rhode Island for two weeks, living a double life—morphing from a smart, high-achieving Catholic-school girl from Maryland into just another rebellious teenager. My friend and I would dress up, tease our hair, slather on the eyeshadow and mascara, and go out looking for a party, riding with her older brother or one of his friends, chugging beer in the back seat. We'd go to a house in a neighborhood I'd never been to, with the Rolling Stones blaring from the living-room stereo; or join a bunch of cars parked on a cul-de-sac or beside a less-traveled road, one of the car radios blasting the Kinks or the Dave Clark Five. Besides plenty of beer, there were boys, of course—cute boys, cool boys, boys I wouldn't have had the nerve to talk to without a couple of cans of Budweiser coursing through my veins. Not much of significance came of these encounters—a smile, a look, a joke, an arm slung carelessly across my shoulders during a conversation—and, once, a couple of kisses. But that heady illusion of something about to happen, of a door just starting to open, a momentous threshold waiting to be crossed: that sustained my high-school self through the other fifty weeks of the year.

And now I was riding that same giddy feeling of possibility. But I wasn't a teenager anymore. At some level I knew that beneath the feverish excitement lay a dark void, a blackness like the cold water beneath the skin of ice on a pond in early winter. Beneath my restless boredom lay a feeling of worthlessness. I had to skate across that ice quickly or I'd be sucked down into the emptiness. I'd been inclined to hurt myself before, more than once since my years of innocence; and I'd acted this out in various ways, often involving men. Now, thanks to my recent experiences on the wards, that worthless, self-injurious feeling was oozing back. That night I kept the abyss at bay by telling myself I just needed a change of pace, a little adventure. If I could just kick over the traces for an evening, everything would be fine.

The wall of noise slammed into me when I entered The Fish. I snagged a seat at the bar and sipped my National Bohemian draft, mulling over the path I'd chosen. Medicine was intellectually stimulating, for sure: the pursuit of a diagnosis, combing through medical texts and articles, seeing how a "mystery" patient's symptoms, physical findings, and lab results turned out to fit with some exotic disease you hadn't considered at first. There was also the great satisfaction of helping another person: finding the right medication for their illness; removing a tumor in the OR (or, more accurately, holding retractors while the resident and attending removed the tumor); even drawing blood and starting IVs. I had to believe that the rewards of my work would eventually outweigh the lonely nights, the ill-defined yearning and masked despair that drove me to The Fish.

As I ruminated, a trim, gentlemanly person around my age sidled up to me—medium build, short brown hair with a neatly-trimmed reddish beard, and wire-rim glasses.

"What's a beautiful young maiden like you doing in a place like this?" the stranger asked. He bowed like a courtier in a Shakespeare play. Startled, I laughed at the cliché and blushed at the compliment. He bent over my hand and kissed it—a far cry from the atmosphere of the surgical service at Baltimore City Hospital.

The man introduced himself as Max, ordered a beer for each of us (my second), and continued his campaign.

"I love your hair," he said, picking up a strand and stroking it.

Soon we were joined by a slightly taller, beardless blond guy whom Max introduced as his roommate, Reggie.

"Hey, Max, looks like you hit the jackpot this time," Reggie said, looking me up and down. It seemed I was being courted by two men at once, a first for me.

The flattery flowed freely with the beer. My new companions and I checked out a few more bars in the course of the evening. Riding around with them in Reggie's car, I had a delightful sense of freedom, of living on the edge, mixed with a frisson of apprehension: could they be abducting me? I laughed inwardly at my overblown sense of the dramatic. I'd forgotten what it was like to have fun; and now, thanks to Max and Reggie, I remembered. Right then, that was all that mattered.

Eventually we arrived at their place, where my alcohol-induced high was augmented by some fine weed. Before I knew it, Max was kissing me stirringly, with a hand underneath my top. While he worked on my mouth and breasts, Reggie unzipped my jeans. Then they switched places.

It took me awhile to remember where I was when I woke up next to Max in the morning. The room was dark and close, rank with the smell of stale pot. Food wrappers littered the scarred desk, along with a half-consumed plastic cup of beer. Reggie, to my relief, was nowhere to be seen. I blushed to the roots of my hair when I remembered my wantonness of the previous night, but I also felt a guilty thrill. *I know I was starved for affection*, I reflected. *I know my femininity was in serious need of validation, but—two guys at once?* I felt a confused mix of embarrassment and pride in my adventurous spirit, what some would call recklessness. No doubt about it, I was a liberated woman.

Cynical as I'd become, I wondered if I'd been the object of a dare or a bet the two guys had made before they ever set foot in that bar. Or was it one of those things that "just happened?" Max, the quieter and seemingly more sensitive of the two, was the one I'd been attracted to from the beginning, so I was glad to find myself in his bed rather than Reggie's. I shook my head a few times to try to clear my mind. It didn't help.

I'd been involved in several sexual relationships after losing my virginity in college, a few of which had been one-night stands. I'd certainly done some less-than-wholesome things related to sex over the previous six years, but this was the most transgressive by far.

While I pondered my checkered past, Max yawned and stretched.

"Hi, beautiful," he said with a smile.

"Hi yourself." I smiled back.

He propped himself up on an elbow. "So you're a medical student, huh?"

"Yeah, third year."

He grinned. "Wow, I caught myself a medical student!"

I laughed.

"What's it like, being a girl in medical school? Most of your classmates are guys, right?"

"Oh, yeah. To be honest, it kind of sucks a lot of the time, especially where I'm working now. The guys are all from Hopkins, and they think they're hot shit."

He laughed. "Bet you don't have any trouble setting them straight."

"If only that were true." I shook my head ruefully.

After a brief pause, I asked, tentatively, "So, what is it you do?" I was embarrassed that I'd forgotten what he'd told me in the heat of the previous night.

"I'm working at a pizza place right now, but I'll be starting respiratory therapy school in the fall."

"Good for you," I said. This was a first for me, dating someone with significantly less education, but I was favorably impressed that he aspired to work in a field related to medicine.

That was how I ended up with a boyfriend for the rest of the surgery rotation: the last week of general surgery and the subsequent 4-1/2 weeks of surgical subspecialties—namely, orthopedics, urology, and ear-nose-throat. The subspecialties brought me back to University Hospital, where there were no more Hopkins residents and no more night call, and more time for socializing.

But Max wasn't someone I wanted my friends to meet. It wasn't just the embarrassing circumstances of that first night together, nor was it the fact that he was less educated. It was Max himself. His courtly veneer soon wore off, and he turned out to be crude, ignorant, and stubborn. In his own way, he was at least as much of a misogynist as the men I encountered on the wards. He considered it his responsibility to show me the error of my ways concerning the relative position of the sexes. In his view, a man was supposed to dominate a woman, whether she was a medical student or not. My unwavering contention of gender equality was, in his words, "a load of crap."

I stayed because he was good in bed. Max knew how to kindle my lust, but he was also surprisingly tender. We would laugh and play as well as have hot, athletic sex; but outside of bed, we'd wrangle like toddlers fighting over a toy. Then he'd do something nice, like drive me to the hospital in the morning so I didn't have to take the bus, kissing me goodbye like a devoted husband—and the cycle would start all over again.

Uncomfortable as I was with this weird situation, I tried several times to break things off with Max, but somehow, I just couldn't stay away. I'd come home from the hospital determined to spend the evening in my room studying; then Max would call and cajole me, even plead with me, to spend the night. I usually acquiesced when this happened, spending two or three nights a week at his place. Once I got there, we couldn't keep our hands off each other. As soon as we started to make love, I descended into a place of subterranean darkness where I didn't have to be responsible for anyone, didn't have to care about anyone or anything other than my own pleasure.

The last few months of medical school had beaten me down. I'd had a rude awakening to the stark reality of sickness, old age, and death in a way I hadn't previously, even at the death of my own mother. I was helping to take care of women and men for whom death would have been a welcome release, yet my job was to contribute to the team's effort to postpone the inevitable—a task made more painful by the fact that I'd watched my mother go through a similar ordeal. Besides feeling objectified as a woman, I felt like a cog in a machine as a medical student. The patients seemed like cogs in a machine, too—a great mechanism of suffering and despair, the same one that had consumed my mother several months earlier. I was furious about all this; but the worst part of it was that I could see myself starting to view my patients and my colleagues as objects, too—patients who had inconvenient needs at inconvenient times, residents who seemed to exist solely to make my life miserable. Perhaps that was why

I couldn't resist the pull of this other kind of objectification, a relationship with a man I didn't love or even like very much—who could, however, make me feel like a woman in the most fundamental way.

The chaos and anarchy of this relationship that I couldn't own, that I believed I had to keep as much of a secret as possible from anyone I cared about, was somehow gratifying—it validated the sense of life's hapless disorder and lack of meaning that my recent experiences of loss and sickness and death had left in their wake. In Max's bed I wordlessly acted out my anger—anger about my mother's death, anger about the hard lessons of medical school, and especially anger, even hatred, toward every man who'd ever abandoned me.

One weekday morning, Max fixed breakfast while I got ready to leave for the hospital, something he'd never done before. He set a plate of scrambled eggs and bacon in front of me with a flourish.

"Aw, Max—how sweet! You didn't have to do that."

"Hey, I'm feeling generous today." We ate in companionable silence, which was unusual for us. I picked up my things to leave.

"Whoa, whoa, not so fast! You need to wash the dishes," he said.

Tilting my head, I squinted at him. "You know I have to be at work in 20 minutes, right?"

"Too bad. I made breakfast, so you have to clean up." Max frowned at me, arms crossed.

"Are you kidding? There's no way I can wash the dishes now. I can't be late, I just told you." My voice rose despite my effort to control it.

"I'm not kidding. If you don't do the dishes now, I'm going to break up with you."

Shaking my head in disbelief, I couldn't help but laugh.

"Oh, for god's sake, Max! I'm going now—I'll call you later." I even kissed him on the cheek as I left. Though I was angry about the dish-washing ultimatum, I was still touched by his fixing me breakfast.

But the minute I got out the door, I felt a dizzying sense of freedom. If he never called me again, it would be just fine with me.

Our affair limped on for a few more weeks, but that showdown over the dishes marked a turning point. Max became increasingly truculent, and I became increasingly intolerant of his bantam-rooster posturing. The darkness and anarchy, and the need for mutually exploitative sex, had played themselves out. As the end of the third year of medical school came into view, I was ready to move on.

13

SECOND CHANCE

On Tuesday, July 6th, the day after the bicentennial Fourth of July weekend, I started my summer externship. Early that morning I parked the VW Beetle in the Union Memorial Hospital parking garage and, with sweating palms, made my way to the personnel office. I'd eagerly signed up in March for this job, my chance to redeem myself after my mediocre performance at the VA Spa—and then I'd put it out of my mind for more than three months. Now the day of reckoning was at hand.

After the requisite filling out of forms, the administrative assistant handed me my temporary ID with a smile. "Hope you enjoy your time here," she said. "Let us know if you need anything." My shoulders relaxed a little in response to her kindness.

Underneath my name was the word "Extern," which meant I was a fourth-year medical student doing the work of a first-year resident, aka an intern—admitting patients to an internal medicine ward and assuming responsibility for their care. This was a dry run for the following summer when I would actually *be* an intern. A surge of pride shot through me: I was almost a doctor! Externship was a kind of apprenticeship; I'd be more closely supervised than someone who'd just graduated. But I would receive a modest stipend for my work, which was exciting. I was grateful for this remedial course in internal medicine, this second chance.

With my ID clipped to my chest pocket, I went to meet my colleagues on the ward where I'd be working. Our team consisted of a resident, an intern, and me. For the first few weeks, my supervising resident was an Egyptian man, Dr. Qatoush, who took a dim view of women in medicine. "So, we have a girl extern this month," he said with a pained smile. I heaved a sigh and steeled myself for conflicts to come. Craig, the intern, shot me a look out of the corner of his eye as he tried to suppress a grin. He was the polar opposite of our superior—a California native with a laid-back attitude, long black curls, and a Freddy Mercury mustache, who drove to work in a sweet little burgundy Triumph.

The ward where I worked was a busy one—sicker patients were hustled on gurneys to the ICU while recovering ones returned in wheelchairs; nurses scurried from room to room. Eventually I'd be responsible for an average of eight or ten patients on any given day. Most of my charges were elderly men and women with chronic illness, so their medical charts were several inches thick. It took a while to get used to finding the highlights in these masses of paper in order to put together a coherent medical history. I always hoped the previous intern had assembled a good discharge summary, but this wasn't always the case.

My work involved combining the patient's account of the current problem with a distillation of their past medical history from the chart; doing a physical examination; formulating a list of likely diagnoses and a comprehensive treatment plan; and, finally, presenting all this in a concise fashion to the supervising resident and the attending physician. This was an art, a skill requiring a lot of practice. It took me a long time to master it, because I often got lost in the sea of detail. But I got plenty of practice that summer, and I managed to learn a lot of medicine with considerably less humiliation than I'd experienced at the VA Spa and Baltimore City Hospital.

I was so absorbed in learning how to care for patients that it was difficult to turn off the hustle and bustle of the ward when I got home at night. There'd been some changes in my living situation: I remained at 1210 Bolton Street, but I no longer shared the third-floor front apartment with Isabel. After their wedding at the beginning of June, Michael had officially moved upstairs with her, and I'd moved into the small second-floor apartment he'd vacated.

The first floor of the building was occupied by Lily, a first-year social work student. Lily was a few years older than me, slim and blonde, with a pretty face and clear blue eyes, pleasant and easygoing. She'd lived there with her husband, Gene, for several years. But once Lily had finished supporting him financially while he completed law school, Gene left her for another woman, making him *persona non grata* in the eyes of Isabel, Michael, and me. The three of us had become good friends with Lily over the past year, and now that she was a lonely divorcee, we spent more time with her. As the one member of our trio who was single, I grew especially close to her. I looked forward to becoming her roommate in August, when her lease on the first-floor flat would be up. We planned to move into the third-floor rear apartment together.

But for most of that summer, I had an entire apartment to myself, a novel experience. The place was very small; half the second floor had been annexed to the landlords' neighboring townhouse, so there wasn't much room for my living/dining area, tiny bedroom and bath, and minuscule kitchen, where an old-fashioned casement window overlooked the back alley. But it was cozy, and I really enjoyed having my own space.

Some nights I went upstairs for an after-dinner mug of peppermint tea with Isabel and Michael. Others, I visited Lily in the first-floor apartment. Sometimes I just grabbed something out of the refrigerator and attempted some reading from my *Harrison's Principles of Internal Medicine* before I crashed. I seldom cooked for myself; cleaning up afterward was too much work. I barely had enough energy to maintain my little apartment. When I dozed off over my textbook in the evening or went to sleep at night, I often dreamed about happenings on the ward.

Sleep deprivation loomed large in a way it hadn't previously, not even on the medicine and surgery rotations. I was on call every third night, which was standard on an internal medicine ward. My nights on call were more like 32- to 34- (or even 36-) hour days, since I was expected to work a full day post-call and to stay until the work was done. Since I seldom got more than four or five hours of sleep, sometimes as little as one or two, I wasn't very efficient the next day. The necessary paperwork of patient care took twice as long as it did when I came in fresh after a good night's sleep.

The one day that was neither call nor post-call could last anywhere from eight or nine hours to twelve or more, depending on how busy the ward was and how long it took to finish up. I could have cut corners by writing a more cursory note or leaving work I should have finished for the colleague to whom I signed out my patients. But there would be a price to pay for that, along the lines of the Golden Rule: what you did unto others, they would likely do unto you. There was enough for any of us to do at night—new admissions, problems with current patients, tests that had to be done at certain hours, IVs to restart—without having to finish someone else's leftover scut-work.

This schedule took a greater toll on my physical and mental well-being than I'd anticipated. After my first middle-of-the-night admission, I skipped breakfast so I could work on my patient presentation for morning rounds. Soon I was tremulous, cranky, and paranoid, and I even started to cry when a conflict arose over the discharge of one of my patients. My own low blood sugar had sabotaged my attempt to make a good impression on my colleagues. From then on, I always managed to snag a bagel or a muffin from the hospital cafeteria before rounds.

Then there was the quintessential medical student's dilemma, which became even more irritating when I hadn't had enough sleep. One resident did things one way and another resident— the one I was on call with that night—did them a different way; and I, at the bottom of the medical pecking order, was caught in the middle, knowing that someone would be pissed off no matter what I did. Dr. Qatoush was particularly intransigent in this regard; he took me to task one day for ordering an ECG on a man with pain below his rib cage that was clearly due to acid indigestion. When I explained that I'd only been following the night resident's orders, he just glared at me.

There was an upside to this situation, though. It helped me find my own way, my own style of practicing medicine, by observing how these different approaches played out in the actual care of patients. But it took a long time to gain this perspective, a lot of being chewed out by one medical superior or another and feeling like I couldn't do anything right. I didn't suffer this conundrum gladly. It brought all my self-doubt to the fore. I felt stupid, and then angry with myself for feeling stupid.

But I had enough insight even then to realize something important: in medicine at least, the words "You're wrong" are often code for "I don't agree with you"—a subtle difference, but a crucial one. Still, I found it difficult not to perceive a correction or criticism as a personal attack, especially with my internal-medicine and surgery colleagues. While my own hypersensitivity and thin skin accounted for much of this, some of it was due to the lack of tact and finesse these hard-charging individuals brought to their interactions with just about everyone, including patients—and especially with us lowly medical students. My responses to the situation ranged from second-guessing myself to angry defensiveness, with a steady undercurrent of resentment.

That summer I started to have nightmares which recurred for many years. In these dreams, I lost my teeth—sometimes a few, sometimes all of them, sometimes they would even shatter in my mouth. Taking my cue from Freud's *Interpretation of Dreams*, I attributed these nightmares to the problems I was having as a fledgling doctor with initiative, assertiveness, and self-confidence. Many years later I learned more interpretations for such dreams: stress due to impending major changes (like moving on from medical school to residency); attachment issues and a wish to be nurtured (I had that one in spades!); ambivalence that makes difficult decisions even more so (indeed); and the suffering that accompanies personal growth (yup, that too).

The second half of my tenure at Union Memorial proved to be a lot more enjoyable than the first. My new colleagues were both named Jim. Jim Carroll, the intern, had just graduated from the University of Maryland Medical School, as I would within the year. He was tall, trim, and blond, with a somewhat less formidable mustache than Craig's. Carroll was the scion of several generations of physicians and had all the self-assurance of someone born to medicine. He was practical, efficient, and commonsensical. He wasn't particularly warm and fuzzy, but he was not unkind, and he had a good sense of humor. Our supervising resident, Jim Elliott, was very different. He was a big, ungainly teddy bear of a guy with lank brown hair, round pink cheeks, and wire-rim glasses without which he was virtually blind. If Carroll was a doer, Elliott was a thinker. His style matched my own; he pondered things deeply and was often tentative.

While I found Carroll intimidating and envied his decisiveness and his supreme comfort in his doctor-role, I appreciated Elliott's guileless good nature and his wickedly wry sense of humor. Carroll helped me gain confidence in procedures like starting IVs and in the difficult process of cutting to the chase when presenting a patient on rounds. Elliott was a gentle, patient teacher who helped me think my way through diagnostic dilemmas. Carroll once called us the Three Musketeers, but I thought of us as the Dream Team.

One evening the Dream Team was confronted with an elderly woman whose sodium and potassium levels were out of whack, most likely because of her diuretic medication. This was a fairly common scenario among older folks with high blood pressure or heart disease, but the degree to which this woman was affected was unusual. She claimed that the clock on the wall was watching her and that people were talking about her over the PA system (which was in fact blaring commands like, "Dr. Schmidt to the ICU, STAT!").

Unfortunately for her and for us, such changes in a patient's mental status can't be attributed solely to medication issues until other potentially life-threatening conditions, like meningitis or brain hemorrhage, have been ruled out. Mrs. Doe would require a lumbar puncture, also known as a spinal tap. Since she was physically agitated as well as hallucinating, shouting at us and cursing us out, this would be no easy task. Try as we might to get her to hold still and lie on her side for the procedure, she was having none of it. Sedating a patient for a spinal tap wasn't an option since this could be dangerous in someone with an altered mental status. We couldn't just skip the procedure, because the consequences of missing a case of meningitis were dire. The three of us looked at each other. Carroll shook his head. Elliott sighed deeply.

I think it was Carroll's idea. He picked up a roll of heavy white cloth tape and began taping Mrs. D.'s legs to the bed. Her shouts and curses rose to an ear-splitting volume as Elliott and I joined in, taping the poor woman to the mattress, snickering like kids in a classroom who've put a whoopee cushion on the teacher's chair. We agreed that Elliott, the most senior among us, would be the one to insert the spinal needle. Carroll gathered our taped-up patient into the requisite C-shape, her spine facing the lumbar-puncturist, while Elliott scrubbed his hands and donned sterile gloves. Similarly scrubbed and gloved, I set up the instrument tray for him. Mrs. Doe's squirming increased with the intensified effort to restrain her, and our laughter became harder to stifle. I felt bad about our mirth, but I knew we were laughing about our own predicament as much as our patient's; and we were pretty sure Mrs. D. would recover once she received the treatment she needed.

Elliott inserted the needle with some difficulty. To our relief, the spinal fluid was clear. Twelve hours of intravenous saline and potassium chloride was all she needed. The three of us were a little embarrassed the next day when Mrs. Doe, her electrolytes now in balance and her faculties restored, asked us cautiously if she'd been talking out of her head.

Those weeks with Carroll and Elliott gave me my first real taste of the camaraderie that can happen among people working together in medicine, and that time remains one of my fondest memories of medical school. It was hard to say goodbye to the men of the Dream Team. I would miss them—the first time I'd ever felt that way about finishing a medical rotation. Besides the joy of that experience of fellowship, I'd spent that summer learning—ever so gradually and mostly by default—how to take care of myself as well as how to take care of patients. As the autumn of the fourth year of medical school loomed, that critical time of decision, I went into the next phase with a little more self-understanding and self-compassion.

• • •

Halfway through August, I reconnected with my former lover, Preston. To my pleasant surprise, he'd called me when he returned from his sabbatical in Europe. As I watched him walk from his car to my door, he seemed slimmer, more compact than I remembered; even his Afro was cut closer to his head. There was a youthful spring in his step, an ageless quality about him. He seemed trimmed down to the essentials of himself.

As we exchanged stories about the year since we'd last seen each other, it occurred to me that our relationship was now one of near-equals rather than parent/child or mentor/student. My experiences on clinical rotations had matured me in a way I hadn't been aware of until I shared them with him that evening. We ate dinner at our favorite Chinese restaurant and went back to his place for the night. His fervor and expertise in bed were refreshing and invigorating. After those tempestuous weeks with Max in the spring, it was wonderful to be with someone with whom I had a much deeper connection than sex alone. I marveled at the chocolate brown of his skin, once so familiar, against the sun-deprived pallor of my own.

• • •

As summer ripened into fall, I moved upstairs to the third-floor rear apartment with Lily, and we became closer now that we were roommates. She was still depressed about her ex-husband's desertion; sometimes she was so ruminative that I worried about her. But when she wasn't brooding about her own troubles, she was a good sounding-board for my relationship problems. One evening she made chamomile tea and we sat on opposite ends of her orange corduroy sofa, sipping the calming beverage and talking about men. Lily tucked one foot under her and gave me her full attention, as though no one else existed.

"So, that night with your old boyfriend bummed you out, huh?"

"Yeah." I sighed. I'd had a major attack of loneliness after the evening with Preston. "It was great, but it reminded me of what I've been missing. I'd like to see him again, but I'm afraid I'll just get hurt." I shook my head. "I just can't seem to sustain a relationship with a man. Maybe it's time to go back into therapy again."

Lily nodded and took a sip of her tea.

"That's a great idea. I've been in therapy since Gene and I started having trouble, long before the divorce, and it's helped me. I'm sure it could help you, too."

But there was one thing I found jarring about Lily's behavior. Bereft as she was after losing Gene, she now had a boyfriend who slept over a couple of times a week, even though she confided to me that she didn't love him. Unhappily single myself, I found this baffling.

• • •

Halfway through September, I had a few weeks of hard-earned and much-needed vacation, which I used for residency interviews and visits with family and friends in New England. My first stop was my maternal grandmother's home in Natick, Massachusetts. Gram, now eighty, had begun her slide into dementia before my mother's death three years previously, but the descent had accelerated in the last several months. It took longer than I remembered for her to arrive at the back door when I rang the doorbell. When she let me in, it was hard to conceal my dismay at her appearance. She looked much older than she had the last time I'd seen her. Her hair, usually done up in a neat French twist, was slightly disheveled.

"Hi, Gram. It's so good to see you!" I reached for her, and she pulled me close.

"Well, hello there, darlin'!" We hugged each other tightly. Shuffling a bit, Gram led me through the kitchen with its sloping yellow linoleum floor, through the dining room with its dark furniture and cabbage-rose-patterned rug, and into the back parlor where she spent most of her time. The old brown horsehair sofa was still there, the one that always made me itch when I sat on it. Her venerable Singer sewing machine was ensconced on a square card-table with a basket of fabric scraps next to it. The windows were open, the gauzy curtains billowing in the warm September breeze. Gram led me over to the mantel where she kept an assortment of family pictures—her "rogues' gallery," she called it.

"Mary sent me a picture of the kids last week," she confided. I noticed a recent-looking picture of my cousins on the right-hand side of the mantel, but Gram steered me to the other end of the shelf first. "See, here's your mother when she was a little girl," she said, stroking the front of a picture I'd seen there for as long as I could remember. She pointed to the next photo and said, "Let's see, is that Walt Sr. or Walt Jr.?"

"That's Uncle Walt, Gram. It looks like he was in the army

then." I leaned toward her, my hand resting lightly beneath her elbow.

"Silly me! Of course." Gram shook her head slightly. "And this must be Phil." She pointed to a picture of my father from the early '50s, when he was about the age Phil was now.

"No, Gram," I said softly." That's my dad, not my brother."

A look of frustration crossed her face. "Darn it! I seem to be striking out all over the place, don't I?"

At that point I gently guided her to the photo at the far end of the mantel. "Gram, is this the picture you were telling me about, the one Aunt Mary sent you?" My five cousins were lined up in order of age, with 15-year-old Dottie on one end and 6-year-old Billy on the other.

"Why, yes, there it is!" Gram picked up the picture, beaming. "Hard to believe Dottie and Geoff are teenagers, isn't it?"

I was aware of a kind of double vision as I watched my grandmother struggle with the photographs. It was painful to witness the effort with which she husbanded her wandering faculties; it was all I could do not to cry. But caring for the old guys at the V.A. hospital had taught me how to deal with Gram's forgetfulness in a compassionate, matter-of-fact way that helped both of us. Putting on my doctor persona interposed some distance between her obvious decline and my own sadness, the grief I felt for the person she'd once been. This kind of objectivity hadn't been available to me when my mother was dying at the start of medical school.

A mile or so from Gram's house was the cemetery where my mother and grandfather were buried. I'd planned to visit my mother's grave on previous trips but had always lost my nerve. Now I spent a long time at her headstone, crying a little and talking softly to her.

The cemetery was warm and still in the September sun. I watched as a woman drove up, weeping, to place a single rose on the grave of her son who'd died the previous year at the age of 21. How much the headstones told us, and yet how little—like that of a 17-year-old boy whose epitaph read, "A song of sunshine, love and peace."

After I touched my mother's gravestone and said goodbye, I wandered over to the spot where her father was buried, the headstone carved with the names of both my grandparents. I wondered how long it would be before Gram's date of death would be filled in.

A few days before my residency interviews at Rhode Island Hospital in Providence and at Yale-New Haven Hospital, I was visiting a friend in New Hampshire when I found out that Gram had been hospitalized. She'd fallen on the sidewalk outside her home, and a kindly neighbor had helped her and called an ambulance. I returned to Natick to spend time at her hospital bedside before leaving for my interviews. After our visit, my uncle Walt accompanied me to her house and told me to take whatever items I wanted, since she would be going to a nursing home after her discharge. I chose a few small things and the gate-leg table from her front parlor. Both of us were sad. Gram's "rogues' gallery" looked forlorn without her.

At the end of September, I returned to Baltimore to start an elective rotation in pediatric hematology and to take Part 2 of the National Boards, that rite of passage required for medical licensure. The countdown to residency, the next phase of my medical training, had begun. With Match Day now only five months away and anxiety mounting about the next step in my career, I haunted the offices of my advisors, looking for counsel and support. There was a lot to be said for getting out of Baltimore and starting over in a new place, but it was a difficult decision. There'd been so much involuntary change in my life in the last three years—did I really want to pull up stakes and start over in a whole new city? In the evenings I sat by the casement window of the apartment I shared with Lily, looking at the turning leaves and weighing my options. Whenever I heard ships' horns blowing in the nocturnal October mist, I thought wistfully of lost love, wondering if I'd ever find someone to share my life with.

One bright spot in that solitary time was my growing friendship with our new neighbor, John, who'd moved into the small second-floor apartment when I moved in with Lily. He was an accountant, a decade older than me, and a newly divorced father of two school-age children. He was of medium height and build, with straight brown hair, blue eyes, and a thick mustache. His features were plain, but he had a great smile.

John invited me in for a chat and a drink one evening. It felt strange to sit in one of his tastefully upholstered wing chairs in the living room I'd recently vacated. His well-matched furnishings were a far cry from my Goodwill odds and ends. Previously, I'd confided in him about my romantic difficulties, encouraged by his warmth and openness. On this visit, he was talking about his divorce.

"I was completely blindsided." he said, taking a sip of scotch. "She never really told me what went wrong, and I still haven't figured it out." He shook his head. "I feel worse for the kids than for myself. They've both had trouble in school this year."

Though John had been wounded by his divorce and was not ready for another relationship, he had a curious, exploratory attitude that I deeply respected. He seemed determined to make the most of his new-found freedom, painful as its genesis may have been. He went to concerts and the opera regularly and checked out a couple of singles gatherings, and I accompanied him on some of these jaunts.

I was struck by the contrast between John's response to an unwanted divorce and Lily's. Unlike John, Lily had leapt head-long into another relationship, yet she spent much of the time second-guessing herself about her marriage and wishing her ex-husband would return. I wondered how much of the differ-ence in their attitudes was unique to each of them, and how much of it was because Lily was a woman and John was a man.

In the middle of October, a few weeks after I returned from my New England trip, Gram was discharged from the hospi-tal and Uncle Walt brought her to his family's home in western Massachusetts before moving her into a nursing home. On her first night with her son's family, she didn't answer the call to din-ner and was found unresponsive on the bed: she'd had a massive stroke. She died twelve hours later.

I was deeply saddened by Gram's death, but I didn't attend the funeral. Though I wanted to be there, I planned to drive to Cincinnati and Pittsburgh for residency interviews in a few days—a longer drive than I'd ever done by myself, and into unfa-miliar territory at that. I mourned my grandmother as I pored over road maps and tried to figure out how much time to allow for each leg of the trip. For the time being, at least, anxiety and anticipation about interviews eclipsed my grief.

On the appointed day, I packed up the VW Beetle and set out. By the time I got to Breezewood, Pennsylvania on Interstate 70, I was in full road-trip mode, singing along with Boz Scaggs' "Lowdown," the car radio cranked up to full volume. My sponta-neous euphoria must have disoriented me, because I was halfway to Cleveland before I realized I'd turned north instead of south on Interstate 71! It was a good thing my interview at Cincinnati

Children's Hospital wasn't until the next day.

After my morning interview in Cincinnati, I drove 300 miles to my next interview at Pittsburgh Children's Hospital. That night I stayed at a Howard Johnson's Motel that featured worn sheets, a thin mattress, and even thinner walls. Worse yet, there were a couple of new bug bites on my legs when I got up.

Once the next morning's interview was over, I realized I was ill. I'd been fighting a cold for a week, but now my primary symptom was fever, with its attendant feeling of weakness and rapid heartbeat. As if feeling miserable weren't enough, it began to rain right after I left Pittsburgh for the final leg of my journey, the drive to Connecticut. I planned to stay with my paternal grandmother, now my sole surviving grandparent, while I did a month-long rotation on the infant ward at Yale-New Haven Hospital. Grandma's Southport, Connecticut home was about forty-five minutes from New Haven, a reasonable daily commute.

A few hours out of Pittsburgh, I wondered if I'd ever get there. I was driving through an unremitting downpour, made worse by the great sluices of water from passing truck-tires that threatened to capsize the Beetle. And I was feeling lousier and lousier, popping aspirin and downing cups of coffee, keeping Grandma posted by pay phone at my frequent pit stops. A drive that should have taken eight hours ended up taking more than twelve.

When I finally arrived in the middle of the night, Grandma took one look at me and went to her medicine cabinet for the thermometer. When she took my temperature, it was 103. She fussed over me, urged me to drink some water, and fetched the Tylenol. Aching and exhausted as I was, it felt good to be taken care of. After a few more minutes of conversation, I took a couple of pills and stumbled off to bed.

Wretched as I felt that night, I had no idea how much worse

things were about to get.

14

BOOKENDS

Partially rejuvenated by a few hours of sleep and Grandma's breakfast of eggs, bacon, and strong coffee, I dragged myself to Yale-New Haven Hospital (YNHH) the next day for the start of my three-and-a-half-week rotation. When I checked in at the Pediatrics office, the department secretary peered at me over her glasses.

"You're the University of Maryland student?" she said. "One of the first-year residents had to make a schedule change, so you're to report to the adolescent ward instead of the infant ward."

My face fell. I'd looked forward to an opportunity to gain some experience starting IVs and doing other procedures on the little ones before pediatric residency. But that was not to be.

Most of my adolescent patients had cancer, were on dialysis for kidney failure, or were otherwise afflicted with serious chronic illness, much like the adult patients I'd taken care of for the last eight months. My most recent rotation at University Hospital had exposed me to kids with cancer, but I was still intimidated by the prospect of caring for these near-adults, who weren't much younger than I was. Kids weren't supposed to be chronically ill; that was the province of old people. With a sigh of resignation, I sat down to read the charts of the teenagers who'd been assigned to my care.

After a couple of hours, my body told me I wasn't ready to assume my ward duties. My temperature rose again, accompanied by fatigue and malaise. I excused myself to the ward resident and drove back to my grandmother's house in Southport early in the afternoon.

"You look awful," she said. When I took my temperature, it was 104.2. I took to my bed and sipped the glass of water she brought.

I called in sick for the next two days, even though I was embarrassed about "wimping out" at the very beginning of a rotation, especially this one. I'd been dazzled by Yale at my interview the previous month. If I left Baltimore for residency, Yale-New Haven would be my first choice—though it was a long shot, considering my unremarkable performance thus far in medical school. Missing two and a half days of my first week on the adolescent ward certainly wouldn't help my chances; but my temperature was still 102 to 104 degrees. Grandma wasn't very reassuring about my decision to stay home. With characteristic bluntness, she asked, "Aren't you afraid they'll think you're goofing off?"

I sighed. "No, Grandma, I don't think they want somebody who's sick with a high fever around their immunosuppressed cancer patients." At that point I felt too crappy to care.

By Friday my temperature was almost normal, but my legs had broken out in ugly boils. Though I still didn't feel well, I assumed my ward duties for the first time. When there was a lull in the action, I swallowed my embarrassment and asked the resident, Luke, to look at the rash on my several-days-unshaven legs.

"Wow, those lesions look nasty," he said. He needled one of the pustular sores to send for a bacterial culture and prescribed an antibiotic for staph infections, which I started to take as soon as I could get the prescription filled at the hospital pharmacy.

Fortunately, I didn't have to be on call until Sunday, which happened to be Halloween. After the day's work was done, Luke and I had dinner and braced ourselves for the evening to come.

Sure enough, there were some unusual admissions to the adolescent ward that night, including a 15-year-old boy who couldn't or wouldn't open his mouth.

"Trismus!" Luke exclaimed—meaning lockjaw, the hallmark of tetanus; he could barely contain his excitement. But the boy's mother claimed he was fully immunized, making tetanus unlikely. His toxicology screen was negative, too, thus eliminating the first diagnosis we had to rule out in any teenager with just about any acute problem: drug ingestion. The boy probably freaked out when a friend injured himself by biting into an apple with a razor blade inside. (To my relief, somebody else got to care for that kid.) We made sure to obtain a psychiatry consult soon after the boy was admitted to the ward. This was my first encounter with that kind of Halloween cruelty. Who *did* stuff like that?

Over the next two days, I got to know my patients on the ward. First was Albert, a chubby and very depressed fifteen-year-old boy with kidney failure due to multiple urinary tract infections in infancy. He'd recently received a kidney transplant, so his face was bloated from the steroids he took as part of his regimen to avoid organ rejection. Whenever I tried to engage him in conversation, he crossed his arms and turned away, perhaps because I was the one who had to draw his blood twice a day—a very difficult procedure because of his tiny, scarred veins. I took extra care to keep his family updated on his condition and to listen empathetically to their concerns about his mental state.

Then there was Eileen, a freckle-faced fourteen-year-old

whom I admitted late one afternoon from the hematology/oncology clinic for newly diagnosed non-Hodgkin's lymphoma. The girl didn't seem to realize she had a life-threatening malignancy, but her parents looked like they'd been run over by a truck. They knew all too well how grave the situation was.

The morning after Eileen was admitted to the ward, she needed a bone marrow aspiration to see whether the cancer had invaded her marrow as well as her lymph nodes, which would affect the oncologists' choice of therapy. A large-bore needle would be inserted into the top of her hip bone, drawing out some of the thick blood-rich fluid within—a painful procedure, but not a complicated one. I'd done a couple of these with supervision during my summer externship, and I'd even done one on a school-age child during my pediatric hematology rotation. Since I was Eileen's primary doctor on the ward, I assumed I'd be doing the procedure, but the oncology attending physician thought otherwise. Yale medical students, it seemed, were not given the kinds of clinical opportunity we took for granted at Maryland.

In fairness to the oncologist, I'd only been at YNHH for a few days. He had no way of knowing how "strong" a student I might or might not be; and, because of the system he worked in, he was not accustomed to medical students taking that kind of initiative. After a tense discussion in another room, I was allowed to perform the procedure. Fortunately, it went smoothly.

On the evening of Thursday, November 4th, I arrived at my grandmother's house tired but elated. I'd been on call the night before and hadn't gotten much sleep, but I'd received my first positive feedback from the attending on the ward after presenting my admission from the night before. Things on the adolescent ward were finally coming together, and I was starting to feel like I belonged. My spirits were further buoyed by an early birthday card from my father and stepmother, signed "with all our love," just like my mother used to do.

Shortly after dinner, the phone rang. Grandma answered it and handed me the receiver with a questioning look. "It's for you, says his name's Michael."

"For me?" I wondered why my Bolton St. housemate would be calling me now. "Hi, Michael, what's up?"

"Kay, I've got some really bad news." He paused. "I don't know how to say this, so I'll just tell you...Lily took her own life today."

"What?! She *killed* herself??"

By now Isabel was on their extension. "I'm so sorry," she said. "We just got back from the emergency room..."

I screamed. Grandma took the receiver from my hand and hung up the phone. I cried and pounded my fists on the floor.

"My God!" Grandma said, gripping my shoulders. "*Who* killed herself?"

"My roommate!"

Grandma turned on her heel and left the room. She returned in a few minutes with a cup of tea. Then she patted my head awkwardly and murmured sympathetically while I sipped.

After an hour or so I was calm enough to call Isabel and Michael back. Grandma hovered in the background in case she had to hang up the phone again. It took a while for the story to emerge; they were only slightly less distraught than I was.

Lily had driven to the home of a friend whom she knew was gone for the day, closed herself in the garage, rigged up a hose from the exhaust pipe to the driver's-side window, and asphyxiated herself with carbon monoxide. She'd left a note in her friend's kitchen.

"When we saw her in the ER, I couldn't believe she was

dead," Michael said. "She didn't look blue at all."

As medical students, we knew that carbon monoxide poisoning left a person's skin pink rather than the usual bluish-white hue of death; but medical knowledge just didn't stand up to scrutiny in a situation like this.

After I hung up the phone, I noticed Grandma's quizzical frown. "Come to think of it," she said, "you had a call last night while you were at the hospital. It was a woman, but she didn't say who she was or what she wanted. It must have been your roommate. I'm sorry." She reached over and squeezed my hand.

Somehow, I managed to get through the next day on the ward. On Saturday the 6th, my birthday, I had the day off. I spent a lot of time talking on the phone with family members who'd called to wish me happy birthday. They were all shocked to hear my news and offered condolences and support. Grandma bought me flowers and a birthday cake when I drove her around town in her huge mint-green Lincoln Continental doing the Saturday errands. When I had some time to myself in the evening, I confided my thoughts to my journal, trying to make sense of Lily's suicide.

Besides being shocked at the sudden loss of a good friend, I felt guilty. As her roommate and confidante (or so I'd thought), I'd probably seen more of the despondency beneath her bright, pleasant façade than most people had; but I hadn't realized how serious the situation was. Being no stranger to despair myself, I'd assumed Lily would manage to get through that difficult time. Even at my most depressed, there'd always been a part of me that wouldn't give in, that refused to let the bad guys win. I'd thought Lily felt the same way, but I was wrong. I never expected her to kill herself.

After that awful period at the end of my first year of medical school, I knew what it was like to feel trapped, caged, boxed in so tightly by depression that suicide looked like a viable option. But I just couldn't do that to the people I loved: my father, my brother and sisters, my friends. What if one of them were to *find* me, as Lily's poor friend had found her? No, I couldn't do that to anyone. I'm not sure I could even have done it to a shitty ex-husband like Gene.

After the guilt came the anger. Lily *had* been in therapy. More psychologically astute minds than mine, or Isabel's or Michael's—and they were planning to be shrinks, after all—had missed whatever signs had been there. How could Lily have done this awful thing, this self-murder; how *could* she? How could she treat her friend with the garage that way? How could she do that to her parents, who would likely never recover?

But it's impossible to know the depth of someone else's suffering, especially if they can't or won't communicate it. Lily had been a human being in pain, greater pain than any of us had realized. For whatever reason, she thought things would never get better. She gave up. And *that* was terribly sad.

And there was the simple fact that I would miss Lily's friendship. I'd felt unusually close to her, considering how short a time we'd known each other. I'd experienced my share of loss and knew very well how it felt to be lonely, so I'd tried to convince her that things would get better, that she could use that awful time after the divorce as a stepping-stone to real growth. And I'd had genuine confidence in her ability to do that. It would take a long time for me to fully understand that I would never again see her, speak with her, hear her laugh, be the recipient of her unique warmth. And so I continued to cycle through grief, guilt, anger, and sadness.

The following week at work, I had to make several trips to

the on-call room throughout the day just to cry for a while. It was a lot like having a stomach virus and needing to use the bathroom urgently at inopportune times. After one particularly trying day on the ward, I learned from Grandma that someone from Lily's family had called for me. I dialed the number she'd written down.

"Oh, Lily really wanted to kill herself, no doubt about it," her sister Cheryl said. "There was an empty bottle of Valium on the passenger seat of the car. The car exhaust was just insurance."

That made it even worse. I could no longer assume Lily had capitulated to her demons in a moment of weakness. This was truly premeditated. I cycled back into anger.

After I got off the phone with Cheryl, I called my house-mates. Isabel and Michael had attended the memorial service that day, and Isabel vented her own anger about the suicide. John from the second-floor apartment told me that he'd talked with Lily the night before she killed herself. Though the conversation had seemed unremarkable at the time, he could see it in retrospect as a good-bye, and he was struggling with his own guilt about missing the real message. He wanted to know when I would be returning to Baltimore so he could be sure to be there, which warmed my heart.

I went to the living room to say good night to Grandma, who was watching a news show at top volume on the TV. She sat on a barstool a few inches from the screen to compensate for her macular degeneration. Tilting her head to the side, she peered at me with her peripheral vision.

"I'm starting to worry about you," she said. "You've been spending an awful lot of time talking to people on the phone since that girl killed herself. How do you ever get any studying done?"

I sighed deeply. "Grandma, I appreciate your concern. But you've got to understand. I can't just wave a magic wand and instantly get over this. Lily was a good friend, and this is an awful shock. I just have to get through it the best I can. Trust me, I know what I'm doing."

Grandma cocked an eyebrow. "Well, okay, if you say so." Then her skeptical tone softened, and she reached out to pat my arm. "I just wish there was something I could do."

I smiled. "Thanks, Grandma. It's good just to have you here." When I came home from work the next day, she kissed me—an unusual move for her—and told me she was sorry I had to go through such an awful thing. I hugged her gratefully. From that point on, she was nothing but supportive.

Five days after Lily's death, I presented Albert's case at the weekly psychiatry conference. Sam, the team's social worker, pulled me aside after the meeting to speak with me privately. I'd been a little nervous, but I thought the presentation had gone well. Had I left out something important?

Sam smiled. "Do you know what a fine job you're doing? People have noticed how good you are with Albert and his family. You've done better with him than most of the residents, even though he's so depressed and challenging."

I must have been beaming even as tears sprang to my eyes. "Thanks, Sam. That really means a lot to me."

Later that afternoon, I was finishing my notes when Dr. Greenberg, Sam's supervisor and the psychiatrist who headed the team, pulled up a chair next to me. He reiterated Sam's praise and then said gently, "I can't help but notice that you've been looking a bit sad for the last few days. Is everything all right?"

His face held no trace of judgment, only kindness and concern—qualities that were in short supply in my experience as a medical student on a hospital ward, especially at YNHH. Before I knew it, I'd told him all about Lily's suicide and my mother's death three years earlier, the traumatic events that bookended my time in medical school. It helped so much to have a sympathetic yet professional listening ear. I was grateful to Dr. Greenberg and told him so. As I lay in bed that night, I replayed our conversation, savoring his kindness and compassion. Perhaps it really was time to go back into therapy.

The last week of the YNHH rotation was a trying one. Sitting around the residents' conference room on my Saturday on call, I heard the residents—all male—praising another fourth-year student—also male—to the skies. This might not have been so bad if they hadn't acted as though I weren't there—no one had even looked up when I entered the room. I felt invisible, as if I had no place there. The old boys' network was every bit as operative among the Yale pediatric residents as among their surgery counterparts at Johns Hopkins. This didn't surprise me, but it still stung me and left me deeply discouraged.

A few days later, I cried throughout the entire 45-minute drive from New Haven to Southport. Albert's body appeared to be rejecting his transplanted kidney, which was very bad news; and I realized that, irrational as it was, I felt somehow responsible for Eileen's lymphoma. Battered by chemotherapy, her sunny disposition faded a little more with each clump of hair she lost. I'd grown attached to her, even though I knew her prognosis was abysmal. The fact that her malignancy happened to be the same one that had killed my mother only made it harder.

The next night, Lily's sister called just as I was drifting off to sleep. Cheryl was a talker. I learned more about Lily's family and childhood in that hour than I'd ever heard from Lily herself. She'd pretty much led a charmed life, at least as a child; and the family had been, according to Cheryl, a very happy one. Until this.

Cheryl's take on the suicide was, "Lily is now out of pain," an interpretation that made me cringe. That may be true, I thought; but what about their parents? Cheryl herself? The rest of us? I found it easier to accept Cheryl's contention that no one but Lily herself could have done anything to prevent it. Cheryl was dealing with the tragedy by trying to focus on remembering the good things. I had to admire her determination to stay positive. But I was saddened by much of what she told me about her sister.

"Lily used to be an artist, you know," she said. "Painting, pottery, you name it. And she loved classical music. But she seemed to lose interest in all that stuff after the divorce."

I'd had no idea. Come to think of it, I'd never seen her use the pottery wheel in our living room. After that late-night phone conversation with Cheryl, Lily's death felt utterly real and irrevocable in a way it hadn't before.

I stayed home from work the next day. Raw emotion and sleep deprivation were not a good mix, and I knew my limits. I was growing more anxious with every passing day, dreading the return to my Baltimore apartment. A lot of Lily's stuff would still be there, waiting for Cheryl to retrieve it in a few weeks. Would the place feel—haunted? Thank god she hadn't killed herself *in the apartment.*

The last three days of the rotation couldn't have ended soon enough. My predominant emotion had shifted from tearful sadness to anger. On my very last day and night on the YNHH adolescent ward, everything that could go wrong went wrong: lost X-rays, phones that were always tied up, and an operative permit I hadn't known I needed to get, occasioning a chewing-out by one of the surgeons. I did a lot of slamming of phone receivers and charts that day.

The real cause of my anger, of course, was Lily's suicide, and particularly its egregious timing from my own selfish point of view. I figured the events of the past three and a half weeks had pretty much guaranteed that I wouldn't get into the Yale residency program, Sam's and Dr. Greenberg's glowing recommendations notwithstanding. I knew it was ridiculous to think this way, but it felt as though Lily had killed herself at that particular time just to obliterate my chances of landing a spot in a top-tier residency program!

The Yale rotation culminated in one final tragedy in the wee hours of that last Saturday morning: the demise of a delightful cerebral palsy patient, a sort of ward mascot, who choked on his own vomit and died despite the best resuscitative efforts of our adolescent medicine team. The surgical intern had been especially attached to the boy and was furious about his death.

Later that morning I drove from YNHH to Southport for the last time, in a daze of exhaustion and sadness. Having a child die on my last night on call was a terrible way for things to end. Also, I knew I would never find out what happened to Albert or Eileen. A first-year resident, or perhaps another fourth-year medical student, would assume their care after I left, and that would be that.

After a few hours' sleep at Grandma's house, I threw my belongings into the Beetle, kissed Grandma good-bye, and got the hell out of there, leaving Yale-New Haven Hospital in the dust. "A Fifth of Beethoven" blared from the car radio as I crossed the George Washington Bridge, glad to put the state of Connecticut behind me for the foreseeable future. In no hurry to face my Baltimore apartment, I'd arranged to spend the weekend with my good friend Sadie in New Jersey.

She met me with open arms, and we hugged for a long time. I debriefed her about the Yale rotation and Lily's suicide over cups of tea instead of a joint, since we were in her parents' home. That evening we went to a bar, where Sadie brought me up to speed on developments in her own life over a couple of Piña Coladas. It really felt good to laugh and talk about those crazy weeks with an old friend who'd helped me through so much in the first difficult years of medical school. We lingered over brunch the next day, sipping coffee and savoring croissants. Late on Sunday afternoon, I couldn't postpone the inevitable any longer. Sharing one last long hug with Sadie, I fired up the VW for the final leg of the journey.

Appropriately enough, a cold November rain pelted the windshield as soon as I hit the city limits. Isabel and Michael were holding dinner for me, and once again it was a great comfort to be with old friends. We shared Michael's coq au vin and talked about recent events, especially Lily's death, for a long time.

Then I headed down to John's apartment for a brief visit. True to his word, he'd stayed in that evening so we could talk whenever I was ready. He was sitting upright in one of his wing chairs, facing the TV. He got up to give me a quick hug when I came in, turning the volume down as he did so.

"How are you holding up?" he said.

"So-so. How about you?"

We compared notes about the last few weeks. Then John turned the TV up again for a program about out-of-body experiences and the speculation they engendered about the possibility of life after death. We looked at each other wide-eyed when the title flashed across the screen. It seemed uncanny, that particular program airing on that particular night, just as John and I were sharing our struggles to come to terms with Lily's death.

Finally, I said goodnight to John and dragged myself upstairs to spend my first night alone in the apartment I'd shared with a now-dead roommate. The hardest part was opening the door to Lily's room. Thankfully, a lot of her stuff was packed up or gone, leaving some cardboard boxes on a bare mattress and box spring. It was a forlorn sight, but not the frightening image I'd somehow anticipated. Once I'd closed the door to her room, I found I could get to sleep if I kept a light on.

The next day was the Monday of Thanksgiving week and the start of the six-week ambulatory rotation. This was an obligatory part of the fourth year of medical school in which each of us would rotate through a doctor's office out in the community, in keeping with the University's mission of training physicians to deliver primary care throughout the state. For this short week of classes, we would undergo a general orientation before dispersing for our respective ambulatory experiences. After my surreal interlude at YNHH, I had to laugh at the irony of the term "orientation:" I couldn't have felt more *dis*oriented on my first day back at University Hospital. It took a while for the once-familiar halls to lose their aura of unreality. I confided in one of my advisors about Lily's death, which helped me regain my footing. My friend Louis, who'd lost a close friend to suicide himself, volunteered to become my new roommate, sealing our verbal agreement with a handshake and a kiss.

Before going home for Thanksgiving, I dealt with my grief, anger, and confusion by cleaning the apartment from top to bottom and then packing what I would need for my six-week ambulatory stint in Cumberland, Maryland, three hours from Baltimore. I would stay there during the week and return to the city most weekends.

Cumberland in 1976 was a good-sized but still very rural

town tucked into the scenic Allegheny Mountains of western Maryland, in a narrow part of the state's panhandle, with roughly seven miles between Pennsylvania to the north and West Virginia to the south. It was about as different from Baltimore as it could be, a refreshing change of scenery. Driving over the mountains in winter was a challenge, but watching the sun set over those mountains was an experience not to be missed. There were plenty of woods to hike in, and I took full advantage of the opportunity, which proved to be a balm for my soul.

As a medical student, I was assigned a place to live for the off-campus rotation, a nice little apartment that I shared with Melissa, a soft-spoken second-year pediatric resident from University Hospital with a musical Southern drawl and a thick braid of waist-length auburn hair. She and I, along with Rob, my friend from the Pediatric Tracking Program, were working with a four-person (all male) pediatric practice led by Dr. Bill Brigham, a graying, energetic man in his fifties. I would see a few of Dr. Brigham's patients, with and then increasingly without Melissa, and report to him with my findings and ideas about diagnosis and treatment. Intimidated by the man's hurried and brusque manner, I'd often run my cases by my resident first, just to make sure I wasn't too far off base.

Dr. Brigham delighted in teaching us the nuts and bolts of office practice and medical politics as well as primary care pediatrics. He also seemed to enjoy being a father-figure and counselor to those in need of one. Demoralized as I was after the Yale fiasco, I confided in him about my difficulties with medicine and with life in general as I slouched toward Match Day. Unfortunately, his fatherly persona was tainted with sexism. He advised me against applying to any programs that were "too academic" and to steer clear of any of the acute-care subspecialties, lest these choices interfere with having a family. *Wait a minute*, I thought. *How come nobody tells* men *who want to have a family to avoid certain areas of medicine?*

One of his suggestions was that I give myself a break by taking a year off before residency to do some research. I'd considered this option myself, even before Dr. Brigham brought it up; but I was a little afraid I might not go back. At one point, he assured me that I was one of the best female medical students he'd worked with. I tried not to roll my eyes in response. Why did this man, like so many others I'd encountered, regard women as a separate species? Separate, and *not* equal. I often felt, in these talks with Dr. Brigham, that something was being given to me with one hand and taken away with the other.

My rotation in Cumberland was interrupted by Christmas break, during which I finally acquired a new roommate. Louis had been unable to get out of his dormitory contract; but Isabel had managed to hook me up with Debra, a classmate with whom I'd been good friends since our second year. Debra was petite yet solid, with long, honey-colored hair and glasses; she had a quirky sense of humor and a wonderful capacity for outrageousness. Transporting all her worldly goods from her previous digs to my apartment required several trips and a lot of rope for her mattress, which rode precariously atop the Beetle.

I used the first few days of the Christmas break to attend my last residency interview, riding with my good friend Paul to the Children's Hospital of Philadelphia. We made it there in record time in his snazzy little burnt-orange Datsun 510, swapping stories and commiserating about medical school the whole way. I met a couple of Wellesley classmates who were interviewing, too; and I projected a super-motivated, enthusiastic persona at my interview—which felt like a complete fraud, but I was proud of myself for carrying it off so well. The following week I kept an appointment with my former therapist, Karen, to ask for a referral to a male therapist, preferably a psychiatrist. Working with a man, I reasoned, might help me with my relationship problems in a way working with a woman hadn't. This was a step I'd been contemplating for months and felt good about finally taking.

The ambulatory rotation ended in the middle of January 1977. The night I got back from Cumberland, Debra was at her parents' house, so I was alone in the apartment once more. I settled myself on a cushion on the living room floor, lit a candle, and gazed out the frost-rimmed casement window at the urban night sky as I meditatively smoked a joint. It had been one hell of a year.

I hoped my last semester of medical school would be better.

15

EVERGREEN

At the turning of the year, before the last semester of medical school began, I completed my form for Match Day. After Lily's suicide, I felt I didn't need any more upheaval, so I'd placed the University of Maryland's Department of Pediatrics at the top of the list and eliminated any programs that weren't in Baltimore. Goodbye, Yale-New Haven Hospital, Children's Hospital of Philadelphia, *et al.* It was a relief to have that decision behind me. The die was cast.

Starting in mid-January, we spent six weeks immersed in the specialties of radiology, ophthalmology, and anesthesiology. The good news about these rotations was that there was no night call; the bad news was that they consisted almost entirely of lectures. Sitting through lectures as we'd done for the first two years of medical school was difficult after the previous eighteen months of active, hands-on clinical rotations. I squirmed in my seat in the morning and tried not to fall asleep after lunch.

On January 14, 1977, I had my first session with the therapist whom Karen the social worker had recommended. Dr. Alan Epstein graduated from the University of Maryland Medical School at the end of my first year there. He was now completing his chief residency in the University's psychiatry program, which included seeing patients like me through the Student Health Service. He was also a candidate at the Baltimore-Washington

Psychoanalytic Institute, which meant he was in training to be a psychoanalyst as well as a psychiatrist—a more demanding curriculum, since it involved being a psychoanalysis patient himself.

With Dr. Epstein, I'd be embarking upon psychoanalytic psychotherapy—more challenging than the counseling I'd had with Karen earlier in medical school. This brand of therapy sounded like a sort of psychoanalysis lite: you didn't have to lie on a couch or have sessions five days a week, and the therapist would talk with you more than an analyst might. But the work still relied heavily on the process of free association, where you said whatever came into your head—much more difficult than it sounds, I would soon discover—and the therapist helped you probe the deeper meanings of your fears, obsessions, and behavior.

At the heart of this process was the transference. The psychoanalytic psychotherapist, more than other therapists, revealed as little of him- or herself as possible, which was supposed to make it easier to relate to them as you would to significant others in your life—parents, siblings, friends, and lovers. This would help you learn more about how and why those relationships hadn't been working well and, hopefully, how you could make them work better.

On that first Friday morning, I approached Dr. Epstein's office, conveniently located at University Hospital, with considerable trepidation. My previous experiences with therapists had been mixed. I'd had one session at the college student health service with an exceedingly surly middle-aged man, followed by a few sessions with a more sympathetic middle-aged woman whose favorite expression was, "Don't let the bastards get you down."

Then there'd been Karen, the social worker with whom I'd worked after my breakdown toward the end of the first year of medical school and for several months afterward. With Karen's help, I'd pulled myself together after my mother's death so I could continue with my studies. She'd been very helpful in some ways, but she'd never understood my difficulty with sexism in medical school. Plus, she was often late and canceled a few sessions at the last minute. I wondered with some anxiety what kinds of problems—if any—I would have with Dr. Epstein.

I arrived several minutes early and fidgeted in the small waiting room, drumming my fingers on the arm of the worn but comfortable upholstered chair. When Dr. Epstein stuck his head out the door to tell me it would be a few more minutes, I was surprised at his unassuming appearance. When I entered the office and shook hands with him, I realized that my therapist was an inch or two shorter than me, and he even stammered a little. It was comforting to think that he might be nervous, too. I showed my own anxiety by grinning like a fool for at least the first half of the session. And I'd been flummoxed at having to decide which of the two patient's chairs to sit in—the one closer to him or the one farther away. (I chose the closer one, wondering how he would interpret my selection.)

Some of his biographical questions felt awkward, particularly his queries about my living situation. He and my roommate Debra, a soon-to-be psychiatry resident herself, knew each other from her psychiatry elective. Somehow it felt like a breach of confidentiality to mention my roommate when talking with my shrink. I observed myself with a kind of amused disbelief through all this. Having been a junior therapist-in-training during my third-year psychiatry rotation, it felt strange to be answering these kinds of questions instead of asking them. In reply to the stock question, "What is it that brings you here today?" I said, "I hope that being in therapy with a man will help me with my problems in relationships with men."

"And how do you think having a male therapist will help?" Dr. Epstein asked.

Once again, I was at a loss. After a good half-hour of struggling with my awkwardness and embarrassment, we finally came to an understanding of why I'd shown up in his office in the first place. First, since this was therapy and not a dating situation, I wouldn't be vulnerable to rejection and abandonment the way I'd been in romantic relationships. Second, a therapist would not undermine my self-esteem as many of my boyfriends had done; and he would not be perfectionistic and demanding, like so many of my elders in medical school. Finally, I was hoping that this therapy would bring my anger—at rejecting lovers, male-chauvinist superiors on medical wards, and the dehumanizing process of medical training itself—down to a manageable level, much as my therapy with his predecessor had made my feelings of worthlessness and depression more workable.

Dr. Epstein nodded. "I can tell you've thought a lot about this," he said. "I think we can work well together." I was inordinately pleased.

Soon I was telling this stranger about my childhood, the psychoanalyst's stock-in-trade, especially my problems with my parents—the loving but demanding mother who'd lived vicariously through me until her life was cut short; the father whose approval seemed so difficult to attain, much like the attending physicians I encountered on the wards. Though I'd taken on this therapy with a sense of enthusiasm, even excitement, at first—finally, I might be able to get somewhere with my relationship problems!—it wasn't long before it started to feel like the Spanish Inquisition. I saw that it would be scary and difficult to reveal the depths of my fear, anger, and pain to this stranger. I'd had similar feelings with Karen at first, but they seemed to be stronger with

Dr. Epstein. Was it because he was a man?

Between my fear about revealing so much of myself so soon, and my hostile—though obviously unfounded—expectation that my therapist would pick apart my feelings and ideas like an attending physician picking apart my diagnosis of a patient, I'd established a rip-roaring transference in our very first session.

Within a week, I had developed a terrible crush on Dr. Epstein, or Alan, as I now thought of him, aka "my hero." There was something about revealing my most intimate thoughts and fears to this stranger, excruciating as the process often was, that made me feel a kind of desire for him. It was a weird paradox. This sort of self-revelation is what one does with a lover; but a therapist, by definition, can never be a lover, will in fact always be a stranger, no matter what. I had chosen this kind of therapy and this particular therapist with a complete understanding that there could never be any mutual exchange as there would hopefully be with a boyfriend. But knowing the value of this process, how it could help me in future situations where mutual love could develop, didn't diminish my painful longing for Dr. Epstein himself.

All of this came to a head about three weeks after the start of therapy. It was a Saturday morning, the day after that week's therapy session. Debra and I were in the grocery store, doing our weekly shopping. I was also looking forward, with mixed feelings, to a date that night with my old lover Preston, who'd called me unexpectedly earlier in the week. As I pushed our basket toward the front of the store, I saw a familiar face in the checkout line.

"Omigod, Deb, it's *him!*" I gasped.

"Who?"

"Epstein!" I hissed. "There! In aisle 4!"

"Yeah, so? Epstein is buying groceries, just like we are." The corner of Deb's mouth twitched a little as she tried to suppress a smile. Obviously, I wasn't conveying the urgency and significance of the situation.

"Deb, he—he eats!" I spluttered. I didn't know how else to communicate the miracle of seeing my hero in such mundane circumstances—in the Giant on a Saturday morning, of all places!

Deb finally had to laugh. "Well, yeah, he's a human being, not a robot. What did you expect?"

She toned it down when she saw the look of longing on my face. Having committed herself to a career in psychiatry before she even started medical school, Deb had more experience with therapy and the vicissitudes of the transference than I had. As I was driving us back to the apartment, she said, "Look. Having a therapeutic relationship with a shrink is a very intimate thing, and you *have* to fall in love with the person to justify revealing all that stuff. It's really hard, especially in the beginning, but it'll pay off in the end." I felt a little better.

That evening's date with Preston turned out to be an unmitigated disaster instead of the respite and relief I'd hoped for. Our lovemaking was very pleasurable at first, and the familiarity of his touch was a homecoming. But gradually I became aware that something about him had changed. It felt like his expertise had become purely technical. I'd been broken open in therapy, sharing my most private thoughts with my therapist in a way I hadn't shared them with anyone since—ironically—the early days of my affair with Preston himself, now more than three years ago. While I'd softened and opened, he'd grown some kind of shell that I couldn't penetrate. To my sorrow, I realized that no amount of good sex could close the chasm that now yawned between us.

This, of course, gave me plenty to talk about in the following Friday's session, though it was painfully difficult to get started. I looked at my hands, scraped imaginary dirt from under my nails, even talked about the weather at first, vainly hoping that my therapist would come to my rescue and start pulling things out of me, and then feeling angry when he didn't. I was discovering that the process of therapy was often a kind of oscillation between talking too little when there's something to say and talking too much when there's little to say.

Eventually I began to tell him about the disastrous date with my ex-lover, how lovemaking hadn't been able to bridge the gap between us. Once I'd gotten into that, I couldn't sidestep the incident in the Giant. As I became more fully engaged in the session, I realized there was a lot of fear behind my childish anger with Dr. Epstein—fear of failure in relationships, fear of loneliness, and fear of failing to marry and have children, which, rightly or wrongly, I equated with fear of being a failure as a woman. Citing himself as an example, Dr. Epstein pointed out the way in which I alternated between deifying the objects of my affection and devaluing them. I devalued them because it was humiliating to feel so vulnerable to rejection, to need anyone that much.

That session ended with a moment that forever endeared him to me: having arrived two minutes late, Dr. Epstein told his secretary, "Two more minutes" when she called to tell him time was up. This scrupulous fairness seemed like a small thing, but it showed me I could trust him and rely on him. It was a great comfort to me, especially after my previous therapist's casual attitude about cutting appointments short. Moved as I was by this, I was also emotionally exhausted. I could hardly concentrate on ophthalmology lectures that afternoon.

That night, I went to Liberated Singles, a gathering held in a Unitarian church basement a few blocks from my apartment. It was not the kind of pickup joint I was used to; there were no barstools or jukeboxes. Wine and light snacks were served, and recorded classical music played softly in the background. Every Friday night, a few dozen well-dressed people in their twenties and thirties assembled there to seek companionship in a more upscale environment than their local watering-hole. I had accompanied my downstairs neighbor John there on one of his forays several weeks earlier. On this particular Friday, I met two interesting guys, one of whom took me to Fells Point for a drink. Perry wrote down my phone number and said he would call me, and we went our separate ways before ten o'clock. I congratulated myself on my ability to follow conventional dating protocol for once. Therapy was having a salutary effect already.

The end of February brought with it a clinical rotation, a month on an internal medicine ward at Mercy Hospital, several blocks north and east of University. I was pleasantly surprised at how much more knowledgeable, skillful, and confident I felt compared with previous rotations. Perhaps those difficult weeks at Yale-New Haven Hospital had paid off, after all. Taking care of patients at Mercy was less arduous than at University Hospital, the VA Spa, or Baltimore City. The nurses usually started the IVs, and technicians drew the patients' blood for labs. There was more time to read up on my patients' conditions and to actually think about the diagnostic possibilities. My first week at Mercy felt like a Goldilocks rotation—the workload was neither too much nor too little, but just right.

I managed to get back to University Hospital every Friday morning for therapy, except once when there was an emergency at Mercy. The first time I went to therapy in my "doctor suit"—white jacket, stethoscope, etc.—I felt as though I'd been replaced by an alien: who *was* this high-functioning adult who projected professionalism, competence, and authority? I started the session by talking about my experiences taking care of patients. It felt weird, but in a good way. Epstein was very supportive of my doctor persona, saying things like, "Being an authoritative adult is very appropriate for a doctor."

Another topic that elicited more of his bland but pleasant therapy-speak—"I hear that you're feeling better about yourself"—was my growing closeness with Perry, the guy I'd met a few weeks earlier. So far, we'd had a couple of chaste dates and spent a lot of time talking on the phone.

Perry arrived at my place for our third date a bit early, to take me to a play. I was touched by this show of eagerness on his part. As I put the finishing touches on my makeup, I knew I was ready to take the relationship to the next level, and he seemed to be ready as well.

The play, an early production of the innovative Baltimore Theater Project, struck a chord in both of us. Perry seemed to share the sense of life's beauty and brevity that the play evoked within me. We strolled back to my place with our arms around each other's waists, the first time we'd done more than hold hands. When I invited him in, he took my face in his hands and kissed me tenderly. He ended up spending the night. He was passionate, and his need to be held, touched, and cared for seemed to match my own. We felt right together. It was wonderful.

Perry was in his early thirties. He was about an inch shorter than me. His light-brown hair was on the long side, his brown eyes snapped with lively intelligence, and he had a full, sensuous mouth that I enjoyed kissing. He'd been born full-term but small for gestational age, he told me, and had spent his first few weeks in the hospital—not just because he was underweight, but also because of a collapsed lung at birth, something of which he spoke proudly, as though it were a badge of honor. He'd also had polio as a child which, while it didn't leave him with any apparent disability, had affected the growth of his legs, accounting for his short stature. Perry was finishing up a master's degree in political science and supporting himself by tutoring teenagers at a rehabilitation hospital for people with disabilities. He was divorced, with no children. He lived in East Baltimore in the row house near Patterson Park that he'd shared with his wife.

One morning I awoke before the sun was up, facing Perry in his bed. He smiled at me and then rolled onto his back, staring at the ceiling with an arm across his forehead. He chuckled a little and said, "I just had a really weird dream. I was at work with a bunch of my students in their wheelchairs, and I was yelling because my back hurt. I felt really stupid, because *they* were the ones in the wheelchairs, and here *I* was, complaining about my back. What the hell?"

"Maybe the pain wasn't actually in your back." I hadn't been seeing a shrink for the last two months for nothing.

"You think?" He turned toward me with a frown. "So my back pain was psychosomatic?" He sounded skeptical.

"Could be. It's not that unusual, especially with back pain."

"Yeah, maybe so. During the last year of my marriage, we fought a lot, and that was hell on my back."

When I got to Mercy Hospital for work that morning, I was overwhelmed by sadness without knowing why. Then I realized that, as often as we laughed together, Perry's laughter was often tinged with sorrow, and I was picking up on that feeling myself. Plus, I was having second thoughts about falling in love again.

Being so closely attuned to someone else's emotions was fraught with pain and risk, therapy notwithstanding.

Naturally I discussed all this with Dr. Epstein during that week's session.

"It sounds like you're feeling about Perry the way you said you felt about me a while ago," he said. "Like I've been replaced." A small smile played at the corners of his mouth. It was true. I now regarded Dr. Epstein as a counselor and mentor rather than an unattainable love-object. It was a pleasant surprise to see that my romantic allegiance had shifted completely to someone with whom I could actually have a relationship.

• • •

Monday, March 14: Match Day, the much-anticipated culmination of medical school. Ever since the formation of the National Residency Matching Program in 1952, Match Day has been an annual rite of passage for medical students. It's the day all fourth-year students in the United States learn simultaneously where they will continue their training for the next few years. While the advent of the internet has brought about some changes, the basic procedure remains the same. During their last year of medical school, students register for the Match in the fall. Once they've visited and interviewed at programs they're interested in, they submit a rank-ordered list of the programs they've chosen. Then the programs work through their own rank-ordered lists of applicants and matches are made.

On that milestone Monday in March, all 166 of us, culled from our various rotations, gathered in the lecture room in Howard Hall, the very place we'd been held captive for the first two years of medical school. If we were on call that night, as I was, we were given the afternoon off for the big event. Most of the married students were accompanied by their spouses.

Many folks were dressed up. The room was abuzz with nervous excitement as we took our seats—raucous laughter, exchanges of friendly insults, and a lot of shifting in chairs.

The Dean of Student Affairs called us up to the podium one at a time, announced where we'd matched, and handed each of us a small plastic placard with our name followed by the letters "M.D.". This last touch was an unexpected foretaste of the thrill of being able to write those two letters after my name. When my turn came, I held my breath as I made my way to the podium. "The University of Maryland in Pediatrics," the dean intoned, indicating that I'd matched with my first choice. I let my breath out in a whoosh and grinned.

There's a two-page spread in the yearbook dedicated to this momentous day. Several of the photos show people holding plastic cups in their hands. (I abstained from the celebratory libations, since I'd be on call that night.) While my classmates matched with programs from one end of the country to the other, about a quarter of our class would be doing residencies at the University of Maryland in various specialties. I was happy to learn that some of my friends from the Pediatric Tracking Program would join me as co-residents.

My yearbook's spread of Match Day photos had its poignant aspects. The popular guy in the plaid shirt halfway unbuttoned to reveal his chest hair, drink in hand and sweater slung over his right shoulder, would be the first member of our class to die just a few years later—the first of several to succumb to AIDS. The couple sitting in the row in front of me, gazing into each other's eyes, would be divorced before she finished her residency. The camera took pictures of us from several angles, thus managing to capture most of the class. While many of the photos show smiles, backslapping, and plastic cups raised in salute, there are a few somber faces in the group, a reminder that not everyone was happy with the results of the Match.

While I was basking in the glow of Match Day that month, I was also having a wonderful time with Perry. The trees were starting to unfurl their leaves, displaying that beautiful shade of nascent green that reminded me of a forest after rain. A love-song called "Evergreen" got a lot of air play that spring and seemed to fit our situation. We had long, lively talks about politics—Perry was an ardent socialist—culture, families, and everything else under the sun.

We even talked about our feelings. Perry was not as reluctant to share these as most of the men I'd been involved with. To my delight, he called me his girlfriend, which of course gave me license to call him my boyfriend. When he said he loved me I was thrilled, even though it first happened while we were having sex. We spoke a lot in bed, usually in whispers, and we laughed a lot too. We developed a wonderful rhythm, both in lovemaking and in day-to-day life—a give-and-take that I'd rarely experienced.

His aura of sadness from the early days of our relationship evaporated, along with my ambivalence about falling in love again. Perry seemed to be every bit as in love with me as I was with him. There wasn't the kind of power imbalance I'd experienced with other men; rather, it was a feeling of mutuality and reciprocity, of equal standing in the relationship. This sense of equality was new to me, and it was delightful. It made me proud of the growth I'd attained through my work in therapy. My emotional ups and downs became less intense. It was great to have less drama in my life.

By the end of March, Perry and I were seeing each other two or three times a week. The last week of March was my spring vacation. I'd arranged, months earlier, to spend it in Minneapolis with my youngest sister, who'd transferred from MICA to the Minneapolis College of Art and Design the previous August. Perry stayed with me the night before my Monday departure. We would be apart for a whole week. Much as I looked forward to visiting Mary Alyce, it was hard to leave Perry. As I bustled around the apartment fixing breakfast that morning, he put his coat on, then gave me a quick hug.

"Leaving already?" I asked.

"I figured I'd stop at my place on the way to work."

"I thought you were staying for breakfast, honey. I made pancakes." Tears sprang to my eyes, surprising me as much as they must have surprised him. When I couldn't suppress a sniffle, he took me in his arms again.

"Oh, babe, I'm sorry. Of course, I'll stay." He kissed my cheek and stroked my hair. A few minutes later, as I was turning the pancakes, I noticed that he was facing away from me and dabbing his eyes with a handkerchief.

Being happily involved in a love-relationship affected my therapy with Dr. Epstein in interesting ways. Now that I had a bona fide boyfriend to love, I could see my therapist as an actual human being rather than a godlike figure, or even a parental one. I no longer expected Epstein to pull my problems out of me like a dentist extracting teeth, and I was better able to take the initiative in expressing my thoughts and feelings as they arose. I was finally starting to take responsibility for my own healing instead of passively relying on my therapist to fix me. We had a lot more eye contact now, and we were even able to laugh together occasionally, which I especially enjoyed.

One day I said, "Now that things are going so well with Perry, I'm actually wondering if I still need to be in therapy."

His eyebrows shot up, but he didn't say anything.

"Don't worry," I added hastily. "I *know* it's a bad idea to terminate therapy just because I'm in love." His face relaxed; I thought I saw a twinkle in his eye. "And besides, I'm really going to miss our sessions after graduation."

"Just because you're graduating doesn't mean we have to terminate therapy," he said. "Why don't you consider staying on when you start residency?"

"You mean I can do that?" I was greatly relieved to hear this; but there was still a vestige of pride or vanity in me that kept me from agreeing on the spot. I left the topic open for future discussion, though I'd pretty much made up my mind to stay. It seemed like a good idea not to have too many endings at once.

Early in April, Perry and I spent a weekend camping together in western Maryland. A number of things came to light that weekend. As we huddled in front of a campfire the night we arrived, Perry said something about his first wife.

"Your *first* wife?" My eyes widened. "How many times have you been married, anyway?"

"Two," he said sheepishly. "And, um, I'm not divorced yet from my second wife, just separated."

I didn't say anything, but my mind raced as I pondered this new information. It was one thing for him to have had one failed marriage, but *two*? He might be a great friend and lover, but I had to seriously question his suitability as a marriage prospect.

Embarking on a cooperative endeavor like camping led to other revelations as well—like how disorganized Perry could be; we had to buy a flashlight because he'd forgotten his at home. I also discovered that he was a man of fervent but brief enthusiasms and bursts of energy, rather than a person of sustained and steady application. And he could be quite inflexible in his opinions, even downright authoritarian, though he was quick to apologize if he offended me by coming on too strong. When he started trying to educate me about socialism by quizzing me, I explained that this Socratic approach reminded me too much of medical school, so he backed off.

Shortly after the camping trip, Perry told me he'd been thinking for some time about moving to New York City to live in a socialist commune. In fact, he planned to visit this commune the following weekend when he went to NYC for a conference.

I was livid at this news. Had the last six weeks been a hallucination? How could he possibly talk about moving away *now*, when we were having such a good time together and—I'd thought, at least—were so much in love? Reading the same sentence in my *Harrison's Internal Medicine* text over and over in the medical-school library one day, I seethed about Perry's revelation. I had to leave the book in the carrel and run up and down the concrete fire-stairs several times to keep from screaming myself hoarse. By the time we got together that night, I was able to talk rationally about the situation, though I made no attempt to hide my displeasure.

"Jeez! You couldn't have told me about this earlier? What the hell, Perry?"

He ducked his head slightly, then shrugged. "Would that have made any difference?"

I just glared at him.

Something had shifted, a subtle balance disturbed. It wasn't just Perry's talk about moving to New York; it was also the fact that he'd been married twice. I loved him as much as ever. But the blinders were off, the honeymoon was over. I now loved him as an actual human being—limited, flawed, and fallible, as well as unique and lovable. He was not some ideal partner, not my missing half. He was just a man.

Though the serpent had entered the garden, we continued to talk, laugh, make love, and enjoy going places together. The third weekend in May, we took Debra camping with us at Assateague, the barrier island off the eastern shores of Maryland and Virginia where the wild ponies roam. Having my roommate along prevented us from having sex, which probably contributed to the meltdown I had our last morning on the island. I sat miserably alone in the tent while the other two chased each other around on the beach. Finally, Perry lifted the tent flap and came inside. I was angry with him for having so much fun when I was feeling so out of sorts. I crossed my arms and frowned.

"What's the matter?" he asked.

Suddenly the anger was swept away by the sadness it had been masking all along. Out of the blue, I felt my mother's loss like a blow to the stomach: she wouldn't be there to see me graduate from medical school. "I want my mother!" I wailed.

"Oh, honey." He took me in his arms and held me tight. Snuffling loudly, I said, "I'm really going to miss her when I go up there to get that damn diploma. It's just not fair that she doesn't get to see that!"

He rocked me until my tears subsided and sniffled a bit himself. Then he pulled away and gave me a funny look. "Jesus, you should see the snot on your face!" He started making pig-like snorting noises, and we both cracked up. I forgot about missing my mother for a while.

Though our good times continued, talk of New York City cropped up with increasing frequency. Perry seemed to be waffling about the move as he got closer to finishing his master's degree. Should he pursue the teaching opportunity at Morgan State, right here in Baltimore City, or the comparable position at City College of New York? (Did he really have to ask?)

I tried not to interfere in his decision-making process, though it wasn't easy to keep my mouth shut. My position was abundantly clear. But I truly did want him to be happy, even if that meant moving to NYC to live in that commune he was obsessed with. I didn't want to hold him back, much as I wanted the relationship to continue as it had. I pointed out to him that I could transfer to a pediatric training program in New York after my first year of residency. I wasn't crazy about the idea of leaving the University of Maryland, but I was willing to do whatever it took for us to stay together. Dr. Epstein had reminded me that relationships had been known to survive a year apart.

It was hard to be on tenterhooks with Perry just when my own life would be changing so much, moving into the next phase of medical training. Thanks to therapy, I found myself able to sit tight and not force the issue.

16

ATTAINMENT

The final card of the Major Arcana of the tarot is called "The World" by some, "The Universe" by others. It depicts a female figure dancing within an oval-shaped braid of laurel leaves, a victory wreath. She's in perpetual motion; her garment billows around her and her long hair waves to one side. Yet she appears exquisitely poised, in perfect balance, much like "The Hanging Man"—one foot on the wreath, the other leg behind her, arms extended, a slender wand in each hand. Many of the interpretations of this image fit well with the conclusion of medical school: Realization of a much-desired goal. Recognition and rewards for hard labor. Successful endeavor. The end of a long journey. Finishing one phase and starting another. A change in status. Mastery, completion. Attainment.

But as the last week of medical school finally arrived, like an overdue train after a lengthy track repair, I found myself fighting sadness and despondency—the same feelings I'd had after finishing that final physiology paper at the end of my first year. By now I recognized these feelings as a harbinger of the loss of meaning once a goal is accomplished, a sort of post-partum phenomenon, and I knew I wouldn't feel this way forever.

The cause of some of my sadness was the fact that several of my friends of both sexes were receiving prizes or awards for various sorts of excellence in medical school—and I was not. For the first time in my life, I would graduate without any kind of special recognition. It was a far cry from the last weeks of college—hearing my mother's delight when I phoned her in the middle of the afternoon to tell her I'd made Phi Beta Kappa; attending the Sigma Xi reception with several of my pre-med friends; seeing my name in the commencement program under "cum laude" with asterisks for the two honor societies.

Now there would be no awards beyond that hard-won degree, Doctor of Medicine; and there was no Mom either. Ever since my meltdown with Perry at Assateague, I felt her loss more acutely as graduation approached than I had since that awful spring after she died. Also, I could now see the toll my mother's death had taken on my own drive and motivation. If she'd lived, would I have been able to do as well in medical school as I'd done in college?

What I did realize, even then, was that what I *had* achieved was remarkable. Despite the vicissitudes of medical school itself, and in spite (perhaps because) of all that had happened to me during that time—from my mother's death to Lily's suicide—I'd actually come through medical school stronger and more together than I'd been when I started. Even as I worked hard to attain my degree, I was also working hard to become my own person, though it sometimes felt like the two were in conflict.

I was sad that my particular kind of achievement was not recognized by any sort of award or honor society, but I still had a sense of pride about what I'd accomplished, and I knew that the people I cared about most—my family, Perry, Debra, and other friends—recognized my accomplishment as well. Perry said, "Not getting any awards at graduation might be the best thing that ever happened to you. Maybe now you'll finally get off the treadmill of achieving for other people and start doing it for yourself." I hadn't thought of it that way before.

The official last day of school was May 27th, the Friday of Memorial Day weekend. Perry and I spent the holiday weekend at his house in East Baltimore. Though he'd helped me feel better about the lack of awards, there was still some sadness about the ending of medical school and the losses I'd experienced—deaths, lost friendships and love-relationships, and my various failures in and out of school.

We spent much of the weekend cleaning out Perry's basement and packing up his stuff—yet another foretaste of an ending. His house would go on the market in a few weeks, and he'd rent an apartment while he finished his course work for his master's degree before moving to New York. As with our camping trips, spending the weekend together in a domestic setting proved to be good practice for living together. We got on each other's nerves more than we ever had in the course of a single night, or even a weekend camping trip; but we managed to displace most of our hostility by means of good-natured teasing and physical rough-housing. Perry was proficient at using humor to defuse anger, a valuable skill that I picked up quickly myself. (Being married twice must have taught him something after all.)

On Sunday morning I picked a fight with him when he didn't want to go back to bed with me. I felt rejected and hurt, and I didn't hesitate to let him know it. Perry's work ethic kept him from lying around in bed, even on the weekend; he had to be up and doing—reading, studying. He made it up to me early in the evening, coming up behind me at the kitchen sink to slide his hands under my shirt and nuzzle my neck. Afterward, his books called to him again as I lay basking in the warmth of his bed, so I banished myself to the living room to read a book while he put in a few more hours of study in his bedroom. Later that night, we walked arm in arm around Patterson Park. The air was cool and fresh, our love was strong and steady, and I felt a warm, secure fulfillment deep inside which persisted throughout the rest of the night, one of the last we spent in that house.

• • •

Wednesday, June 1, was the senior banquet—an evening of dining, dancing, drinking, and general celebration. There's another two-page spread in the yearbook for this event. Most of the women wore long dresses reminiscent of high-school prom gowns. The men's attire ranged from plaid sports jackets to three-piece suits with the wide ties of the '70s. One guy even wore a white suit with flared pants, like John Travolta in *Saturday Night Fever*. I don't appear in any of these pictures, but I remember the long dress I wore, with its dark floral print, ruffled hem, and smocked bodice—a quintessential '70s garment. (I also remember the hairpins digging into my scalp, in the attempt to wear my long hair piled up on my head.) Perry's eyes lit up when he saw me all dressed up.

Glasses were raised; faculty members danced as enthusiastically as members of the class. This was one of the few times in my medical-school career that I came to a major function with a date. While Perry and I shared most of the slow dances, he turned me loose to dance with classmates, too—including Louis, my dear friend who'd almost been a roommate, and Paul, my friend since the Stricker St. days, who'd accompanied me to Philadelphia for our residency interviews.

And then there was Blake. I hadn't seen him since our second year, but I knew he was headed to the Midwest for his internal medicine residency, so I was unlikely to see him again. When I caught sight of him dancing with one of his nursing-school friends, I got that old feeling in my chest, like birds' wings against my rib cage. When the music stopped, I asked him for the next dance. He obliged, and I lost track of Perry for a while.

After catching each other up and talking about our destinations for residency, I said, "You know, I'm with a guy I really like now. But I have to tell you, it always does something to me when I see you. I guess that's good for your ego if nothing else, right?" I flashed him a smile.

"Yes, it sure is!" He laughed.

"By the way, I'm sorry I gave you such a hard time second year," I said.

"Oh, jeez, if anybody needs to apologize, it's me. I know that was a horrible time in your life."

Then he said, "Kay, I'm really glad I had a chance to know you."

"Me, too." The color rose in my cheeks. I felt a rush of affection for him.

As the party wound down, Perry came back and took my hand. I introduced him to Blake. Perry kept my hand in his while the three of us chatted. As the last song came to a close, I gave my other hand to Blake, and we stood that way for a moment.

This time, I was the one who let go.

• • •

Friday, June 3, 1977, was exquisite, one of those long, luminous days before the heat and humidity take over—no longer spring, but not quite summer, either. The previous day, I'd cleaned the apartment, picked my sisters up at the airport, and organized everything for the family party we would have at our place after the graduation ceremony. Debra was at home with her parents in Silver Spring so my sisters could stay with Perry and me on Bolton St.

Before going downtown for graduation, I spent some time

by myself, lying on the bed and looking out the casement window. Like a soldier preparing for battle, the gravity of the situation had just dawned on me. After today, I would have the letters "M.D." after my name for the rest of my life, meaning that I would be responsible for others' lives in a way that few people were. It felt like what I'd learned in Catholic school about the sacraments, that they left an indelible mark on your soul.

Once my heartbeat slowed and my stomach stopped cramping, I picked up the black academic gown in its dry-cleaner's plastic and took off for the nearest bus stop. I was so preoccupied as I walked down the hill that I didn't hear Perry calling my name to wish me luck.

The festivities began with the 170th Pre-Commencement Convocation in the Francis Scott Key ballroom at the Baltimore Hilton Hotel (now the Radisson Hotel Baltimore Downtown), a block northeast of the place where we'd receive our diplomas. After we processed into the ballroom, there was a prayer and a welcome by the Dean, followed by the presentation of honors and awards. To my pleasant surprise, I didn't feel any envy or rancor when my friends' names were called, only joyful excitement on their behalf. While we already wore black mortarboards and gowns trimmed in green velvet to symbolize the discipline of medicine, each of us would be hooded prior to reciting the Hippocratic oath: one of the deans would place a long piece of green velvet fabric over our heads and fit it snugly against our throats with the remainder trailing down our backs, a remnant of the academic hoods of earlier centuries. Deb offered her own psychodynamic interpretation of that heavy fabric right up against our throats. Leaning forward from the row behind me, she whispered, "It's the fingers of medicine tightening around our necks."

Then we stood to recite the Hippocratic Oath.

"I do solemnly swear by that which I hold most sacred, that I will be loyal to the profession of medicine…that I will lead my life and practice my art in uprightness and honor…that I will exercise my art solely for the cure of my patients…"

The ancient words sent shivers down my spine as we took our places in a line of tradition that reached back for millennia.

After the convocation, we headed across the street to the Baltimore Civic Center. This event space, more recently known as the Royal Farms Arena, is a 14,000-seat facility with a distinctive roofline made up of triangular structures which give it the appearance of a giant piece of white corrugated cardboard. The scene outside the arena on that June day was electric—more festive than the banquet, even without the alcohol and dancing. We milled around in our caps, gowns, and hoods for what seemed like hours. There was much kissing and shaking of hands. I kissed both the deans who'd helped me through that previous difficult autumn and exchanged many hugs with my closest friends. To my surprise, my old friend Eric came up and kissed me. And the handshakes… We were lined up alphabetically, and I lost track of how many times I shook hands with the guys directly in front of and behind me.

Finally, we were shushed and told to queue up, faces front. The time had come to enter the auditorium with all due pomp and circumstance. We filed past row upon row of folding chairs as we made our way to the front of the arena, refraining from waving to families and friends in the bleachers. But once we'd taken our seats, any sense of ceremony was abandoned, at least for a while. A couple of guys in my row resumed the card game they'd been playing while we waited outside. Debra kept up a lively repartee with one of her fellow psychiatry residents-to-be, a guy who'd been dubbed "The Phantom" during the first year because of his spotty attendance at lectures.

After an interminable series of speeches, it was finally time to get our diplomas.

When my big moment arrived, I firmly shook hands with the Chancellor, took my diploma from him with the correct hand, and responded, "Thank you!" in a strong, enthusiastic voice when he congratulated me. As I walked down the steps with that precious piece of paper, I raised my diploma-bearing fist in a militant power salute of triumph. God, it felt good!

Once all the degrees had been conferred for all the schools that made up the University of Maryland at Baltimore, it was time to greet the family. I'd had a lot of anxiety about whether my father, brother, and sister-in-law would be able to find Perry and my sisters in the crowd.

I scanned the bleachers for my people. A balding man in a light blue suit waved to me—was that old guy really Dad? Yes, it was; and there was Perry next to him, grinning from ear to ear. Unlike my boyfriend, my family members were quite reserved in their greetings. I couldn't help but think that my mother would have been all over me with hugs and kisses, and I had a piercing moment of missing her.

But that was soon forgotten in the festivities back at the apartment. Deb and her parents were there when we arrived. There were flowers from my stepsiblings, a luscious chocolate cake from my stepmother, and six long-stemmed red roses from Perry. My dad walked into the kitchen just as I was kissing my boyfriend, roses in hand; he laughed about "catching us in the act." (To my relief, he and Perry hit it off despite their divergent political views.) After snacks, drinks, and conversation, Dad took us all to dinner. When the party broke up, I thanked everyone for coming, Dad thanked me for graduating, and we all laughed. Perry and I hung out with Deb for a while back at the apartment. Then my boyfriend and I finished that never-to-be-forgotten day with our own private celebration.

• • •

Perry and I had one last weekend of camping in western Maryland before I started residency. We joked and teased each other on the three-hour drive, stopping for supplies along the way. After pitching the tent, we drank some beer and took a nap to recover from the drive. Then it was time for dinner—canned chili warmed on a Coleman stove—and a fire to take the evening chill off, for which Perry chopped an impressive quantity of wood. He rested his head in my lap as we gazed into the flames. Later that night, we laughed when the air mattress started to leak while we were making love.

There was something wonderful about drifting off to sleep accompanied by a full insect chorus on the other side of the tent canvas. And what could be better than waking up to leaf-filtered morning sunlight flooding the front door? After a morning hike to the falls, we returned to the tent to make love again, accompanied by the sounds of a basketball game a few hundred feet away. As we relaxed before the fire that night I said, "Man, this is the life! I wish it never had to end."

"I've got an idea," Perry said. "Whenever you have Saturday and Sunday off, I'll come up here Friday night to set up camp and you can join me for the weekend when you're done signing out."

I'd done enough night call by this time to know that was probably unrealistic; but I was touched that he'd thought of it.

When the subject of New York came up, as I knew it would, I reminded him once more that I could transfer to a residency program in New York City after my first year so we could be together. Perry seemed open to the idea.

But when I started my first rotation as a pediatric resident, he went AWOL. I knew he was finishing his own course of study at the end of June and getting ready to move to New York; but I never expected him to just stop calling. There were no calls when I was home at night, and Debra didn't report any when I was on call. I had no idea what had happened. And for the next several weeks, I would be too busy and too exhausted to find out.

17

BAPTISM BY FIRE

On the day of my orientation as a first-year pediatric resident, the roiling of my gut rivaled what I'd experienced three weeks earlier at graduation. We PL-1's—Pediatric Level 1 residents, aka interns, aka newbies—assembled on Thursday morning, June 23, 1977. The venue was the Core Conference room, where we would meet five days a week at lunchtime throughout residency. The room was small, with a podium, a blackboard, and steel-framed plastic chairs.

There were twelve of us, evenly divided between folks who'd taken their medical degree at University of Maryland and those who'd come from other schools. We mingled briefly before the start of the official program, introducing ourselves and exchanging pleasantries.

After a few minutes, one of the chief residents called us to order. Marcia was a tall woman in a skirt and heels who wore her hair in a bun. She explained in general terms what would be expected of us. Then her co-chief resident, Larry, a burly guy with lank brown hair and wire-rim glasses, continued with some housekeeping details. He started with the news that we might not have uniforms or receive paychecks for three or four weeks. Those of us who'd worked on the wards at University as students exchanged knowing smiles. We weren't surprised.

"You get two weeks of vacation, guys," Larry continued.

"That's two *non-consecutive* weeks, because somebody's got to pick up your slack when you're gone. And we'll try to honor your vacation requests, but" he added with a smirk, "this will most likely be impossible." Stuart, one of my medical-school buddies, nudged me and whispered, "Kind of a hard-ass, isn't he?"

The year I started residency was an intermediate stage in the evolution of postgraduate medical training. Most training programs no longer required their residents—also known as house officers—to live in apartments or even barracks on the hospital grounds, as they had earlier in the 20th century; and most specialties, except surgery, no longer required house officers to be on call every other night. But the reforms that limited the consecutive hours residents could work and the number of hours they could work per week were still more than a decade away. As pediatric house officers at the end of the 1970s, we would take call every third night for our entire PL-1 (internship) year, and for much of our PL-2 and PL-3 years. Being on call every third night, which included 24-hour shifts on weekend days, meant working somewhere between 80 and 100 hours a week. Fortunately, I hadn't done the math prior to that first day of residency.

As Larry droned on, we squirmed in our seats, waiting for the big reveal: our ward assignments for the year. Would our first rotation be on the Adolescent Ward on the 8th floor? 5B, the ward for school-age kids? 5E, the infant and toddler ward? The Outpatient Department? For me and another Maryland classmate, Angela, who'd been part of both the Pediatric Tracking program and my Physical Diagnosis group, it was none of the above. We would be starting in the Intensive Care Nursery, or ICN. My jaw clenched at this news. I knew from my third-year pediatrics stint that the ICN was the most challenging rotation of all.

It made sense for a couple of Maryland graduates to rotate through the nursery first. After all, we were familiar with the general layout of the hospital, and we'd had some exposure to the ICN through the Pediatric Tracking program. But—why us? We'd both been average students; surely there were those among us who were better candidates for this baptism by fire. Perhaps the chief residents had drawn straws on our behalf, and Angela and I got the short ones.

The ICN rotation encompassed much more than the premature babies in the Intensive Care Nursery. Though these needy newborns would be the focus of most of our time and energy, we were also responsible for the babies in the Well Baby Nursery who didn't have private pediatricians. In Southwest Baltimore's landscape of urban poverty, this included most of the babies born there. The Well Baby Nursery housed from fewer than ten to more than twenty babies on any given day. We would examine them shortly after birth and once a day until discharge, taking care of any problems that arose.

Then there was the delivery room. One-third to one-half of all deliveries at University were considered "high risk," for many reasons besides prematurity. Among these were lack of prenatal care; diabetes or high blood pressure in the mother; an ominous fetal heartbeat pattern in labor; and meconium-stained amniotic fluid, occurring when a fetus passed some stool before delivery, which could signify fetal distress and cause pneumonia in the newborn baby. Sometimes there was a sudden emergency involving compression of the umbilical cord or separation of the placenta before birth. High-risk deliveries, like all births, happened at any time of the day or night—whether you were trying to start an IV, round on your patients, grab a bite to eat, take a bathroom break, or steal a few moments of sleep. No matter what you were doing when you got that call to the DR, you had to drop everything and run.

Many of the babies from these high-risk deliveries would be healthy enough to go to the Well Baby Nursery rather than the ICN, but this did not necessarily mean they'd escaped the need for intensive care. The first six to twenty-four hours of life are a time of transition. Any infant could still develop respiratory distress, a low blood sugar, or a rising bilirubin level—the chemical in the blood that causes jaundice, a condition that could lead to brain damage if not recognized and treated. A supposedly well newborn could vomit a feeding, fail to pass urine or stool within a reasonable amount of time, start breathing too fast, or have a temperature that was a little too high or low. These signs and symptoms could be perfectly benign, or they could be harbingers of disaster, making the Well Baby Nursery a potential minefield for an inexperienced resident.

The ruler of this domain, the Director of Nurseries, was a neonatologist named Dr. Gutberlet, known to us as Dr. G. He was fortyish, wall-eyed, with unkempt graying hair. He had a wry sense of humor to which he gave free rein in a welcoming letter he'd written in longhand, photocopied, and personally distributed to us at orientation. He exhorted us to pay no attention to any "distorted myths" we might hear from the PL-2s and PL-3s about the ICN rotation.

"Ignore these unconscionable hyperboles," Dr. G. advised, "and come to your rotation with the expectation of having lots of free time, minimal scut work, and"—this was the best part— "a staff that has a deep understanding of and caters to your every personal need."

He continued, "Only 16.8% of your patients will be ill. The remainder will be bouncing baby boys and girls. How pleasant!

If things do not work out as described above, it will only be because you happened to hit one of the few busy months in the nursery (91.7% of the months last year). We welcome you with open arms and remind you that additional clinical nursery time is available on an elective basis at your request."

My anxiety was somewhat assuaged by Dr. G.'s exercise in tongue-in-cheek, and rereading that letter brought me a laugh when I needed it most. I wouldn't feel the full impact of its irony for a few more weeks.

The day after orientation, I assumed responsibility for a handful of patients in the Intensive Care Nursery. The rest were divided between Angela and a PL-2 named Ray, a quiet guy from New Jersey.

When I first set foot in the unit several minutes before 8 a.m. rounds, I felt like I'd stepped into a noisy inferno. Monitors beeped and squawked. The phone rang continually. Nurses moved rapidly back and forth among the four small rooms radiating from a central hub that comprised the unit. The first room I peeked into housed most of the "growing preemies"—those babies who had recovered from their earlier illnesses and would be well enough to go home in a couple of days or weeks. Most of these babies were in bassinettes like the infants in the Well Baby Nursery.

Across from that room was the admissions area—the hottest and noisiest room, where the newest and sickest preemies lay spread-eagled on open-warmer beds, many of them with tubes running through their mouths into their airways so a ventilator could breathe for them, and most of them with catheters emanating from the vestiges of their umbilical cords.

Corbin, a solid, gap-toothed woman who was the head nurse and Dr. G.'s right hand, had just finished weighing a newly admitted preemie who didn't appear to be in much distress. She held the tiny naked girl up with one large hand, crooning, "You're a little split-tail, aren't you, yes you are!" Nurse Corbin's way of describing normal female anatomy—the cleft beginning with the labia and extending back to the top of the buttocks—was a new one on me.

The other two rooms were jam-packed with incubators that kept the premature babies' temperatures within a normal range. Most of these were fitted with banks of blue lights, known as phototherapy, which controlled the inevitable jaundice of prematurity, thus protecting vulnerable infants from the type of brain damage known as kernicterus.

I dabbed at my forehead with my cover-gown. For all this heat and light, there was no central air conditioning. Each room had its own big, noisy floor fan to push the humid air around, its churning blades thick with dust. Since everyone was expected to wear a cloth cover-gown over their scrubs or street clothes, I wondered if anyone ever fainted from the heat; but perhaps the noise level would prevent that. After taking it all in, I stood motionless in front of the nurses' station, wide-eyed and rooted to the spot. The thought of trying to wrangle this noisy chaos struck terror into my heart.

When we assembled for rounds, our supervising PL-3 resident, a bored-looking guy with a squared-off Amish-style beard named Kevin, gave the newbies a whirlwind tour of the unit. After he'd shown us where the supplies were kept, he turned the handle of a door I hadn't noticed before. It opened onto a windowless hallway, walled on one side by a pair of elevators dedicated to servicing the psychiatric ward. The space was empty except for a large, cracked leather sofa along the wall perpendicular to the elevators.

"Behold your call room." He bowed and flashed us a sardonic grin. "You won't be able to sleep in the fifth-floor call rooms at all when you're on the nursery rotation. This luxurious sofa is it, ladies—specially reserved for the intern on call. I advise you to try to get at least one hour of sleep a night whenever you can. Try not to let the psych elevator bother you. And don't worry, it doesn't stop at this floor." I glanced at Angela. She cocked an eyebrow at me.

The rest of that day was spent getting to know our patients. Ray, the veteran among us, took call that night. The next day was Saturday, when I would be on call for 24 hours. I arrived fifteen minutes early, getting a head start on examining my own patients before Ray would sign out the entire group of babies to me. Fortunately, I would be closely supervised on this first day by Pete, a skinny, hyperactive PL-3 with Groucho Marx eyebrows and a wacky sense of humor who, I soon learned, entertained his fellow residents with a large repertoire of foreign accents.

Ray had barely signed out to us when Pete and I heard ourselves being paged over the loudspeaker. "Neonatology, Room 632, stat! Neonatology, Room 632, stat!" We ran to 632 to find a woman delivering a 33-week preemie. Because the mother had a fever, this already-imperiled newborn would also be at risk of infection. The good news was that the little boy weighed four pounds, which was right on target for a baby born seven weeks early, and he was crying and active from the start. Plus, his lungs were more mature than expected; he barely needed oxygen.

The bad news was that he would require a full sepsis workup: a two-bottle set of blood cultures to look for bacterial growth in the blood; a spinal tap to check for meningitis; and a bladder tap to check for a urinary tract infection. (This series of procedures had garnered the moniker, "the three-needle treatment.")

As a student I'd had plenty of experience drawing blood from adults, and I'd even done a couple of adult spinal taps; but I'd had few opportunities to do these procedures in children, much less preemies. That little 33-weeker proved it was a lot harder than I'd expected. And, too late, I realized I'd only filled one of the blood culture bottles—the anaerobic one, which was much less likely to show bacterial growth than the aerobic bottle.

Once my first admission to the Intensive Care Nursery was stable, the day flew by in a flurry of writing orders, starting IVs (as much of a struggle as drawing blood cultures), writing progress notes for each baby, and attending deliveries. Fortunately, there were no more admissions that day or night. Around 3 a.m. I stumbled into the hallway behind the nursery and flopped onto the beat-up leather sofa, pulling an extra cover-gown over myself as a makeshift blanket. The psych elevator clanked at frequent, irregular intervals; I couldn't imagine how anyone could sleep next to it.

But the next thing I knew I was being gently shaken by one of the nurses. "Time to get up," she said. I rubbed my eyes. Her rancid coffee-breath propelled me to my feet. "Pete wanted me to wake you at 4:15 to start doing the bilis."

Shit, I grumbled inwardly. *I forgot about the bilis.*

"Doing the bilis"—short for "bilirubins"—meant doing a heel-stick with a tiny lancet on almost every baby in the Intensive Care Nursery, plus several in the Well Baby Nursery. The procedure required drawing a few drops of blood from the baby's heel into a tiny capillary tube; sealing the tube by sticking one end of it into a small square of clay; and spinning the tubes in a centrifuge that separated the yellowish serum from the red blood cells clumped at the bottom. The serum was then transferred to a small glass chamber inserted into a machine that would give a bilirubin reading, letting us know how jaundiced the baby was. It seemed crazy to tax anyone's fine-motor skills like that when they'd barely had an hour's sleep.

Several other parameters had to be checked on the babies before sign-out rounds: vital signs, intake and output, other lab results. Most of these could be easily found on the nurses' bedside charts, though some calculation would be required. I grabbed a cup of stale coffee from the Labor and Delivery nurses' station to fortify myself for this task. Pete, who'd helped me with the bilis, also assisted with the other pre-rounding work. He was efficient and sympathetic, and he even got me to laugh a couple of times. Even so, we barely got everything done by 8 a.m., when it was time to sign out the patients to the next day's team. Finally, I could go home, rip off my pantyhose, and sprawl in front of the small fan in my room for a while before losing myself in sleep. Though the heat was stifling, my bed in that third-floor apartment was my refuge. It was the only place I felt safe and secure.

Sleep deprivation was a constant companion that month, more than it had ever been in medical school. I was lucky to get an hour of sleep at the hospital on my call nights; and I had to drink upwards of five cups of coffee most days, which didn't sit well with my GI tract. Coffee was ubiquitous: every nurses' station had a pot, other sources being the cafeteria and—a last resort—the vending machines. I didn't know anyone who didn't drink multiple cups a day. Staying awake for the daily noon Core Conference, where the chief residents lectured us on basic pediatric topics, was a real challenge. My head jerked up from my chest at least once per lecture; every time I glanced to my left or right, one or the other of my neighbors was nodding off.

Then there was the issue of food. Meals were usually taken in the cafeteria, but it would often be closed by the time I got there, so I would have to get something from a vending machine. I always made sure to have plenty of change in my pockets.

Since female residents were expected to wear either scrub dresses or the resident's uniform white skirt, wearing pantyhose was *de rigueur*. This was a unique form of torture in a non-air-conditioned environment in July, especially when I was on call for 24 hours.

• • •

It was a busy evening, three weeks into the rotation, right around dinnertime. My last full meal had been breakfast at 6 a.m. I'd just wolfed down a packet of crackers and another Baby Ruth candy bar from the vending machine when I was called to look at a baby whose delivery I'd attended at 4:12 p.m.

Baby Boy Petrovich had been born at 36 weeks' gestation, four weeks early, only slightly premature. He weighed as much as a full-term infant and was vigorous at birth, so I'd admitted him to the Well Baby Nursery instead of the ICN. When I checked him after my quick repast, he was breathing a little fast, but his respirations weren't labored. He was a lovely shade of pink, indicating that he was oxygenating himself in room air without difficulty.

Since I was busy admitting another baby from the well nursery to intensive care for vomiting and abdominal distention and Baby P. looked fine, I told the nurse to keep me informed and went back to my other patient.

A few hours later, in the middle of a series of deliveries, the nurse asked me to see the 36-weeker again. The call came while I was picking up the vomiting baby's X-rays from Radiology on the second floor. This time, little Mr. P.'s breathing was a bit faster and slightly labored, but he was still reassuringly pink.

The night wore on. It was a hectic one, with more deliveries to attend, another admission of a preemie who needed oxygen, and several IVs to restart. Plus, the vomiting baby's X-rays did not look good. I'd consulted the pediatric surgery resident, who agreed there was a bowel obstruction that would require surgery. I drew blood for tests and started an IV on the vomiting baby.

There was yet another call about Baby P. from the Well Baby Nursery. When I saw him this time, he looked much the same to me, but his nurse was concerned. I sighed and told her I would draw a blood gas to check his oxygen level as soon as I returned from the Blood Bank with blood for the surgical baby, who needed a transfusion before her operation. For the fifth time that night, I walked down the stairs from the sixth to the second floor. There usually wasn't time to wait for the elevator.

My errand in the Blood Bank took longer than expected. It was hard to keep my eyes open while I waited, since I'd been up for almost 24 hours. When I got back to the Intensive Care Nursery with the blood, dawn was just starting to streak the brick buildings outside the window multiple shades of pink and lavender, usually a welcome sight signifying that the end of a night on call was near. But this time I stepped through the door to find my worst nightmare playing out before my eyes: Baby Boy Petrovich was on an open warmer bed, surrounded by second-year residents from other pediatric wards who were doing CPR on him.

His formerly pink skin was now a mottled blue-white. There was a tube in his airway through which one of the residents administered oxygen with an anesthesia bag; and there was a large-bore IV catheter in his umbilicus. The scene was organized chaos: the continuous high-pitched whine of the baby's monitor; Bill's staccato orders— "Another 0.3 cc of epinephrine" and the nurse's equally terse reply—"Epi given;" the sound of paper tearing as more syringes were used for drawing up medications; the whooshing sound of the anesthesia bag ventilating the baby.

"Oh, God! What happened?" I cried, covering my mouth in horror.

Bill, the second-year resident who was running the resuscitation, gave me a level, unreadable look. "He crashed in the Well Baby Nursery and Tom rushed him over here and called a code. Where were you?" He sounded pissed.

"I was in the Blood Bank getting packed red cells for the surgical baby. Oh, God." I approached the warmer uncertainly, ready to take over the ventilation or the chest compressions.

"No, you go ahead and get the other kid prepped for the OR. We'll take care of this." Bill's tone softened once he realized I hadn't been slacking off.

Apparently, I'd been lulled into a false sense of security by the baby's good skin color in the Well Baby Nursery. What the hell happened? Then it dawned on me—he probably had an overwhelming infection with a bacterium called Group B strep, or GBS, which he'd picked up from the birth canal during labor. GBS infections usually had little effect on the mother, but they were notorious killers of newborns, especially preemies.

While I was getting the paperwork ready for the OR and struggling to replace the surgical baby's IV which had come out shortly after I returned to the unit, I eavesdropped on the drama unfolding on the bed across from me. Finally, Tom told Bill, "We've been coding this baby for over forty minutes, and we've never gotten a heart rate."

Bill sighed. "You're right. I guess it's time to call it. Time of death, 6:39 a.m."

Somebody turned the monitor off and the whining stopped. The flurry of activity gave way to an eerie quiet. I sat down abruptly on the nearest chair. The room was a mess, littered with emptied vials, discarded syringes, and ripped packaging. The noise of the code still rang in my ears.

Several minutes later, the nurses from the post-partum ward brought the dead infant's mother in to see him. She was a sturdy woman in her late thirties. Her first language was Russian, so I wasn't sure how much she understood.

"What happen to Ivan?" she demanded. "He is fine when born!"

"Mrs. Petrovich, I'm so sorry," I said. "We're not quite sure what happened, but we think your baby had an infection in his blood that his body couldn't fight off."

Mrs. Petrovich just glared at me. "How this happen? My baby fine when born!" she repeated. She touched the baby, shaking her head in disbelief.

I never saw her cry, never witnessed the grief that must eventually have overcome her. While she had no tears at that point, I was struggling to keep from weeping in front of her. She kept shaking her head as she stroked the baby's waxy arm.

Mrs. P.'s nurse escorted her back to her room. As soon as I could, I fled to the coat room at the back of the nursery. A baby was dead because of me—my inexperience, my incompetence. A mother's life would never be the same, and it was my fault.

Dr. G. stole in quietly and sat down beside me while I sobbed and tried not to wail. He didn't take my hand or utter soothing words, but his eyes radiated kindness. He seemed to realize that taking me to task was unnecessary; I was all too aware of how terribly I'd screwed up.

"What do you think happened?" he asked.

"I guess the baby must have had a group B strep infection. I don't know, I—I just wish I'd admitted him sooner…"

"Yes, it's too bad you didn't," he said gently. "Babies with early-onset GBS sepsis are often 35 to 37 weeks' gestation, and they're often pink even when they're having some respiratory distress, because their circulation is getting ready to shut down. Like this baby.

"But you should know," he continued, "that even if you'd gotten antibiotics into him right away, there's a good chance he still would have died."

I nodded, drying my eyes with my cover-gown.

"What else could do this?" He looked at me intently, clasping his hands together and leaning forward with his forearms on his knees.

I shrugged hopelessly. I was totally spent, and I couldn't imagine coming up with a differential diagnosis just then. Without pressuring me further, Dr. G. ran through some possibilities for me.

"He could have had a cardiac problem, like hypoplastic left heart syndrome or critical aortic stenosis, or possibly pulmonary atresia." And he went on to explain how these forms of congenital heart disease could have caused a newborn to be pink for several hours and then deteriorate rapidly.

Eventually I would realize that I'd made a rookie error. This was something that had happened to every PL-2 and PL-3 in the program and would happen to every one of my PL-1 peers over the coming months. Most of these mistakes were not devastating like the one I'd made, but several came close. None of us would emerge from our training unscathed. That was the downside of the learning process, the part nothing—and no one—could prepare you for.

• • •

I never forgot Dr. G.'s kindness to me that day, or the skill with which he turned a catastrophe into a teachable moment. I never forgot the horror of seeing Baby Petrovich go from a pink baby with mildly labored breathing to a moribund baby with the bluish pallor of death.

And I never forgot the lessons that baby taught me. Not just the clinical ones about group B strep sepsis and shock, but about how to be a doctor: Be ever vigilant. If the nurse at the baby's bedside is concerned, assume there's something wrong until proven otherwise. Check it out right away, because that nurse spends a lot more time with the patient than you do.

As in other areas of life, always be ready to question your idea of what's going on as soon as any conflicting data arise. Be open to other possibilities—to all that you've learned and already know, and to things you might not have encountered before.

In other words, be ready for anything.

18

GHOST SHIPS

Finally, that soul-crushing month in the Intensive Care Nursery was over. As soon as I had an opportunity, I phoned Perry. After several unanswered calls, he finally picked up.

"What the hell happened?" I said. "Where have you *been* for the last four weeks?"

"Well, hello to you, too. I told you I'd be finishing classes and painting the house; what did you expect?"

"That's great, but what about your brilliant plan of weekend camping when I wasn't on call?"

After some more wrangling, we agreed to get together that Saturday night. Perry took me out to dinner and a movie, holding my hand while we waited for our entrées and snuggling with me in the theater. He couldn't have been sweeter. Back at his place, he massaged my neck and shoulders, knotted from internship stress—and the stress of wondering where he'd been all that time. He listened sympathetically to the awful story of Baby Boy Petrovich and my subsequent struggles with guilt and feelings of incompetence. Once I'd vented for a while and my muscles relaxed, the massaging turned to caresses.

It was a comfort that he wanted to make love, and I enjoyed it. After our month apart, though, I felt emotionally detached in a way I hadn't felt with him before. I must have been pulling away for a while without realizing it. He was really there for me that night; but his absence during that awful first month of residency had ripped a huge hole in the fabric of our relationship.

On July 28, I started my first rotation at Union Memorial Hospital, the place where I'd done my remedial summer of internal medicine the previous year. Pediatrics at Union consisted of caring for kids in a small inpatient unit and a well-baby nursery, plus attending deliveries and taking pediatric admissions from the emergency room.

While the on-call rooms at University Hospital—which I had yet to sleep in—were barracks of bunk beds, the intern's call room at Union Memorial, located in the "old" hospital, was like a bedroom in a house—there was a window and a single bed, complete with a bedspread as well as a blanket and pillow.

Union Memorial had been founded in 1854. The rooms in the older part of the building, including the call room and the pediatric ward, dated from the turn of the 20th century, while most of the action took place in the "new"—mid-20th century—hospital. This was where the delivery room, nursery, and emergency room were located. You could finish a candy bar in the time it took to walk to the "new" hospital from the call room. We made rounds on the pediatric ward twice a week with a septuagenarian who wasn't very savvy about the latest advances in the field. Fortunately, Tom, our senior resident, kept up with the current journal articles and was an engaging teacher.

The day after the rotation began, I took pediatric call at Union Memorial for the first time. What a change from the ICN! Tom was on call with me that night. Though he was only a PL-2, he was very knowledgeable, so I felt secure with him as my backup. Short and plump, he had a great rapport with the little ones, and his cheerful attitude endeared him to the rest of us. We rounded on the handful of well babies and checked them for jaundice. The lab ran the bilirubins for us, so there were no onerous capillary tubes or finicky glass chambers to fuss with. There were only a couple of kids on the pediatric ward that day, so Tom and I went our separate ways to read in the afternoon, met in the cafeteria for dinner, and sat companionably watching TV for most of the evening.

Around 11 p.m., I got to crawl under the covers of the bed in the intern's call room. What luxury! Of course, I couldn't sleep. What if there was a delivery in the middle of the night, or an admission from the ER? Sure enough, I'd just drifted off when my pager beeped, displaying Tom's number. "I've got a little asthmatic for you to admit to the ward," he said when I answered the page. I rubbed a hand across my eyes and stepped into my shoes, the only thing I'd taken off when I went to bed. Tom met me outside the ER, pushing a small stretcher bearing a cherubic toddler wearing an oxygen mask and a worried frown, sporting an IV in his left hand.

"This is Andre, and this is his mom, Tanisha."

I smiled and introduced myself to the baby's mother. I couldn't help but smile at Andre, too. He was adorable, but he was breathing faster than he should have been, still in some distress even after treatment in the ER. Asthma was one of the most common diagnoses in pediatrics, especially in the inner city. Allergies, second-hand cigarette smoke, and air pollution, whether from industrial processes or car exhaust—any or all of them could have contributed to Andre's condition. The only one that could be mitigated was smoking. Tanisha wasn't a smoker, but other household members were.

"He's had three shots of epinephrine and he's still wheezing," Tom said. "As you can see, I've put an IV in him. So, what do we want to do next? How fast should his IV run?"

Yikes! There was a world of difference between toddlers and ICN babies. The respiratory problems of newborns were different from those of older pediatric patients; and I remembered from my third-year pediatric rotation a few eons ago that figuring out IV fluids was more complicated for children beyond the neonatal period. I felt a little like I had as a third-year student at the VA Spa, when I'd taken care of my first "real" patient under the supervision of Sanctimonious George.

I got out my calculator for the IV fluids and ran the numbers by Tom, who pointed out a minor mistake. Then I chose the correct dose of aminophylline for Andre's asthma, wrote the orders, and got the little guy tucked in for the night. When I checked on him a few hours later, Andre was sleeping peacefully, his breathing comfortable and unlabored.

Those four weeks at Union Memorial were fairly uneventful. There were some scary moments in the delivery room, and we had to prepare a newborn with an intestinal obstruction for transport to University Hospital for surgery; but, having seen worse in the ICN, I took these events in stride. The more challenging aspect, I discovered, was getting the hang of treating the older children, the ones between the neonatal period and the adolescents I'd taken care of at Yale-New Haven Hospital. There was a steep learning curve for starting IVs on toddlers, drawing blood from children who already felt lousy from their illnesses, and figuring out those IV fluid rates.

The night Elvis Presley died ended up being our worst night on call. When Tom joined me in the cafeteria for dinner, he was grief-stricken. "The King is dead! I can't believe it." It was as if he'd lost a relative. Fortunately, there were no medical crises to deal with that night.

While August was quiet at work, my personal life was another story. Perry's departure from Baltimore was slated for late fall; and, after that night when he'd been so loving, he made himself scarce for most of August, just as he'd done in July. I was angry, but I was also mourning our relationship as I watched it slip away. My social life at that time consisted of eating pizza, drinking beer, and watching *Saturday Night Live* with Debra when neither of us was on call. We loved Gilda Radner as Roseanne Roseannadanna and Emily Litella, and we enjoyed the ridiculous posturing of Steve Martin and Dan Aykroyd as "two wild and crazy guys."

Depression started to drag me down after the ICN rotation, so I was receptive to Dr. Epstein's suggestion that we increase therapy from once to twice a week. This was tricky, given my call schedule, but my therapist was flexible and I was motivated. Dr. Epstein's approach during that first nightmarish month of internship had been to back off on the analytic stuff and offer simple support, which I'd deeply appreciated. Now that I wasn't so sleep-deprived and exhausted, I was ready to dig into my grief about Perry and the toll internship was taking on my emotional well-being. Twice-a-week therapy was a mixed blessing. Sometimes it felt like going to the dentist for root-canal surgery, but other times I actually looked forward to it. I wanted to get on with my inner work, to start feeling—and doing—better.

I also took my first mental-health holiday that month: I called in sick on a Friday before a 24-hour call on Saturday. Chores I'd neglected, like paying bills, finally got the attention they needed. My body had been neglected, too. Just taking an extra-long shower and shampoo felt like a spa vacation. It would not be the last time I played hooky during my training. I tried to take my unauthorized leaves of absence when they would be least detrimental to my colleagues. I don't know how many of my co-residents took mental-health holidays, though I'm pretty sure some of them did; but there were times when I knew I would be of no use to anyone if I didn't take care of *me*. I learned early on the importance of pacing myself.

The end of August brought me back to University Hospital for a two-month rotation in Behavioral Pediatrics, a subspecialty in which the University of Maryland's Department of Pediatrics was on the cutting edge. This would prepare us for dealing with common emotional problems of childhood in the pediatric out-patient setting—things like hyperactivity, school phobia, tan-trums, and issues with eating or toilet-training. We would learn how to manage behavioral problems and when psychiatric refer-ral was indicated. I was doing this rotation at precisely the time when my own therapy was intensifying. Working with children's behavioral problems as an intern forced me to continually con-front my own childhood difficulties with tantrums and obsessive thoughts, which made for an eerie convergence of work-life and therapy. Plus, as I was all too aware, I had full-blown symptoms of clinical depression at the time—loss of appetite, difficulty sleeping (except when I was thoroughly exhausted after a night on call), social isolation, and even suicidal thoughts. Fortunately, that terrible spring of 1974 had taught me that my pain would not last forever and that I could get through it.

Therapy wasn't just about early childhood issues, however. One day I stomped into Dr. Epstein's office and threw my white coat on the floor, causing its pockets' contents—stethoscope, Harriet Lane Handbook (a quick reference for residents), sterile packets containing an IV needle, a syringe, and an endotracheal tube for emergencies—to spill all over the room.

"I'm fed up with being jerked around!" I yelled. I was tired of always feeling like I didn't know what I was doing as a resident;

and I was *really* sick of being ill-treated by my erstwhile boy-friend. Perry had become insufferable.

When I'd recently called him up, the conversation started civilly enough; but when I took him to task for not calling as he'd promised he would, knowing I was already depressed and struggling with therapy, he said, "You really ought to give up on this bourgeois psychotherapy stuff. You need to stop navel-gazing and get political, spend that energy on changing the system."

"What?? It's not navel-gazing, it's what's holding me together right now. And how is society ever going to change if individuals don't?"

"There are better ways to go about it. One of my friends in the commune told me about a different kind of therapy..." I rolled my eyes and tuned him out. Him and his goddamn commune! What had happened to the tender, loving Perry from a few short months ago?

As if this weren't enough, he continued: "And you ought to give up on your ideal of conventional marriage. It's simply unrealistic in this society. Nobody in the commune's married. Some people are monogamous, some aren't, and some people aren't in relationships at all."

My grip tightened on the phone receiver. Had I heard this right? Was Perry, who had failed at marriage *twice*, now giving *me* marital advice? Plus, he'd casually mentioned earlier in the conversation that he had a female roommate in his temporary Baltimore apartment. Did that have anything to do with why he hadn't called? It took all the self-restraint I had not to throw the phone across the room.

"But one of the things I find most attractive about you," he went on," is that you don't accept the kind of superficial relationships people are expected to settle for in this society. I admire the way you insist on the real thing. Even if it makes you lonely and unhappy sometimes."

Was this supposed to make me feel better? I thought I'd found the "real thing" with Perry. Now I was "lonely and unhappy," all right—thanks largely to him.

By the time we hung up, I was totally disgusted. I never wanted to hear the phrase "in this society" again. He sounded like a political science textbook, or some callow college freshman spouting socialist platitudes. Who *was* this guy, and what had he done with my boyfriend?

During my Behavioral Pediatrics rotation, I took night call in the pediatric emergency room. The Peds ER was located on the 5th floor, the pediatric floor of the hospital, separate from the main ER on the first floor. Working there at night could present you with everything from the terror of treating a child in cardiorespiratory arrest, to the chaos of standing room only in the waiting room, to a leisurely trickle of colds and ear infections—or anything in between. As a first-year resident, it was all new to me, and I lived in dread of screwing up. It was hard to just let myself suck at being a resident until the time came when I didn't anymore.

Sleepless nights on call were not a given as they'd been on the nursery rotation, but they did happen frequently. By the wee hours, my body would ache all over. A sinus infection I'd acquired the second week dragged on for most of the two-month rotation. Though I knew it came with the territory, I resented the imposition of being called back to see a patient when I'd just settled into one of the bunk beds in the women's call room. Sometimes parents were rude and demanding. Plus, I often felt helpless and frustrated in the face of the intractable problems of urban poverty that most of these families faced, and I knew they had to feel a lot more helpless and frustrated than I did. I felt like Sisyphus, pushing that damn boulder up the hill yet again.

But sometimes it was a lot of fun. Perhaps the stars were in alignment, or maybe I was more rested than usual, but there were some ER nights when the workload was neither too heavy nor too light and everything just flowed. Though I would be up most or all of the night, there was the satisfaction of watching an asthmatic child's labored breathing relax after treatment; the elation of a procedure going smoothly; or the pleasure of diagnosing a straightforward ear infection and prescribing an antibiotic that I knew would give relief within a day or two. When we were in the zone, there was the joy of camaraderie, of working as a team, as though we were one organism. We joked and bantered back and forth while we got the work done. Going home after such a night, I was grateful that I was getting paid to do something I enjoyed so much.

Another source of enjoyment and satisfaction was the one afternoon a week dedicated to seeing my own patients in Continuity Clinic. Children I'd admitted to the hospital or seen in the Peds ER came to the clinic after discharge for follow-up of their asthma or other problems. Those who didn't have their own pediatrician to go to—and there were many—came to our clinic for their immunizations and well-child visits. And I was their doctor. There were issues like those we encountered in the Peds ER and the Behavior Clinic—missed appointments, transportation problems, difficulty reaching families because their phones had been disconnected. But the experience of taking care of my own patients and teaching and counseling their mothers was one of the most rewarding parts of residency.

Early in October, Perry phoned to see if Debra and I wanted to go out drinking the following evening. I was at work when he called, so Deb accepted the invitation for both of us. Then she called me in the ER, all excited. "It sounds like he wants to start seeing you again!" I rolled my eyes, remembering that bizarre phone conversation a few weeks earlier. When I called him the next day to finalize a plan, he sounded so blasé that I almost backed out. I was angry, and I was afraid I'd spend the whole evening sniping at him, which wouldn't be fun for any of us. Did Perry expect us to be "just friends" now? While that was a great idea in theory, I knew I couldn't do it. I wanted things to go back to the way they'd been, and he'd never made it clear to me why they'd changed in the first place. And if we couldn't pick up where we'd left off, then why didn't he just let me go instead of coming back into my life every few weeks? This was turning into the longest goodbye ever.

Instead of going out for drinks, we sat around Deb's and my apartment eating pizza and drinking beer. Deb and Perry traded mock insults and she attacked him with a sofa cushion. I threw a corner of a pizza slice at Perry, which landed in his hair. Gradually my anger dissipated in the face of all this horseplay. Perry spent the night, making love with me as if the last couple of months and all this New York stuff had never happened. Next day I was devastated. I knew he would be leaving soon; but I still loved him, and it seemed like he still loved me. Why on earth couldn't we make it work?

• • •

The Behavioral Pediatrics rotation ended the last week in October. Our attending physician, Dr. Ariana Visconti, invited the other intern and me for beer and pizza in the basement of the Student Union. Dr. Visconti was a warm, vivacious woman in her mid-to-late 30s. My co-intern, Seth, was a hard-charging New Yorker and a genuinely funny guy. We'd bonded early in the rotation over a role-playing exercise where I took the part of a depressed teenager—not much of stretch for me—while he played the concerned pediatrician putting his behavioral-pediatric skills to work. The three of us had become good friends. We were deep in a discussion of what the last two months together had meant to each of us when I was hesitantly approached by a woman in her fifties who looked pale and uncomfortable.

"Excuse me, miss, are you a doctor?" I was wearing my hospital-issue white skirt, while Seth and Dr. Visconti were both in street clothes.

"Yes, I am, can I help you?"

"I hope so. My heart just started pounding really fast, and I don't feel well…"

We sat her down, took her pulse, and ascertained that her heart rate was at least twice what it was supposed to be. "P.A.T.," Dr. Visconti said tersely—the acronym for "paroxysmal atrial tachycardia," a major heart-rhythm disturbance. The three of us got her to the emergency room, where she was put on IV medication and admitted to the hospital. I went to see her on the ward a little while later.

"When I saw your white skirt, I knew you must be a medical student or resident and that you could help. I've never been so scared. I'm so glad you were there."

I held her hand and we spoke of nonmedical things for a while. She told me about her two college-age daughters, and I told her about medical school. The roles of doctor and patient fell away, and we were just two women talking. Our simple conversation warmed my heart.

As I walked home, I realized that, because of that white skirt and what it represented, my life would never be the same. For better or worse, I was marked for life as a physician; I could never *not* be a doctor again. I would forever see people differently—that man on the street with the odd gait must have suffered a stroke; that woman in the hospital hallway with the barrel chest and uplifted shoulders likely had emphysema; that two-year-old with glasses at the grocery store had probably been born prematurely. And, clearly, other people saw me differently as well. The trappings of a physician, whether a white skirt or a white coat and stethoscope, invested me with real authority and a commensurate degree of responsibility.

My next rotation was on 5E, the infant ward—the most technically challenging rotation aside from the ICN. Children between the ages of twenty-eight days and two years were no more able to tell you what was bothering them than newborns were. They could not be reasoned with like older children, and they had a lot more physical strength than preemies, so their ability to fight off our attempts at necessary medical procedures was formidable.

Then there was the noise level. The screams of children in the procedure room could be heard through its closed door; infants in their cribs cried to be fed; toddlers cried when their parents had to leave. IVs in their arms or legs, oxygen masks over their faces, mist tents around their cribs—these therapeutic accoutrements were all sources of discomfort and frustration for our poor little patients. It was heart-rending to listen to all this misery, but we had to become inured to it to do our jobs.

The month of November was a busy one on the infant ward. The first cases of influenza were cropping up; and RSV, a seasonal virus that causes much of the serious respiratory disease in this age group, was shifting into high gear. Like their nursery counterparts, the infants and toddlers required a full sepsis workup—cultures of blood, urine, and spinal fluid (CSF), plus a chest X-ray—to rule out a bacterial infection whenever they had a fever; and they had to be treated with IV antibiotics for at least three days until it was clear that the infection was viral rather than bacterial. Between the needle sticks for blood and urine cultures, the spinal taps, and starting IVs, 5E was Procedure City.

Our resident, Kurt—a soft-spoken PL-3 who was a little older than most of the third-years and a family man with young children—was preoccupied for most of that month with a tragic situation. Jimmy, the toddler-age son of a pediatric social worker, was gravely ill and in a coma, not expected to survive. While a second-year resident presided over his bedside care in the Pediatric ICU, Kurt supported Jimmy's mom and the rest of the family. We PL-1s were not exactly left to our own devices; but the fact that so much of Kurt's energy was taken up with Jimmy's care forced us to rely more on our own judgment, and that of our PL-2 colleague, than we might have otherwise.

This was how I met Queenie, a twelve-month-old girl with a fever that had spiked as high as 106. Queenie had had her full sepsis workup before I made her acquaintance. The chest X-ray had shown evidence of pneumonia, and she'd been on antibiotics for almost thirty-six hours. She was miserable—fretful, restless, unable to eat much, and unhappy about her left forearm being wrapped in gauze like a mummy's to make sure her IV stayed in. Her temperature was coming down, but slowly. Though she wasn't in major respiratory distress, the pneumonia was probably enough to account for her high fever. I renewed her antibiotic orders, wrote for enough IV fluid to keep her hydrated while she wasn't eating, watched her closely all day, and signed her out to the intern on call for the night.

When I returned the next day, Queenie's temperature had plateaued at an unsatisfactory 103.8. She was even more irritable than she'd been the previous day. I was baffled. No bacteria had grown on her original cultures of blood, urine, or spinal fluid. Pneumonia might explain the persistent fever, but what about the irritability? Could she possibly have bacterial meningitis even though the spinal fluid culture was negative? Her current doses of antibiotics were enough to treat pneumonia, but not enough for meningitis. Now I was really worried.

I approached Kurt, who was on the phone with one of Jimmy's family members. *Poor Kurt*, I thought as I waited for him to finish his conversation. Finally, he hung up the receiver, shook his head sadly, and turned his attention to me.

"What's up?" he asked.

"It's Queenie." I told him about the persistent high fever despite the negative cultures. "She's so irritable. Do you think she could have meningitis, even though the first CSF culture was negative? Should I do another spinal tap?"

Kurt nodded. "Sounds like a good idea."

When the preliminary results came back, the spinal fluid was abnormal in several parameters. But when the lab tech mentioned that she'd seen a couple of pairs of bacteria on the microscope slide, I could hardly contain myself. I went down to the lab to look. "Holy shit," I whispered as I peered through the microscope at a few purplish paired dots on the slide. Yes, Queenie actually had bacterial meningitis! My clinical observation and intuition had been borne out by laboratory evidence.

We doubled her antibiotic dose, the standard procedure for treating meningitis, and continued the medication for another two and a half weeks. Queenie recovered completely and, like Andre, the little asthmatic from Union Memorial, she became one of the patients I would follow in my Continuity Clinic for the rest of my residency.

At the end of my 5E rotation, Kurt called me in to chat about the evaluation he planned to write. Not all senior residents did this, but Kurt was a particularly nurturing guy, conscientious about his teaching responsibilities as well as the care of his patients. He looked tired. Jimmy had died the previous day.

"I'm sorry I was so busy with Jimmy. I wish I'd been able to spend more time with you guys," he said.

"Oh, gosh, Kurt." I waved this away. "We completely understand."

"You seem to have done all right anyway—nice job with that little girl with the *D. pneumo.* meningitis."

"Thanks." My face flushed with pride.

Then he shifted uncomfortably in his seat. "Kay, I've noticed that you seem—well, depressed. It doesn't seem to interfere with your doing a good job. Other people have noticed this, too. Are you—getting help?"

I blushed again. "Yes, I am, thanks. I've been in therapy for almost a year now."

He looked embarrassed. Perhaps I'd shared too much. "Well, keep up the good work. You're well on your way to becoming a very solid resident. And—I hope you feel better soon."

"Thanks, Kurt, I really appreciate it." I smiled at him and shook the hand he offered, feeling a surge of gratitude. As I walked back to the nurses' station to finish my progress notes, I considered what he'd said about people knowing I was depressed. I felt both very exposed and very cared for. It would be a while before I would fully appreciate his courage in speaking so honestly. Only years later would I realize the significance of the fact that my depression had not adversely affected my performance.

My next rotation, in December, was in the pediatric outpatient department (OPD). It was a lot like working in the Peds ER at night, which was where I did night call that month; but the hours were better—9 a.m. to 5 p.m.—a considerable improvement over working on the wards like the ICN or 5E, where the hours were 8 a.m. to whenever-the-work-was-done p.m. While sign-out on the wards was at 5 o'clock, paperwork was often completed after handing your patients off to the person on call; and, since I tended to work slowly, that could take a long time. When I worked in the OPD, I was usually able to get home in time to have dinner at a reasonable hour with Deb, if she wasn't on call.

Shortly before I started the OPD rotation, Debra and I had moved out of our townhouse apartment in Bolton Hill to a garden apartment in Ellicott City. We were tired of living downtown; and Marie, my best friend among the first-year pediatric residents, lived in the same complex. I had mixed feelings about making this move with my roommate, even though she was my best friend. We commiserated about residency, especially the myriad humiliations of being a "newbie." And we commiserated about relationships with men. One night over a couple of beers, Debra said, "I'm too scared to be desperate."

I promptly shot back with "I'm too desperate to be scared." I might not have been "too scared" in relationships with men; but I was uncomfortable about moving into an apartment with just one other single woman. Would we end up becoming "old maids" together? Would people think we were lesbians?

Perry and I spent one last night together before he left for New York in mid-December. I took him out to dinner and told him how much our relationship had meant to me. Perry was less emotional than I was, but he did ask several times when I would be visiting him, and he made sure I knew which bus to take to the city. Later, we held each other for a long time after making love. As I gazed over his shoulder at the poster of Picasso's Blue Nude on my wall, I reflected on the intense connection we'd experienced over the months of our time together. We'd been so happy together in those first few months; where had that happiness gone?

I did visit Perry in New York City, just once. It was the end of January, a weekend when I had both Saturday and Sunday off. As soon as I signed out Saturday morning, I left directly from the hospital, excited despite my weariness. Everybody knew about my weekend plans and was rooting for me. The resident I'd signed out to wished me luck. Perry met me at the bus station, and we rode the subway to his new digs. I don't recall meeting any other members of the infamous commune, but I noticed there were a lot more bookshelves and file cabinets than I remembered from his Baltimore house; it looked like he was there to stay. After dinner and a movie, we browsed a bookstore, where he bought me *The Culture of Narcissism* by historian and social critic Christopher Lasch, an idol of his—a book I kept for many years but never read. We had some good talks and even some decent sex; but I finally realized, when I saw him in his new environment, that there would be no bringing back what we'd once had. The roots of our relationship had been severed back in July, when he'd abandoned me during my baptism by fire. Now, six months later, the tree was dead.

• • •

In her book, *Tiny Beautiful Things*, Cheryl Strayed has a lovely passage about the roads not taken in our lives. She says, "Every life...has a 'sister ship', one that follows 'quite another route' than the one we end up taking. We want it to be otherwise, but it cannot be; the people we might have been live a different, phantom life than the people we are...we only know that, whatever that sister life was, it was important and beautiful and not ours. It was the ghost ship that didn't carry us."

The life I might have shared with Perry was the ghost ship that didn't carry me. It wasn't just about the relationship we might have had; it was also about the kind of doctor I might have been. Perhaps I would have provided primary care for inner city children instead of the highly specialized care of the neonatal ICU, where I spent my career. Being a pediatrician in an underserved area would have been a good fit with Perry's socialist politics, maybe even with living in a commune. (I was enough of a hippie sympathizer that communal living was something I might have been willing to try.) More importantly, I knew from caring for my Continuity Clinic patients that a primary care practice in the inner city could have been a good fit with my own ideal of service—and enjoyable, rewarding work.

I never found out why Perry, who'd been so vulnerable and open-hearted at the start of our relationship, withdrew his love so abruptly. Perhaps he couldn't face the prospect of another failed relationship so soon after the implosion of his second marriage, so he had to make a preemptive strike. Or maybe it had more to do with our fundamental differences in outlook. He didn't communicate this in the early days of our relationship; but, to Perry, the political trumped the personal every time. The cause, the struggle, fighting the system to make the world a better place— these were what mattered most to him. Things like romantic love and even one's own personal growth and happiness were unimportant by comparison, maybe even an indulgence this suffering world couldn't afford. But to me, there could be no "political" without the "personal." In my view, a person who wasn't in touch with their inner self, who was indifferent to their own spiritual growth, would ultimately not be of much use in any cause or struggle. I didn't perceive this irreconcilable difference until it was too late.

What I took away from that ghost ship was a sense of finally being an adult in a love relationship—the experience of being a co-captain, an equal partner in the enterprise. I also learned how to use humor in dealing with the everyday slings and arrows of a partner's foibles and imperfections, which proved to be an invaluable life lesson.

But the best part of Perry's legacy may have been his love for the rebel in me—the part of me that was, as he put it, the "accept-no-substitutes fighter," the resister. Having that part of me loved, appreciated, and nurtured, even just for those few months, would stand me in good stead for every struggle I would encounter in the years ahead.

19

PURPLE HEART

In February, the month after that final visit with Perry, I did my second four-week rotation on 5E, the infant ward. My PL-1 year was more than half over, and I had enough of a grasp of the basics that I was starting to chafe under the constraints of internship—the long hours and endless scut work, the sometimes-contradictory demands of my superiors, the feeling of being at the bottom of the pecking order. My acute depression during the first part of the PL-1 year had lifted, but a chronic, low-grade resentment had taken its place.

Fortunately, I was not alone in my disaffection. Marie, the soft-spoken woman from Duke Medical School who was my best friend in the residency program, felt much as I did. Whenever the three of us were not on call—and not too tired to stay up past 7 p.m.—Marie, Deb, and I gathered at our place or Marie's to hang out and commiserate about internship. We'd eat pizza and watch episodes of *M*A*S*H* or *Mork and Mindy*, and sometimes we'd play backgammon, which, under Marie's patient tutelage, became a comforting ritual for me.

One cold February morning I sipped vile coffee from a Styrofoam cup as I looked over my newest patient's history and physical before rounds. I looked up to see 5E's PL-3 boss for that month standing in front of me, arms crossed. He was a wiry, scrappy guy with eyes the color of sea-glass who preferred to be called by his last name, Jamison. I'd caught the sound of his distinctive gait, a kind of swaggering shuffle, when he was still several feet away.

"Guess you got zippity-doo-dah in the sleep department, huh?" he said with a snarky grin. He'd been on call, too, but, unlike me, he'd gotten a few hours' sleep. As the senior resident, his principal task had been accepting patients from the ER and then paging me to do the admission. I glowered at him. No one who'd been on call had a right to look as crisp and fresh as he did—all clean-shaven in a fresh white coat—even if they'd slept all night.

"Aw, come on, don't be a grouch," he said. "It's gonna be a great day—look how sunny it is!" He waved his arm at the grime-streaked window. "Come to the cafeteria with me and I'll buy you a donut."

"Oh, all right," I said. I sighed, stretched, and couldn't help but smile a little as I rose from my seat. Jamison's good spirits were contagious. While we wolfed down our donuts before rounds, I learned that he was married to his college sweetheart and was an avid hockey fan.

But Jamison was rarely this friendly. One day, a pediatric surgery resident had to bail me out after my unsuccessful attempt to start an IV on a nine-month-old scheduled for a hernia repair. The resident muttered, "Damn pediatric interns—you guys are useless!" I turned on my heel and walked out. When I got to the chart room where we wrote our progress notes, I slammed a metal chart down on the Formica countertop. "Goddammit!" I hissed.

"What's your problem?" Jamison looked up at me from the current issue of *Pediatrics*, his green eyes flashing.

"I'm sick of being yelled at by pediatric surgeons!"

"Well, keep your bitching to yourself, please. People are trying to work here. Maybe if you tried a little harder, they wouldn't give you so much shit."

I stalked out and speed-walked up and down the hall a couple times until my breathing slowed down. What a jerk! I knew Jamison wasn't the warm and fuzzy type, but it wouldn't have killed him to show a little compassion.

Jamison may not have been Mr. Congeniality, but over the next few weeks I actually started to like the guy. I had to say this for him—by the end of the month, he'd really whipped me into shape. I was a lot better at starting IVs, and I'd become more efficient at admitting my little patients from the ER at night. Finally, I seemed to be catching up with the other PL-1s, most of whom had gotten the hang of residency a lot faster than me. I appreciated my senior resident's role in this, even though his approach was generally that of a drill sergeant.

"You're coming with me to the Intensive Care Nursery, right?" he asked on our last day.

"Oh, right—I guess so." I'd forgotten Jamison would be the senior resident on my next rotation as well.

"Good!" He grinned. "You've made some real progress this month. I wouldn't want you backsliding because you didn't have me riding your ass," he said with a wink.

I blushed, feeling proud and embarrassed at the same time. I got the feeling Jamison was almost as happy about my improvement under his guidance as I was. His encouragement, rare as it was, felt good. Increasingly I found myself hoping for one of those moments when we shared a smile or a laugh. To my surprise and dismay, I was developing a crush on him.

My second four-week rotation in the ICN started on March 2nd, more than seven months after the first one. Taking care of the smallest and sickest patients was never easy, but I was pleasantly surprised at how much more smoothly things like admissions and procedures went the second time around. Unfortunately, several of our preemies were born at the limits of viability that month, so there were a number of deaths. While the day-to-day work with the babies was easier, sadness hung heavy over the unit.

Marie was also rotating through the ICN that month. One of her patients was a two-month-old preemie with lung disease so severe that she couldn't be weaned from the ventilator. Marie had to place new IVs in her limbs or scalp almost daily. If the endotracheal tube came out of her throat, Marie had to put it back. She also drew blood from the baby's radial artery at least once a day to check the oxygen, carbon dioxide, and acid levels in her blood. This test, known as a blood gas, was a challenging procedure for us and one of the most painful for a baby. Whenever any of us had a patient like this, we tried to help each other out as much as we could. I assisted Marie one afternoon as she drew a blood gas.

She inserted the tiny needle into the infant's artery. As soon as blood appeared in the attached tubing, Marie held the needle in place while I pulled back the minuscule amount needed for the test into a one-mL syringe.

"You got it on the first try this time—good work," I said.

Marie pulled the needle out and applied pressure to the baby's wrist with a small gauze pad. A tear rolled down her cheek, and she turned away from me. After the baby's bleeding stopped, I put my arm around her and steered her into the coatroom at the back of the nursery. We sat together for a few minutes; the only sound was an occasional muted sob from Marie. I broke the silence. "This really sucks, doesn't it?"

"Why are we doing this?" she sobbed. "That baby is in pain practically all the time. We're flogging her, trying to just keep her alive, and for what?"

She broke down, and I cried along with her. I shared her sense of futility. Babies who weren't getting any better, like Marie's patient, were in a kind of limbo. It was very difficult for everyone, from the parents to the doctors and nurses, to accept the fact that a baby wasn't making any progress and was unlikely to survive. The entire medical team's job (especially that of the PL-1) then devolved into an avalanche of minute details—better oxygenation on one blood gas, not so good on the next, on and on for weeks.

And the little ones kept suffering. You couldn't hear them crying, but you could see it in their faces when you drew blood or started an IV. It broke my heart, as it did my friend's; but the work still had to be done. The look on her little patient's face that day had been more than Marie could bear.

One morning I slammed down the telephone receiver after yet another call from the hematology lab. "Arrrgh!" I growled. I would have to draw Baby X's blood for a fourth time, because the specimen had clotted for a third time.

"What the hell is wrong with you? Lighten up!" Jamison barked as he walked past the desk where I sat. We glared at each other while we got control of ourselves. Jamison and I were both short-tempered, and the death-steeped atmosphere of the ICN that month had ratcheted up the usual tension of intensive care.

• • •

Despite the anguish of dying babies in the ICN, my broken heart was beginning to heal from its rupture with Perry. I started spending more time with John, my divorced neighbor from my days at 1210 Bolton St. He'd bought a house north of the city when I was starting residency, and he'd helped Deb and me move into our Ellicott City apartment.

John and I went out to dinner regularly and occasionally to the movies; sometimes we just hung out at his house. One evening in March, while we sat on his sofa watching TV, he drew me close to him and gave me a tentative kiss, and our friendship crossed over into something more. I was ambivalent—wary of letting a good friendship turn into a sexual relationship, having experienced more than once what a minefield that could be. But it turned out that John really enjoyed sex, and our lighthearted intimacy brought out a playful side of him I hadn't seen before. We savored each other's company, as friends and as lovers. Knowing how badly he'd been hurt by his failed marriage, though, I doubted there was any potential for a long-term relationship.

About halfway through the ICN rotation, I had an exceptional night on call. I ran the unit all by myself, without any help from Jamison or any of the other residents, just a couple of phone calls to the neonatology fellow. Everything came together that night, in a way it never had before. Finally, I felt like I belonged in the line of work I'd chosen. For the first time, it seemed like a good fit. Those four uphill years of medical school and eight slogging months as an intern—*finally*, all that work was paying off. By the end of my second month in the nursery, I'd come to appreciate working with Jamison, too. Though his infrequent encouragement usually came with irony or teasing, some of his self-confidence had rubbed off on me, burnishing my new-found sense of capability—and making Jamison seem even more desirable.

April brought a welcome week of vacation. I flew to San Francisco to visit a college friend and her husband—my first-ever trip to the West Coast. I wandered around the city, seeing the sights by myself while my friends were at work. The Bay Area's laid-back vibe was the perfect antidote to the pressures of my medical training back East. As I rode the BART train one balmy afternoon, I noticed a guy about my age reading the *Journal of Pediatrics* as he stood in the aisle. He was casually dressed, without a white coat, but there was a stethoscope draped around his neck. He was probably a pediatric resident like me, but he was so *relaxed*. I envied him his casual air, as if residency were no big deal—so different from my own experience.

The day I returned to work, I discovered that one of the second-year residents had gone on medical leave for a psychotic episode. He was known to have a psychiatric condition, but he'd done well until his behavior became increasingly erratic the week I was gone. Even before my vacation, I'd noticed that something wasn't right—the PL-2s and PL-3s seemed to be spending a lot of energy cleaning up after this guy's mistakes and covering for him. One day he got agitated on rounds and started saying things that didn't make sense, so they had no choice but to get him the help he needed.

I couldn't believe there'd been so much secrecy and denial around the situation. We were pediatricians, for god's sake—one of the "touchy-feely" specialties, the next best thing to psychiatrists when it came to behavioral issues. I was appalled at the system that perpetuated this kind of denial. No one had been willing to confront the guy, much less offer a helping hand. I felt the way I had during my third-year surgery rotation—like we were all cogs in a machine, not permitted to have needs of our own and not allowed to give each other or ourselves the compassion we were being trained to give our patients. I was angry enough to consider tearing up my contract for next year. Plus, I was deeply shaken. As with Leah, my primary patient from the third-year psychiatry rotation, I had a harrowing sense that, with just a little more pressure, that could have been me.

There was a house-staff planning meeting the next day, when the current chief residents would start the transfer of responsibilities to the incoming chiefs. Though this was not a forum to air grievances, I raised my hand, heart pounding, swallowing hard before I could speak.

"Something happened while I was away that really upset me," I began. "A certain member of our house-staff—" I swallowed again and tried to keep the tremor out of my voice "—one of us had a flare-up of a psychiatric illness, and the people who should've picked up on this and helped him out—including the chief residents" –there was a collective intake of breath— "ignored what was going on until they were forced to do something about it."

The room was utterly silent. One of the chief residents blanched; another looked like he'd been slapped. Fighting back tears, I added, "I sincerely hope and pray that nothing like this is allowed to happen next year, or ever again." I lowered my head and wiped my eyes. The room broke out in rustlings and whispers. Jamison whirled around and gave me an are-you-crazy? look. Marie squeezed my arm and smiled at me.

"Thank you, Kay," said one of the incoming chief residents. She looked like she'd rather be anywhere but there; but she said, "You're right. This was a terrible thing. I promise it will never happen again."

This sounded like the kind of reassurance one gives a child, making a promise one might not be able to keep; I wondered if anything would really change. I also wondered if they knew I'd basically been advocating for myself, but I didn't care. Speaking truth to power that day lifted a weight from my shoulders, and I stood up a little straighter after that.

I myself was not immune to the stigma around psychiatric issues, particularly the prevailing attitude toward psychotherapy. My friend Seth from the Behavioral Pediatrics rotation was taking call with me in the pediatric ER one April evening when I reminded him that I would be gone from 5:30 to 6:30 for a therapy session.

Seth groaned. "Aw, come on. What a pain in the ass!"

I stared at him. He, of all people, should have been more understanding, having been privy to my depression when we were on that earlier rotation together.

"Well, excuse me for being a pain in the ass." My voice shook a little, but I stood my ground. "I work hard in therapy so I can get better—not just feel better but do better at my job. And it's helping. This doesn't just benefit me, it benefits you guys, too—all of you."

Joe, another PL-1 who was a good friend of Seth's, watched this exchange with interest. When I finished, he grinned at me and said, "Fuckin'-A!" I did a double take and then broke into a grin as well. Later that evening it occurred to me to be proud of the way I'd stood up for myself. And nobody complained again about my taking an hour a week off for therapy.

At the end of April, I rotated to 5B, the school-age ward. One of our patients had Reye's syndrome, a grave illness requiring one-to-one nursing care and mechanical ventilation. Kids with this disorder have a serious liver malfunction which leads to severe neurological problems, culminating in coma and often death. All of us on the school-age ward spent many night-call hours in the pediatric ICU (PICU) with this boy.

One night I returned from a quick dinner in the cafeteria to find Max, my ex-boyfriend from the third year of medical school, doing a routine check on my patient's ventilator settings. I stifled a gasp. He didn't look any different—same neatly-trimmed reddish beard, same glasses, same everything, only now he was wearing the royal-blue scrubs of a respiratory therapist. I was glad that Max had attained his goal, but—how bizarre it was to encounter him at work! Not to mention the fact that I'd be writing orders for him to carry out.

"Hi, Max," I said. "How are you?" I tried to keep the astonishment out of my voice.

"Just fine. How about you?" He smiled noncommittally, as if we'd never seen each other before.

"Great." I did my best to maintain a mask of neutral civility.

"When do you want me to run another blood gas on this kiddo?" he asked.

"Probably in another hour. We've made some progress with his ventilator settings today. I'd like to keep moving on that tonight."

"Okay, will do." Max nodded, then finished making notations on his clipboard and left the unit. I shook my head, stunned by the weirdness of our encounter. The time we'd spent together a mere two years ago seemed like part of another lifetime—so much had happened since then, and I'd grown far beyond those fevered weeks with him. I marveled at the way the divergent waters of our lives had flowed on, closing over our time together as though it had never happened.

• • •

It was a quiet Sunday night in early May, and I was on call. There was a TV in the playroom where the Child Life team conducted play therapy sessions with ward patients during the week. Since the playroom was next to the pediatric ICU, it was a good place to spend our downtime while we waited for lab results. I was watching *The Rockford Files* when Jamison came in and plopped down next to me. I'd hardly seen him since the end of our ICN rotation a few weeks earlier. After we finished catching up, he inched closer on the well-worn sofa. A minute or two later, he had an arm casually draped behind me. I stole a sideways glance at him. Jamison was married. He hadn't approached any of the other women PL-1s this way, as far as I knew. Did he know I looked up to him and even had a bit of a crush on him? I hoped I wasn't giving off flirtatious vibes.

"I really miss you," he said. "It was great, having you around for those two months. You made things interesting. And you're...really sexy. Wanna sneak off to the call room with me?" He moved in as if to kiss me.

"Whaaat?? No!" I pushed him away. "Are you nuts? I—I have to stay close to my Reye's syndrome kid." *And you have a wife*, I added silently.

He sighed gustily, got up to leave, and gave me a sad-puppy-dog look. "Feel free to change your mind at any time," he said.

I gave my head a quick shake. I'd thought I would miss him when he finished his residency, but now I was relieved that he'd be gone in another six weeks. And yet... while part of me was offended, another part of me was flattered. I tried to ignore the fact that I really wanted him.

Agitated, I walked beside Marie as she carried a blood gas to the respiratory lab. I had to tell someone.

"Jamison propositioned me," I said.

"What? He's married!" She spun around to stare at me and nearly dropped the ice-filled cup and its specimen.

"I know."

Marie and I clucked and tsk'd about it for a while. Her

indignation helped me maintain my resolve, but I couldn't get over the fact that a guy I worked with was expressing interest in me as a woman—something that hadn't happened since Blake had approached me in medical school. Confused and conflicted as I was, there would be little sleep for me that night, even though things were quiet in the PICU.

Jamison wouldn't take no for an answer, however, and I found his blandishments increasingly hard to resist. Several times over the next couple of weeks I caught him looking at me; he'd smile knowingly when he caught my eye, and I'd turn away as the color rose in my cheeks.

One evening at the end of May I heard myself being overhead paged while bolting down dinner in the cafeteria with Scott, a former classmate who was now an internal medicine intern.

"Hey, they're paging you, Kay. 3524—isn't that a men's call room?" Scott's eyes lit up with prurient interest.

"Nah, that can't be right," I said. My face on fire, I excused myself and picked up the nearest phone to answer the page—which was, indeed, Jamison paging me from one of the men's call rooms. "Way to go, Jamison—really smooth!" I muttered, as I strode down the hall, adrenaline pumping. I walked in determined to shut down his advances, clinging to the door handle as if to a life-raft.

"You overhead paged me to a *call room*? Are you crazy? What will people think?"

He looked sheepish. "I guess I didn't think about that. I just wanted to talk with you alone. Privately." His gaze was hypnotic, like that of a predatory animal. "I've seen the way you blush when I look at you," he went on, lowering his voice to a confidential purr. "Won't you sit next to me?" He patted the bed. My resistance oozed away like motor oil down a repair-shop drain.

I couldn't fight my own desire when it was so obvious that he wanted me, too.

I went to him as if in a trance. He lifted my shirt, unhooked my bra, and cupped my breasts—at which point the spell broke.

"No, no." I pulled away. "We can't do this."

"Oh, all right." He sighed. "But I can tell you want to." A little smile played around the corners of his mouth.

Silently I put myself back together and slipped out of the room, closing the door softly behind me, more conflicted than ever.

A few evenings later, he was serving me margaritas from a glass pitcher in his well-appointed apartment while his wife was away on a business trip. I hadn't been able to get the call-room incident out of my mind, and Jamison had pressed his advantage at every opportunity, sidling up to me in Core Conference or the hallway to whisper something or squeeze my elbow. When he called me at home to invite me over, I finally gave in. We made small talk, avoiding anything to do with work. I spent the night.

Once in Jamison's bed, I had instant buyer's remorse; guilt canceled any pleasure I might have experienced. I knew I'd ended up here because I'd managed to conflate sexual flattery with being respected as a doctor. Jamison had witnessed—and fostered—my growth as a resident. I'd wanted so much to believe that, like Preston Hayward a few years earlier, he felt a mentor's pride and affection, that his feelings for me as a woman went beyond mere lust.

And yet I saw clearly, even while I was still in his arms, that I was acting out a self-destructive pattern. For the first time, I could admit to myself that, Jamison's campaign notwithstanding, this was something *I had chosen to do*, not something that was happening to me out of the blue. Afterward I realized that, though I'd fought it at first, I'd walked into the situation with my eyes open, even though I knew better. I didn't blame anyone but myself; yet I didn't beat myself up about it. I simply acknowledged that I'd made a mistake and took responsibility for it. This was something new for me.

Jamison called me a few days after our night together to advise me not to get "emotionally involved."

"I'm sorry we got into the sex thing," he said. I fought back tears of hurt and frustration; then I got angry.

"Well, you *should* be sorry. And don't lecture me about getting emotionally involved—what a bunch of crap! Don't worry, I'm not going to impose myself on your perfect little life."

Jamison didn't seem to understand that I'd been "emotionally involved" with him long before we'd had sex, even before I'd known he had the slightest interest. I'd fallen for him when we were on rotations together, over those weeks of prodding and shaping me into something a little closer to his own image, which was also the image of a competent physician. He didn't realize that it wasn't the sex that created the emotional involvement; it was the emotional involvement that allowed the sex to happen.

After that phone call, I went for a drive on a quiet two-lane road near my apartment, radio blaring, and I screamed. And screamed and screamed some more. I screamed out all my hurt, anger, and frustration about Jamison and my own folly. When I got home, exhausted and hoarse, I remembered there was one man who'd never used me, betrayed me, or hurt me—a man who'd been a true friend since our days as housemates on Bolton Street—and a man I hadn't seen in a couple of weeks because of all the nonsense with Jamison. I called John.

"Can I come over?"

"Of course, I'd be delighted. It's been a while."

"I'm sorry." I felt like a heel.

"Don't be sorry. I'm just glad you called."

When I got to John's house, it was nearly sunset. His roses were in bloom and a few birds called back and forth in the lengthening shadows. It felt like home. We sat in his garden, and I told him briefly what had happened with Jamison, how foolish I'd been, and how betrayed and used I'd felt.

"In fact," I said, "I've felt betrayed and used at some point by pretty much every guy I've ever gone out with, except you. And now I've treated you badly. I'm sorry."

His plain features opened in a gentle smile, and he waved a hand dismissively.

"No need to apologize. I care about you and respect you, and you seem to feel the same about me. And we have a lot of fun, right? I think that's enough for now, don't you?" He stood up and extended a hand to me. We strolled across the lawn and walked into the house with our arms around each other's waists. John accepted me the way I was; and that acceptance showed me how friendship could grow into love.

• • •

On the third Saturday in June, I smiled at my reflection in the mirror as I brushed my hair. Two weeks from now, I'd be a PL-2, a second-year resident. And now I was getting ready for a party Dr. Visconti, my Behavioral Pediatrics attending, was throwing for the residents at her house. Mercifully, Jamison had left town right after finishing his final rotation as a PL-3, so there wouldn't be any awkwardness on that score. As I applied mascara, I recalled the highlight of that week. Vivienne, one of the PL-3s, had trotted up alongside me on our way to Core Conference, her high heels clicking on the linoleum hallway floor.

"Kay, I have to tell you something," she said in a rapid-fire stage whisper. "You've come a long way this year. I think you're the most improved resident of your group."

"Thanks, Vivienne." I beamed. Vivienne was a petite, intense woman who took her teaching duties as a PL-3 very seriously. I'd been the recipient of lots of advice and criticism from her over the previous eleven-plus months. Coming from her, this was high praise.

The party was festive, yet intimate. Wine flowed freely, and Dr. Visconti's homemade lasagna was delicious. After we'd had our fill, she distributed awards to each of the PL-1s, little items she'd made herself. Mine was a heart she'd fashioned from cotton batting covered with purple fabric, stitched with large stitches, and attached with a bit of green yarn to a tag that read "Purple Heart Award." I smiled as I thought of the woman with the cardiac arrhythmia whom we'd helped back in October.

I held the little fabric heart in my hand, turning it over, squeezing it. I marveled at how it was firm and soft at the same time. Then I grasped the true significance of the little heart. Dr. Visconti had really *seen* me. She realized that I was one of the walking wounded, and that I'd changed and grown into my role of physician in spite of my suffering. Her "Purple Heart Award" honored me as a wounded healer.

• • •

My last night on call as a PL-1, I sat in the spacious call room at Union Memorial Hospital and reviewed the events of the last few weeks. Marie was packing up her apartment, moving back to Raleigh to pursue a residency in psychiatry; I would really miss her. Earlier that week, I'd sat in the chief residents' office, reading the year's written evaluations by all the PL-2s and PL-3s I'd worked with. Larry and Marcia busied themselves at their desks to give me some privacy.

I drew in my breath sharply when I got to Jamison's. He'd given me scathingly bad reviews for both the rotations I'd done with him, the bastard—an unpleasant surprise, to be sure, but a perfectly fitting end to our association. I wasn't sure when he'd written them—before or after our night together. (Clearly, no one could accuse me of sleeping with him to get a good recommendation!) Shortly after that ill-advised encounter, before I'd seen his crappy evaluations, I'd slipped him a letter in which I took him to task for his behavior with me and advised him not to make a habit of taking advantage of infatuated underlings.

• • •

In light of the recent explosion of revelations about the sexual exploitation of women by men in positions of power over them, I've given a lot of thought to the difference between my experience with Jamison and my relationship with Preston—two decades older than me and a professor when I was a medical student. Though Jamison was close to me in age and only two years ahead of me professionally, the power differential between us was actually greater than that between Preston and me, since Jamison was responsible for evaluating my performance as a resident. But there was a much more important factor than age difference or power differential at work here: while Jamison, like Preston, had been a mentor whom I'd looked up to and respected, he'd exploited his position in a way that Preston, who genuinely cared for me, never did.

• • •

Later that evening, I placed my stethoscope on the chest of an eight-year-old girl with asthma in the emergency room. She'd improved with the usual series of three epinephrine shots, but not as much as I'd hoped. I vacillated between giving her a dose of long-acting epinephrine and sending her home, versus admitting her to the pediatric ward for IV aminophylline. When I still couldn't make up my mind, I called my PL-3 backup, a woman who was quiet and kind, with a gentle teaching style. I was surprised when she sounded more like Jamison than herself. After I told her about my patient, she said, "You know what? You're going to be a second-year resident *tomorrow*. You need to start making decisions by yourself." Click.

Whoa! I looked at the phone receiver as though it were a poisonous snake. Then I took a step back and shook off my hurt feelings. She was right. It was time to fly solo.

I took out my pen and wrote admission orders for my last patient as a PL-1.

And I've mentally thanked that resident, many times over, for her tough love that last night of internship.

That was the night I became a doctor.

EPILOGUE

One Sunday morning in April 2006, I came home from a night on call at the neonatal unit where I worked and looked over the previous day's mail. When I opened the *University of Maryland Medicine Bulletin*, Preston Hayward's obituary stared up at me from the "In Memoriam" page. I gasped and brought a fist to my mouth. I'd known this day would come, but, somehow, I hadn't thought it would happen so soon. The memorial service had taken place the previous day, while I was busy attending deliveries, examining preemies, and writing orders and progress notes in charts. I sat down hard and dabbed my eyes. Then I remembered the last time I'd seen my old lover and mentor.

On a lovely spring day in 1997, I'd just gotten the mail after attending my 20-year medical school reunion in Baltimore. There was a note for me, printed in bold black ink on creamy card stock, from the dean of the medical school—an invitation to a memorial service for a physician a few years older than me who'd been a good friend of Preston's. I was deeply shaken by this voice from the past on a day of voices from the past, and I couldn't help reading into it a message: *Go! This is your big chance!*

I was 46 years old, a mid-career neonatologist working at a large community hospital. I'd been happily—and faithfully— married for over sixteen years, and our three daughters were in middle school. Occasionally I'd run into Preston at a pediatric lecture, and we'd hugged, kissed each other's cheeks, and spent five minutes or so catching up. During these brief encounters, I'd never had a chance to ask him a question that cropped up with increasing frequency as I got older: had our relationship all those years ago had anywhere near the significance for him that it had for me? Or had I just been a minor blip on the radar screen of his attention and affection?

I mulled over the unexpected invitation for a few days before responding. I knew the deceased physician's wife from residency, so it would not be inappropriate for me to offer my condolences—and I *had* been invited. But the thought of being in a roomful of people from that part of my past, many of whom had been my elders and betters in medical school and residency, brought back all those painful feelings of inadequacy that I'd felt as a student and resident. Would I even get a chance to talk with Preston, beyond "hello" and a quick hug?

Fortunately, I'd recently read James Hillman's book, *The Soul's Code*, in which he discusses in some detail the phenomenon of mentoring. According to Hillman, a mentor may see in their mentee a possibility that no one else has seen, and that vision tends to be colored by love in some form—parental, erotic, or simply the love of a friend. (In the case of Preston and me, it was probably all three.) Just as seeing that possibility in the mentee elicits love from the mentor, being truly seen, in a way they've never been before, evokes love in the mentee. In the early days of medical school, Preston had seen a potential in me that I'd been incapable of seeing in myself—the potential to be successful and competent as both a physician and a woman. A potential that, twenty-plus years later, had been realized. Being seen in that way, at that time, was the greatest gift anyone could have given me.

So I dressed in "business casual," put on my best gold earrings, necklace, and wristwatch—all gifts from my husband at various points in our life together—and drove to Baltimore for the memorial service. As I'd suspected, Preston was the emcee for this nonsectarian celebration of life. I offered my condolences to the widow and chatted with some of the less intimidating figures from my past. Finally, the crowd around Preston thinned out. I approached him and cleared my throat. I'd rehearsed what I wanted to say, but I hoped my voice wouldn't shake too much.

"Preston, I just want to thank you for mentoring me, while I still have the chance," I said. He was, I was all too aware, more than a decade older than his departed friend.

He hugged me hard, for a long time. As his rough cheek pressed against my neck, I realized he'd lost some height with age. When he released me, his eyes were twinkling.

"Hey, it was easy to mentor you, 'cause I loved you. I didn't love all those other people," he added with a laugh.

Without even having to ask the question, I'd received my answer.

We sat down. He took my hand, entwining his fingers with mine. His hand hadn't grown dry or wrinkled with age. There was something poignant about the contrast between the pink pads of his fingers and the rest of his dark brown skin.

"You know," he said, "the time we had together was beautiful. In fact, I *still* love you." He smiled and gave my hand a squeeze. I told him how much it meant to hear him say that.

Then we went on to talk of other things. He recounted the exploits of his school-age daughter from his second marriage, and some of his physician-wife's accomplishments. I showed him pictures of my daughters, and he exclaimed about their various resemblances to me. He introduced me to his son, now in his late thirties, who rolled his eyes and said, "He's *still* mentoring me."

As he had at our first meeting in his office all those years ago, he punctuated our conversation with little touches and shoulder-squeezes; and, as it had then, this made me feel a little bashful. But I realized that, while I still loved him, I no longer felt any desire for a sexual relationship with him. It felt wonderful just to hold his hand, to laugh and talk with him, and to bask in that glow we once shared that never completely went away, and never will as long as I'm here to remember it.

• • •

One night during my second semester of medical school, when I was deep in depression about my mother's death and my recent breakup with Preston, some friends and I engaged in the Chinese form of divination known as the *I Ching*. Naturally, my query concerned whether I would ever find a man to share my life with. The hexagram that came up when I tossed the plastic sticks told me that my search would be successful, that it would take a long time, and that "there will be no error." Two years later, I received three fortune cookies in a row with a similar message: "You shall gain your wish." "A wish will be granted after a long delay." "Your romance will be a long and lasting one."

I didn't end up marrying any of the men I encountered in medical school or my internship year. But when, several months into residency, I committed to the man who later became my husband, I discovered that those previous relationships had prepared me to trust in my love for him, his love for me, and my own judgment as to his suitability as a life-partner. Our romance has indeed been a long and lasting one. There have been the usual ups and downs, but there has been no error.

• • •

On a gray autumn day a few years ago, I went back to the place where my time in Baltimore began. I parked my car a couple of blocks north of 334 S. Stricker St. and walked to the old rowhouse. The crack epidemic of the '80s and '90s had taken a toll on the neighborhood. There was more litter in the gutters; the pavement was rougher and more pockmarked than I remembered. A surveillance camera, right out of an episode of *The Wire*, blinked unsteadily from a corner. A few of the rowhouses were gone, with only a plot of grass or weeds in their place. Some nearby homes were being rehabilitated. Several of the houses remained as they'd been forty-plus years ago, while others were still standing but derelict.

334 was one of the latter. The marble stoop was gone, the windows were missing, and the inside appeared gutted as if waiting for the wrecking-ball.

Like someone touching the name of a lost loved one on the wall of the Vietnam Memorial, I placed a couple of smooth stones on the doorsill—which, without the stoop, was at chest height—to honor all the people who'd lived here before and after me, as well as the people I'd shared this house with, none of whom I was likely ever to see again. With this gesture I bore witness to the joys, sorrows, and struggles we'd all experienced in this place, and to the fact that each of our lives, however obscure, meant—and means—something.

We were here.

ACKNOWLEDGEMENTS

Many thanks to the fine people at Apprentice House Press: Natalie Misyak, acquisition editor, and the other students at the Maryland Writers' Conference in Fall 2022 who were excited about my work; my first editor, Lorena Ercoline; Rhian Barnes; Claire Marino; Jack Stromberg; and the man in charge, Kevin Atticks.

Deep gratitude to those who graciously agreed to blurb my book: Ariele Sieling, Christine Koubek, Paul Offit, Celia Wexler, and Melissa Scholes Young.

Heartfelt thanks to my writing group buddies, who did so much to help me shape this work: Joel Breman, the late Yvonne Brown, the late Sydney Frymire, Kate Lemery, Myrna Seidman, and especially Naomi Weiss, my writing BFF, who brought me into the group.

Many thanks to Christine Koubek, writing teacher and developmental editor extraordinaire. Much gratitude to Ariele Sieling for her developmental editing and encouragement.

Much appreciation to my other readers: Sarah Drew, Beverli Goldberg, Timothy Burton, Amy Morgan Bakewell, Logan Schmidt, Amy Valentine, Paul Offit, Celia Wexler, Robin Tricoles, Melissa Scholes Young, and Doug Boenning. Elizabeth Drew, Sarah Crosby, Mary Alyce Hare, Tracy Rosenhand, and Ellen Volkman also gave helpful feedback on parts of the manuscript.

Thanks also to writing colleagues including Ann Quinn, poetry teacher extraordinaire, and my fellow students in her class; my friends in the Wellesley Literary Circle poetry group; the DMV Women Writers; Nathan Leslie; Melissa Scholes Young; Caroline Bock; Dan Cuddy; Eve Makoff and the Narrative Medicine Cooperative; and the folks at The Writer's Center and the Maryland Writers' Association. And a special shout-out to Tara Elliott and the other wonderful folks I've met through the Eastern Shore Writers' Association,

Many thanks to other friends who have supported my writing endeavors from the beginning: Beverli Goldberg; Joanie Kelly; Mary and Chuck McQueen and Katie Mencarini; Barbara Nagle; and Laurie Feldman.

My deepest heartfelt appreciation to my friends and colleagues from medical school and residency for kindnesses large and small. During that difficult time in my life, even your smallest acts of kindness made a huge difference and will never be forgotten.

Deep gratitude to my therapists for helping me to grow and, eventually, thrive.

Finally, many thanks and much love to my family. Special love to my siblings, Sarah Crosby, Mary Alyce Hare, and Philip White, with gratitude for their support and for helpfully sharing their own memories of family events. To my daughters, Elizabeth, Amy, and Sarah Drew: you give me so much joy. Gratitude and love to Mel Chayette and Eric Leveridge for their love and support of my girls.

To Glen Drew, the love of my life: thanks for everything.

ABOUT THE AUTHOR

Katherine White, M.D., aka Kay White Drew, is a retired neonatal physician and lifelong writer. After graduating Phi Beta Kappa with honors from Wellesley College, she obtained her M.D. degree from the University of Maryland Medical School in Baltimore. She completed a residency in Pediatrics at the University of Maryland and a fellowship in Neonatal/Perinatal Medicine at Georgetown University Hospital in Washington, DC, was board-certified in both specialties, and subsequently practiced neonatology in the DC suburbs of Maryland. Her writing appears in regional anthologies and journals including *Bay to Ocean Journal*, *This Is What America Looks Like*, *Pen in Hand*, and *Grace in Darkness*; and online journals including *The Loch Raven Review*, where one of her essays was nominated for a *Pushcart Prize; Intima: A Journal of Narrative Medicine*; and *Maryland Literary Review*. She lives in Rockville, MD, with her husband, and enjoys spending time with family and friends; traveling, especially road trips; walking in the woods; and, of course, reading.

Her website is: www.kaywhitedrew.com

Apprentice
House Press
Loyola University Maryland

Apprentice House Press is the country's only campus-based, student-staffed book publishing company. Directed by professors and industry professionals, it is a nonprofit activity of the Communication Department at Loyola University Maryland.

Using state-of-the-art technology and an experiential learning model of education, Apprentice House publishes books in untraditional ways. This dual responsibility as publishers and educators creates an unprecedented collaborative environment among faculty and students, while teaching tomorrow's editors, designers, and marketers.

Eclectic and provocative, Apprentice House titles intend to entertain as well as spark dialogue on a variety of topics. Financial contributions to sustain the press's work are welcomed. Contributions are tax deductible to the fullest extent allowed by the IRS.

To learn more about Apprentice House books or to obtain submission guidelines, please visit www.apprenticehouse.com.

Apprentice House Press
Communication Department
Loyola University Maryland
4501 N. Charles Street
Baltimore, MD 21210
Ph: 410-617-5265
info@apprenticehouse.com • www.apprenticehouse.com

9 781627 2052